The Power of Historical Knowledge

The Power of Historical Knowledge

Narrating the Past in Hawthorne, James, and Dreiser

SUSAN L. MIZRUCHI

Princeton University Press
Princeton, New Jersey

Published by Princeton University Press, 41 William
Street, Princeton New Jersey 08540
In the United Kingdom: Princeton University Press,
Guildford, Surrey

Library of Congress Cataloging in Publication Data will
be found on the last printed page of this book

ISBN 0-691-06725-2

This book has been composed in Linotron Janson Type

Printed in the United States of America by Princeton
University Press, Princeton, New Jersey

For my mother,
the first historian I ever knew,

and my father,
who taught me the value
of scholarship.

Contents

Preface

IN HIS 1879 biography, James describes Hawthorne's historical sensibility, his feeling of being possessed by ancestral spirits. "There is a very American quality," James writes, "in the perpetual consciousness of a spell on Hawthorne's part; it is only in a country where newness and change and brevity of tenure are the common substance of life, that the fact of one's ancestors having lived for a hundred and seventy years in a single spot would become an element of one's morality. It is only an imaginative American who would feel urged to keep reverting to this circumstance, to keep analysing and cunningly considering it." James's observation is noteworthy not only for its description of Hawthorne's living memory, but for its suggestion of the manner in which "an imaginative American" encounters the past. James's Hawthorne must "keep reverting . . . keep analysing and cunningly considering" the deeds of his ancestors. One might say that for Hawthorne, history is a region to be reclaimed through return and repetition.

This study combines theoretical and historical methods to explore narrative reconstructions of the past in *The House of the Seven Gables*, *The Bostonians*, *The Wings of the Dove*, and *An American Tragedy*. Within the act of historical narration, in portraits of characters and narrators attempting to reshape their own and their community's past, struggles for personal identity and political power are waged. My analyses differ from previous views of time and history in American novels by treating Hawthorne's, James's, and Dreiser's narrators as distinct from their authors, strategic voices themselves actively engaged in manipulating characters and readers. Within the novels two kinds of narrative time emerge to stand in uneasy relation: characters' transcendent fables, and a marginalized historical vision containing those elements of the characters' contemporary world which both exploit and thwart their aspirations to transcendence.

Partly in response to critical assumptions about the ahistoricism of American novels, I seek to demonstrate that an awareness of the impulse to flee or defuse historical experience is built into the narratives themselves. If American narrators and characters aspire to the condition of transcendence, they nevertheless keep looking nervously back over their shoulders toward the confinements of the historical past and present inscribed in their texts. These limiting historical factors include the burdens of ancestry (and in particular, the limitations of class origins) as well as the developments of an industrialized consumer society threatening individual identity and the life of the community. The fundamental obsession is always with history, and my readings reveal that struggles against the bonds of inheritance and the submergences of change are repeatedly waged in the act of narration. The attempts of characters and narrators to remake their experience through narration represent challenges to historical progress sometimes so literal as to impede the progress of their narratives.

From the declaration of the romance's freedom from the constraints of time in the preface to *The House of the Seven Gables*, to Samuel Griffiths's mythic envisioning of his new factory near the end of *An American Tragedy*, American narrators and characters have claimed an imperviousness to the cause and effect rhythms of history. Previous studies have taken such scenes as exemplary of the lack of historical vision in American novels. It is the claim of this work that far from omitting society and history, American novels *portray* an ambivalence toward social and historical engagement as a cultural habit. In views of fictional personae resisting evidence of historical change and social relations, or attempting to evade their responsibilities for actions, American novels reveal an awareness of the entrapment of human beings in the social and historical worlds they inhabit. Most importantly, within these novels such attempts become explicitly politicized, as characters strive to control others' perceptions, and to rewrite their own and the culture's memories.

I begin with a theoretical introduction that traces a developing set of assumptions about time and history in American novels. At the same time, it draws upon some of these approaches to derive a method for exploring the representation of history in novels by Hawthorne, James, and Dreiser. Employing such theorists as Barthes on the ahistorical impulse of middle-class myth, Jameson on modernist attempts to "manage" history, and Hayden White on the relativism of historical interpretation, I discuss how historical narration can itself be seen as an instrument for defusing social conflict and political polarization. This leads to the question of whether American novels view the process of narration, in particular the narration of history, as a subversive or conciliatory activity. Of special interest here is the attempt to articulate the author's relationship to his text's politics of narration. Chapter Two then turns to primary and secondary sources on nineteenth- and early-twentieth-century historiography to explore the American obsession with retelling the past in the periods roughly contemporaneous with the literary works under consideration. This view of theories of history writing from the mid-nineteenth century to the opening decades of the twentieth enters into a dialogue with ideas about historical narration found in the novels read in later chapters.

For my readings, I have selected examples from a range of novelistic genres: Romance, Realism, and Naturalism.[1] This has allowed me to explore the portrayed relations between narrative repressions of history and the implementation of political power during a historical era—that saw the parallel developments of the

---

[1] For the most part, however, generic distinctions will not play a prominent role in the discussions that follow. Examining a variety of texts has enabled me to demonstrate that my questions would, I hope, illuminate a wide range of American novels. But the differences among my examples have seemed to me more matters of degree than kind.

American novel and of industrial capitalism—namely, 1851 to 1925. One of the aims of my study is to demonstrate that the line from Hawthorne through James to Dreiser is both more aesthetically probable and more politically revealing than has been recognized. The inclusion of two novels by James was warranted by the differences between his early and late works.

Moreover, it was specifically these novels by Hawthorne, James, and Dreiser that prompted me to conceptualize the central questions of this study. The works that I examine prominently feature repetitions of all kinds, from stuttering sentences to doublings of characters, scenes, and structure, in ways that seem decisively related to their characters' obsessions with time and history. But it was not until I began to study these works more closely that I saw that the manipulations of narrative time and of perception, variously engaged in by characters and narrators, were means by which political power was acquired, maintained, and rationalized. Manipulations of perception were part of larger strategies to control the accessibility and content of historical information. And control over time and history was exercised narratively, through the action of telling tales of the past.

In exploring the revelation and concealment of history in nineteenth- and twentieth-century American novels, I examine the dramatized efforts of both characters and narrators to manage history, and the ways in which the novels themselves are related to the historical contexts from which they emerge. I emphasize the function of the repression of history—how these novels relate characters' narrative efforts to control and accommodate their experiences of a particular history, and their responsibilities as historical actors, to the nature of political life in America. This is different from a study of the abstract problem of "temporality," or of the human condition in its relationship to the universal category of time.

My project has a dual genesis in the history of American literature and in the history of its interpretation. From my first study of writers such as Hawthorne, Melville, and James, and critics such as Richard Chase, R.W.B. Lewis, and, more recently, Myra Jehlen and Walter Michaels, I have been struck with the politically conservative characterizations of American literature provided by its foremost interpreters, even the most radically historicist.[2] If one trait remained constant in readings of works from different centuries, it was this peculiar temporal disposition—the penchant for transcendent discovery, the substitution of metaphysical for historical questions—which set American literature apart from the claims of social and political realities. American writers favored a detached aestheticism or an eternalized radicalism over the more immediate concerns of contemporary institutional and political life in America.

Many consider this view of the basically ahistorical and depoliticized aspirations underlying American literary forms to be a critical dead horse, an interpretive line now subsumed by "the new historicism"; but its assumptions persist in most of our readings. Although American literature has fortunately fallen into history, views of its relationship to politics and time remain largely unchanged. To be precise, I am assuming the inseparability of temporal perceptions and political stances. Throughout my study, I associate an eternalized perspective with political disengagement, in accordance with my literary examples.

The "return to history" in the 1980s has left us with a relatively traditional view of the political dimensions of American literature. Our analyses have opened out to include a richer sense of the connection between literature and history, but our sense of the ways in which works of American literature engage the political prob-

[2] Of this group, Sacvan Bercovitch is the most convincing on the political complexities of American writers and their works. See, for example, *The American Jeremiad* (Madison: University of Wisconsin Press, 1978). Bercovitch's recent anthology, *Reconstructing American Literary History* (Cambridge, Mass.: Harvard University Press, 1986), indicates new directions for a politically revisionary criticism. In his introduction, Bercovitch asserts the advent of a literary criticism based on "dissensus," rather than "consensus," as well as on the awareness "that language has the capacity to break free of social restrictions and through its own dynamics to undermine the power structures it seems to reflect" (viii).

PREFACE

lems of their eras seems to have escaped similar revisionary challenges.[3] This appears to have something to do with our reluctance
to consider the presence of authorial consciousnesses in literary
works, particularly in relation to political matters. So far, we have
not used our theoretical insights to consider possible models of authorial vision that might escape the dilemmas of the intentionalists
while they avoid dismissive conclusions about "the death of the author." American new historicist criticism typically displays a condescending appraisal of the author's awareness of his text's social
and political implications,[4] as the critic plots the tension between
his own discovery that the literary work is inevitably situated in
history, and the commitment to transcendent experience held by
the work and its author. The critical drama then becomes an effort
to drag the author and the text into a freshly reconstructed historical context, while demonstrating the myopia or pathos of any aspiration to deny historical entanglements.[5]

[3] This is of course changing. But it is noteworthy that although there has been
much recent interest in the need to recover and refine our historical methodologies,
interest in the refinement of our political analyses, as exemplified by the work of
Carolyn Porter, has lagged behind.

[4] An analysis of specific new historicist readings is provided in Chapter One, below. It is interesting to note that British New Historicists (cultural materialists)
have been more attentive to the political and presentist features of the past. Louis
Montrose attributes this to the greater class consciousness of British academicians.
He observes, "In Britain—where class barriers remain more clearly articulated
than in the United States; where, too, radical politics and radical discourses enjoy
stronger traditions and where the coercive pressure of the state upon educational
institutions and practices is now conspicuously direct and intense—there has been
a relatively greater emphasis upon the uses to which the *present* has put its versions
of the past." "Renaissance Literary Studies and the Subject of History," *English
Literary Renaissance* 16 (1986): 7.

It is significant that a greater interpretive self-consciousness coincides with a
more developed radicalism in British society, and that this perspective yields a crit-
icism more concerned with the radical potential of literature itself. Also see Don E.
Wayne's illuminating essay, "Power, Politics, and the Shakespearian Text: Recent
Criticism in England and the United States," in *Shakespeare Reproduced: The Text in
History and in Ideology*, ed. Jean Howard and Marion O'Connor (London and New
York: Methuen, forthcoming).

[5] It should be pointed out that many of the interpretations I am referring to here

PREFACE

For old historicists and New Critics, myth critics and many new historicists alike, works of American literature possess little potential for a critical social stance. At best they represent aesthetically powerful arguments for the value of "eternal questions," at worst they function as doubtful siphons of cultural energies by diverting attention from pressing political problems. In a recent essay on *The Scarlet Letter*, Jonathan Arac describes Hawthorne's "programmatically willed alienation," which he finds fully compatible with the democratic liberalism of his era, a politics that "allowed *issues* no part in the discourse of the two established parties." Arac concludes that the production of literature in the nineteenth century was "achieved through a series of separations and purifications," and ultimately rejects any "metaphoric" links between "political" and "literary" concerns.[6]

The problem with this argument is that political action is defined too narrowly. We need to expand our conceptions of the ways in which our aesthetic modes may shape and alter societies.[7] Moreover, I wonder about distinctions between what is more or less political. It is undeniable that a power struggle in Congress could have global repercussions while a power struggle in an English department might at worst result in the firing of a faculty member. But intensity of effect does not in and of itself define the "political." One of the greatest possibilities of literary study, both in scholarship and in teaching, is that by sensitizing ourselves and others to the way in which language works in power relations, we make available the potential to effect change in larger arenas. I be-

---

are based on the theories of Michel Foucault. For an analysis of this trend in American literary criticism, see Gerald Graff, "American Criticism Left and Right," in Sacvan Bercovitch and Myra Jehlen, ed., *Ideology and Classic American Literature* (New York: Cambridge University Press, 1986), esp. 114–16.

[6] See "The Politics of *The Scarlet Letter*," in *Ideology and Classic American Literature*, 253, 262, 252–53.

[7] Paul Ricoeur raises this question of "the capacity of the work of art to indicate and to transform human action" as part of his forthcoming agenda at the close of Volume 2 of *Time and Narrative* (Chicago: University of Chicago Press, 1985), 160.

lieve that the authors in my study were convinced of literature's potential metaphorical power.

At the risk of oversimplification, let me explain my understanding of two central concepts to which I refer throughout my arguments. I use the term "history" to designate a phenomenon of change over time, conceived in the novels of my study as a linear process. Historical actions and events are always specific and local, tied to a particular time and place, and historical understanding links a series of human actions and social events by a perception of cause and effect, a sense of *why* something happened. Individuals as well as the collectivity can possess a sense of history.

In a book on the rise of capitalism and technology, David F. Noble makes a distinction that helps to elucidate my use of the term "history." Observing that technology has often been seen as something other than human, as a "disembodied historical force impinging on the affairs of men," Noble suggests that such views of technology are important not as "*explanations* of history, but rather as *examples* of a recurring aspect of history: [its] mystification" (my emphasis). Noble goes on to assert that it is the historian's primary task to "demystify history, to render it intelligible in human rather than in super-human or non-human terms."[8] I see my literary examples as representations and critiques of the very process of historical mystification.

---

[8] See *American By Design* (New York: Oxford University Press, 1980), xix. In *Keywords* (Oxford University Press, reprint 1985), Raymond Williams distinguishes between history conceived as "organized knowledge of the past" that includes specific "accounts of past real events" and "less formal accounts of past events and accounts of imagined events"; and history in the Viconian sense "as a continuous and connected process" of change over time, which incorporates Enlightenment views of history as "progress and development," Hegelian views of the "world historical process," and Marxist views of historical forces as "products of the past which are active in the present and which will shape the future in knowable ways" (146–47). My study employs both senses of the term. The view of history as record is the basis for my explorations of the activity of historical narration engaged in by novelistic narrators and characters. The view of history as a phenomenon of change over time approximates my sense of what constitutes historical vision in the societies of my novelistic examples, both as possessed by individuals and as it appears in larger collective and institutional forms.

I use the term "political" to indicate any social exchange between two or more individuals where one exercises influence or control over another. Such exchanges can be achieved subtly, playing off of supposedly shared values, ensuring that the individual being influenced is responding "spontaneously" and of his own "free will"; or such actions can appear blatantly domineering. I seek to expand our notion of what may be conceived of as political in the novels of my study, to see it as potentially encompassing all social relations, including the relationship between narrator and reader. I am interested in nonauthorized forms of power, in the continuous fluctuations of influence and control between individuals and among classes in these novelistic societies.[9]

In brief my project has two primary aims. The first is to demonstrate how American novels teach us to read their social and historical interests, and what they suggest for our present theoretical concerns about the relativity of meaning, the trap of our own historical dispositions, and the politics of interpretation inevitably

[9] Antonio Gramsci separates the function of social hegemony from direct domination. Social hegemony is based on "spontaneous consent given by the great masses of the population to the general direction imposed on social life by the dominant fundamental group." It is a consent that is rooted in history, dependent upon the past "prestige" of the dominant group. "The apparatus of state coercive power," Gramsci continues, is in place for "those groups who do not 'consent' either actively or passively" and for the "whole of society in anticipation of moments of crisis" (*Prison Notebooks* [New York: International Publishers, 1985], 12). Both types of power are in evidence in the novelistic societies of my study. Kate Croy of *The Wings of the Dove*, for example, is adept at manipulating the consent of others, whereas *An American Tragedy* pictures a world in which such "spontaneous" forms of control are no longer operative. The breakdown of political hegemony in the society of Dreiser's novel corresponds not incidentally to the breakdown of narrative sequence seen throughout the novel. For another perspective on the idea of the "political," see Sheldon Wolin, *Politics and Vision* (London: Allen and Unwin, 1961). Wolin's definition of political activity includes: "a) a form of activity centering around the quest for competitive advantage between groups, individuals, or societies; b) a form of activity conditioned by the fact that it occurs within a situation of change and relative scarcity; c) a form of activity in which the pursuit of advantage produces consequences of such a magnitude that they affect in a significant way the whole society or a substantial portion of it" (10–11). For a discussion of various interpretations of the concept of power by contemporary social scientists, see Stephen Lukes, *Power* (New York: Macmillan, 1974).

raised by such assumptions. The second aim is more self-consciously methodological: to try to combine close attention to novelistic structure, and theories that inform it, with historical analysis. This latter effort has allowed me to see the connections between narrative power and political power as it is inscribed in the novelistic societies of Hawthorne, James, and Dreiser, and as it points to larger power relations in the societies from which their works emerge.

One final point concerns my own sense of historical "progress" or "change" over the range of my examples. I suggest an increasing commitment to the idea of the relativism of historical knowledge from Hawthorne to Dreiser. The breakdown of narrative sequence, which can be seen in the sporadic repetitions of the chimney-corner legends in *The House of the Seven Gables* and in the overall multiplicity of warring tales in that novel, seems elaborated and fixed by *An American Tragedy*, where the protagonist's downfall is inseparable from his inability either to shape a plot for his life or to offer an authoritative narration of his past. The move from Hawthorne to Dreiser also suggests a growing awareness of the alignment of political power and the powers of historical interpretation. In this sense, Dreiser's novel seems to point to the loss of faith in historical narration that characterizes our current generation of literary theorists. Indeed, Hawthorne, James, and Dreiser were as skeptical as many of us about the accessibility of the past: aware that the pursuit of the past can be as delusive and politically distorted as any more overt form of self-inflation or tyranny. Nonetheless, the logic of their works suggests the power of historical knowledge to effect personal insight, and in personal insight, so empowered, to effect political action and social change.

Acknowledgments

IT IS A pleasure to acknowledge those who supported this project.

Emory Elliott has been a source of inspiration. I am indebted to him for his energy and intelligence as a teacher and critic and his humaneness as an advisor.

At Boston University, I am fortunate to be surrounded by a group of exciting scholars who have taken time from their own work to read mine. I am grateful for the generous criticism of Aaron Fogel, Jon Klancher, Jack Matthews, Michael McKeon, David Suchoff, Cecelia Tichi, William Vance, and Carolyn Williams.

I am also grateful for the advice of my brother Mark, a trusted colleague and friend.

I wish to thank the following, whose invaluable suggestions improved the book in many ways: Jonathan Arac, Sacvan Bercovitch, Terrence Des Pres, Philip Fisher, Virginia Jackson, Victoria Kahn, Robert Milder, Mark Seltzer, Carl S. Smith, and David Van Leer.

The contributions of two friends, Nancy Schnog and Robert Muratore, and my brother David, go beyond the bounds of academia.

I could not have asked for a more kind and encouraging editor than Robert E. Brown, nor a more shrewd copyeditor than Sherry Wert.

I would also like to thank John Pearson and the Graduate School of Boston University for expert work and financial assistance in preparing the index.

ACKNOWLEDGMENTS

Parts of Chapter Four first appeared in my article "The Politics of Temporality in *The Bostonians*," © 1985 by The Regents of the University of California, reprinted from *Nineteenth-Century Fiction* 40, no. 2 (September 1985): 187–215, by permission of The Regents.

The Power of Historical Knowledge

ONE

The Problem of History in American Literature

THE PROTAGONIST of Jorge Luis Borges's tale, "Pierre Menard, Author of Don Quixote," is possessed by the desire to rewrite *Don Quixote*. In pursuing this task, he comes to believe that the least interesting means of accomplishing his aim is to exchange his own identity for Cervantes's. "To be, in some way, Cervantes and reach the *Quixote* seemed less arduous to him . . . than to go on being Pierre Menard and reach the Quixote through the experiences of Pierre Menard." Rejecting the possibility that "the history of Europe between the years 1602 and 1918" can be forgotten, Menard proposes to recover within himself the version of *Don Quixote* enabled by the modern world; in the process of recovery, he muses, "History, the mother of truth: the idea is astounding. Menard, a contemporary of William James, does not define history as an inquiry into reality but as its origin. Historical truth, for him, is not what has happened; it is what we judge to have happened."[1]

Borges's insistence on the hermeneutic circle of historical understanding illuminates the portraits of characters and narrators revising the historical past in the American novels of my study. Like Borges, Hawthorne, James, and Dreiser are interested in the idea of historical consciousness as the path of becoming for the romantic ego. The hope that the self can be reconstituted, or the community unified or affirmed, through an encounter with its point of origin is invoked throughout my study. Yet the belief that some confrontation with the historical past can lead to self-reali-

[1] Jorge Luis Borges, *Ficciones* (New York: Grove Press, 1962).

zation or social integration is complicated by another "truth" about history registered by these "imaginative Americans"—that the act of historical interpretation is invariably the site of our most embattled psychological and political struggles.

In exploring the representation of historical narration in selected American novels, I am concerned with how such representations help us to conceptualize the problem of literature and ideology.[2] This chapter explores the ideological issues raised by portraits of characters who narrate history in nineteenth- and twentieth-century American novels. I focus on four central questions. First, how does my subject fit into the continuing debate over American literature's resistance to history and politics? Second, how might the combined use of cultural-historical and narratological methods expand our conceptions of the historical and political engagement of American novels? Third, what effects do historical narratives have in these novelistic worlds? Does the activity of narrating history lead to awareness of the power and responsibility of human agents? Finally, how can the author's relationship to the politics of narration inscribed in his text be conceived?

Historical Resistance in American Novels: Fact or Fiction?

Like any body of writing, American literature comes to us as "the always-already-read."[3] Our re-examination of American literature in history must therefore confront the series of authoritative read-

---

[2] Can literature resist ideology, or does it inevitably reproduce the ideological assumptions of its historical moment? Do some works resist more than others, and if so, how is this resistance manifested? For a collection of recent work on this subject in American literature, see Bercovitch and Jehlen, *Ideology and Classic American Literature*. Anthony Giddens provides a helpful historical survey of social scientists' uses of the term in *Central Problems in Social Theory* (Berkeley: University of California Press, 1979), ch. 5; see especially pp. 165–79 on "Ideology and Consciousness."

[3] Fredric Jameson, *The Political Unconscious* (Ithaca: Cornell University Press, 1981), 9.

ings that have guided our previous "responses" to the texts. Such a survey will also help us to understand the logic and persistence of interpretations that regard American novels as indifferent to matters of immediate historical and political interest. These sorts of arguments characteristically underestimate interplay between the social and aesthetic properties of texts. For example, *Main Currents in American Thought* (1927, 1930), Vernon Parrington's study of the American social novel, criticized Hawthorne and Henry James for their perceived failure to evoke social reality.[4] Their excessive aestheticism, the argument ran, precluded their view of social concerns.

The New Critics of the 1950s took an opposite approach in elevating the fiction and criticism of their "aesthetic" mentor Henry James to a literary standard. Yet their isolation of literary texts from contexts ultimately affirmed Parrington's claims and helped to further the split between "social" and "aesthetic" writers.[5] It was not simply that any one writer's work was confined to a single critical method. Rather, this binomial opposition between formalistic and social questions divided critical approaches themselves. Critics who focused on questions about social and historical context rarely concerned themselves with formalistic questions, and those who considered formalistics usually ignored historical and social issues.

The Anglo-American New Critics were contemporaries of another group of scholars, later known as the "myth critics," who concentrated specifically on American cultural studies. By locating the uniqueness of American cultural forms in their resistance to social problems and in their preference for symbolic transcendence over historical engagement, critics like R.W.B. Lewis (*The*

[4] *Main Currents in American Thought*, 3 vols. (New York: Harcourt Brace and Jovanovich, 1927, 1930). For more on the "social" and "political" motivations behind Parrington's magnum opus, see Richard Hofstader, *The Progressive Historians* (New York: Knopf, 1968), 350–57 and passim.
[5] For a discussion of the politics of New Criticism, see Frank Lentricchia, *After The New Criticism* (Chicago: University of Chicago Press, 1980).

5

American Adam, 1955) and Richard Chase (*The American Novel and Its Tradition*, 1957) affirmed the separation of aesthetic and cultural-historical questions. Their influential works inspired many studies in this vein, including works as different as Richard Poirier's *A World Elsewhere* (1966) and Quentin Anderson's *The Imperial Self* (1971). Such analyses emphasized strains in the American literary impulse that led out of history and into atemporal realms of heroism, romance, style, and neuroses.[6]

More recently, Sacvan Bercovitch has described a uniquely American messianic impulse, which he terms the "Myth of America." This collectively held cultural myth functions as a force for social integration in American society and can be found in writings from the time of the Puritan settlers to the present. Though Bercovitch points to the need for exploring "the changing relations between reality and myth in American culture," his study is more concerned with "an ideological consensus . . . a series of rituals of socialization, and a comprehensive, officially endorsed cultural myth." What differentiates Bercovitch from the myth critics is his analysis of the political effects of these transcendent impulses. Implicitly rejecting Lawrentian claims for the eternal subversiveness of classic American writings, he offers a complex view of ideology's function.[7] America's classic writers, he observes, were "radical in a representative way that *reaffirmed* the culture, rather than undermined it." For Bercovitch, the thwarted history of American radical sentiment reveals the incomparable cooptative power of American ideology. American ideology refutes and absorbs subversive cultural energies, "harness[ing] discontent to the social enterprise . . . by *drawing out* protest, by actively encouraging the contrast between utopia and the status quo." In America, then, the rhetoric of discontent is merely that, a rhetoric that conserves rather than challenges existing political arrangements. And classic

---

[6] Carolyn Porter elaborates this list in *Seeing and Being* (Middletown, Conn.: Wesleyan University Press, 1981), xiii.

[7] *The American Jeremiad* (Madison: University of Wisconsin Press, 1978), especially ch. 8.

American literature provides a central example of this rhetoric at work.

Bercovitch's interpretation is based on the assumption that American writers were incapable of a "historicist relativistic perspective." They could not envision their own society in relation to other possible forms of social organization. "What our major writers could not conceive," he writes, "was that the United States was neither utopia at best nor dystopia at worst . . . that in *principle* no less than in practice the American Way was neither providential nor natural but one of many possible forms of society."[8] But it is precisely their vision of the *boundaries* of political perception in America that registers the radicalism of our classic writers. As I shall demonstrate using Hawthorne, James, and Dreiser, American writers launch their most penetrating social critiques through their depictions of what American ideology reveals and conceals.[9]

[8] "The Problem of Ideology in American Literary History," *Critical Inquiry* 12 (Summer 1986): 644, 646. However much Bercovitch's analysis of a developing rhetorical vision in American writings has been questioned by those dissatisfied with his self-admitted tendency to "simplify social and economic conflict, psychic tensions, and regional disparities," his claims for an especially powerful middle-class hegemony in American society are incontrovertible. See *The American Jeremiad*, especially pp. xii-xiii, and passim. Though I am in agreement with Bercovitch's overall description of "an increasingly pervasive middle-class hegemony" in America, I think it also crucial to recognize the extent to which nineteenth-century American novels themselves serve commentary on the actual limits to this consensus. Therefore, I am less convinced by Myra Jehlen's consensus analysis of the American middle-class novel. Her argument that American literature exemplifies its society's rejection of what Raymond Williams calls "oppositional" or "alternative" cultural formations as inimical to "the very process of national emergence" seems to me unsupported by the recurrence of such forms in works by Hawthorne, Melville, and others. In my view, American literature reveals the hegemony of the "dominant" middle-class culture to be much less complete than Jehlen allows. "New World Epics: The Novel and the Middle Class in America," *Salmagundi* 36 (Winter 1977): 51–52.

[9] Anthony Giddens's distinction between "conflict consciousness" and "revolutionary consciousness" helps to pinpoint the difference between Bercovitch's reading of American writers and my own. He would, I think, associate American writers with what Giddens terms a "conflict consciousness," which is class consciousness formed in opposition to the interests of other classes, a vision that basically affirms the overall organization of society as a dynamic balance of oppos-

CHAPTER ONE

Other critical studies appearing in the past decade have also taken significant steps toward reassessing the political dimensions of nineteenth-century American literature. Employing Georg Lukács's theory of reification, Carolyn Porter (in *Seeing and Being*) reconstructs the implicit social commentary in writings by Emerson, Adams, James, and Faulkner. Her combined use of narratological and cultural-historical analysis leads to a more radical appraisal of the political tenor of American works. Rather than fleeing their contemporary worlds through their art, Porter argues, American writers were confronting the most profound social challenges of their times.[10] Her broader methodology shows that American writers were far more engaged with society and politics than is usually recognized.

But the radical transcendent line of interpretation has also reemerged in deconstructionist readings such as John Carlos Rowe's

---

ing interests. I align these writers with "revolutionary consciousness," which involves "a recognition of the possibility of an overall reorganization in the institutional mediation of power" (113). The most important impetus to revolutionary consciousness is the awareness of the *relativity* of experience within a given system of production. This awareness of relativity within the system leads to the envisionment of alternative systems of social organization. This point is especially pertinent to my Dreiser chapter, where I argue for the characters' *differential* experiences of determinism. Anthony Giddens, *The Class Structure of the Advanced Societies* (London: Hutchinson, 1973), 112–17.

[10] Prior to Porter, one of the few systematic efforts to rehistoricize American literature was made by Harry Henderson in *Versions of the Past* (New York: Oxford University Press, 1974). Distinguishing between a "progressive" conception of "history as . . . measurable change on an absolute scale," and a "holist" conception characterized by "a relativistic view of time-bound man, and by a belief that historical change is not measurable except *in terms of the period under consideration*," Henderson aims to reveal "the self-awareness and complexity of the historical imagination of American writers" (14, xviii). The trouble is that Henderson confines his study to works that explicitly highlight history. By focusing on self-proclaimed historical novels such as *Satanstoe* or *The Scarlet Letter*, or those which use actual historical incidents, Henderson perpetuates the chasm between the occasional American work that includes history and the more characteristic work concerned with larger philosophical ideas. Moreover, the possibility that the novelistic aesthetic might be absorbing contemporary historiographic concerns is never broached.

8

Through the Custom House: Nineteenth-Century Fiction and Modern Theory, which aligns major nineteenth-century authors, including Poe, Thoreau, Hawthorne, Melville, James, and Twain, with like-minded theorists, such as Freud, Heidegger, Sartre, Derrida, and Nietzsche.[11] American works, Rowe asserts, subversively resist the limiting conventions of social discourse, as evidenced by their repeated invocations of the arbitrary signifier. By unraveling the "various repressions at work in different cultural codes," the arbitrary signifier violates efforts by political authorities to reduce meaning to any one system of thought. Though Rowe acknowledges the social and political play of literary signification, however, his readings are uniformly ahistorical. His claims for the eternal subversiveness of great literature lead him to overlook the particular historical concerns of his examples.

Rowe's argument for the radicalism of American literature is undermined by his universalist categories. What is convincing about Rowe's readings is their sensitivity to the workings of language. And the continuing power of deconstructive studies like his seems to lie in the failure of cultural-historical interpretations to provide a similarly sophisticated grasp of how literary narratives work. Too often content with merely placing texts within some readily detachable historical milieu, cultural-historical critics reduce texts to reflections of historical reality.[12]

Our sense of the historical contexts from which literary works emerge needs refining. On the one hand, we must recognize that history itself is primarily accessible through other texts. This recognition complicates the critical process since the interpreter must not only judge the relation between the literary work and its historical milieu, but must also direct a critical eye toward the reconstructions of that milieu available in works by historians and social scientists. On the other hand, such skepticism toward historical

---

[11] *Through the Custom House: Nineteenth-Century Fiction and Modern Theory* (Baltimore: Johns Hopkins University Press, 1982).

[12] On this point, see Raymond Williams, *Marxism and Literature* (New York: Oxford University Press, 1981), 21 and passim.

information confers a greater authority upon the literary work. It frees us to listen to what literature itself has to tell us about the past, and about ways of recovering it. A greater skepticism toward history books may allow us to view literature as a more compelling representation of the past. This is especially true for novels, which, more self-consciously than any other literary form, are concerned with human experience in society over time.

Refining our conceptions of history's accessibility will enlarge our sense of the complex representations of history contained in American novels. History can be seen not as an external background to be reconstructed as some alienated source material, but as reproduced within the narrative aesthetic. History is an integral part of the narrative process, recomposed as the world of the novel. Far from being a monolithic body of knowledge to be applied to any set of works from a commonly defined "period," history is particular to the novelistic source that gives it life.[13]

In addition to the insights to be found in contemporary historiography, there remains the task of bridging historical and political methods with those of narrative theory. The combined use of these methods should expose what I term the "political aesthetic"

---

[13] Here we must remind ourselves of Hayden White's prescient remarks in *Tropics of Discourse* (Baltimore: Johns Hopkins University Press, 1978). White observes that "the presumed concreteness and accessibility of historical milieux, these contexts of the texts that literary scholars study, are themselves products of the fictive capability of the historians who have studied these contexts" (89). Two important recent discussions by historians on the theoretical dimensions of historical analysis are Dominick LaCapra's *Rethinking Intellectual History* (Ithaca: Cornell University Press, 1982), and Michael Kammen's edited collection, *The Past Before Us* (Ithaca: Cornell University Press, 1985); see especially essays by Kammen, 19–46, and Robert Darnton, 327–349. Also pertinent is Michel Foucault's essay, "Nietzsche, Genealogy, and History," where he distinguishes between "the surreptitious practice of historians, their pretension to examine things furthest from themselves, the grovelling manner in which they approach this promising distance," and "an effective" historical sense that is "explicit in its perspective and acknowledges its system of injustice." *Language, Counter-Memory, Practice: Selected Essays and Interviews*, trans. Donald F. Bouchard and Sherry Simon (Ithaca: Cornell University Press, 1977), 156–57.

of American novels.[14] Indeed, the nineteenth-century novel's well-known obsession with temporal limits might well be seen as the aesthetic reproduction of prevailing fears of an ungovernable historical reality. With specific reference to American novels, the tensions aroused by the novel's temporal progress offer dramatic registers of the fears of historical engagement shared by fictional personae and readers. At this point, the tentative answer to the question posed as the headnote to this section—are American novels resistant to the claims of some historical reality?—is that we need to expand our view of how literary texts both incorporate and represent history. Let me be clear here about my argument. I am suggesting that an important historical aspect of American novels is their meta-historical dimension. Demonstrations of how American novels belie or evade historical reality offer only half the picture. Nineteenth-century American novels are most fully recognized as participants in a cultural dialogue on how history should be viewed and written. As my survey of nineteenth- and early-twentieth-century historiography in Chapter Two reveals, American novels are significantly illuminated by attention to contem-

[14] But our selections from among the vast array of theories on history and narration must be carefully made, for certain theorists, such as Bakhtin, Lukács, Williams, the early Barthes, and Jameson, lend themselves more readily to analyses centrally concerned with the problem of ideology.

One feature of the novel that has concerned theorists is the sense of urgency generated by its circumscribed temporality. In *The Theory of the Novel*, for example, Georg Lukács argues that the novel's "entire inner action . . . is nothing but a struggle against the power of time." Many narratologists have analyzed ways in which the novel resists ending. Lukács, *The Theory of the Novel*, trans. Anna Bostock (Cambridge, Mass.: MIT Press, 1971), 122. Also see W.J.T. Mitchell, ed., *On Narrative* (Chicago: University of Chicago Press, 1981), especially the essays by Le Guin, Ricoeur, and White; and Walter Benjamin, *Illuminations*, ed. Hannah Arendt, trans. Harry Zohn (New York: Schocken Books, 1969), 101.

Gerard Genette's comprehensive effort to articulate the signposts of narrative temporality allows for greater recognition of the power of time in narratives. His categories provide a narratological basis for viewing reading as a temporally coercive activity with possible historical and political ramifications. See also Peter Brooks, *Reading for the Plot* (New York: Knopf, 1984), 20 and passim.

porary historiographic debates. Products of a culture consumed with questions about reconstructing the past, American novels offer intricate portraits of the relationships of their characters and narrators to history.[15]

It has often been observed that the social texture of classic American novels is fundamentally different from that of contemporaneous French or English novels. Yet the ritual gesture of apology for the "comparative meagreness" of American novels has obscured an important dynamic in their portrayals of "social reality." Far from ignoring history and society, American novelists dramatize their subjects' ambivalence toward social and historical contingency. And their works offer subtle and complex arguments for the inescapability of social and historical engagement. However often individuals, or whole communities, aspire to the repression of certain pressing historical details, time and again in American novels these facts reassert themselves. The locus for such historical dynamics is found in portrayals of individual and collective narrations of history. The novels by Hawthorne, James, and Dreiser that I examine depict both the pressures of social and political entanglements, and the impulses of characters and narrators

[15] Widespread interest in history is found in previous centuries. But the obsession with historical knowledge, particularly as a malleable and potentially exploitable body of facts to be investigated, was in great part a project conceived by the nineteenth century. This issue will be further elaborated in Chapter Two. The best general sources for a beginning look at the rise of the nineteenth-century historical imagination are Hayden White, *Metahistory* (Baltimore: Johns Hopkins University Press, 1973); and Lionel Gossman's essay, "History and Literature," in *The Writing of History*, ed. Robert Canary and Henry Kozicki (Madison: University of Wisconsin Press, 1978). For the nineteenth-century European connection, see Hans Aarsleff, "Scholarship and Ideology: Joseph Bedier's Critique of Romantic Medievalism," in Jerome McGann's *Historical Studies and Literary Criticism* (Madison: University of Wisconsin Press, 1985), 93–113; Nicola Chiarmonte, *The Paradox of History* (Philadelphia: University of Pennsylvania Press, reprint 1985); and the fascinating overview of recent work on history and memory with directions for future points of exploration by Richard Terdiman, "Deconstructing Memory," *Diacritics* (Winter 1985): 13–36. Nancy Struever explores Renaissance views of history in *The Language of History in the Renaissance* (Princeton: Princeton University Press, 1970).

to transcend those pressures by subsuming them in story. The repetitive, mythical histories woven in these novels serve as means of translating historical experiences into eternal terms. These novels expose a tension between an eternalized conception of time as essentially static and immune to human intervention, and a specific conception of history as a process of change effected by individual and collective agents.

The House of the Seven Gables, The Bostonians, The Wings of the Dove, and *An American Tragedy* can be seen as meditations on the psychological, social, and political effects of viewing specific historical problems as questions on the philosophy of time. The characters and narrators of these works pay homage to time's unchallengeable powers. But their laments are always framed within the structures of specific historical worlds. Within each novel, various narrative strategies (repetitions of phrases or events, ominous doublings of characters or of entire narrative sequences) expose this discourse of temporality as a rhetoric that belies the characters' circumstances as well as their responsibility for action. In these works then, denials of the immediacy of time become evasions of social and political concerns. And history itself is the inert material, the pull of necessity, that resists the characters' coherent designs.[16]

My readings attempt to build upon a tension that pervades con-

[16] In *The Political Unconscious*, Fredric Jameson offers a model useful for exploring the presence of history in nineteenth- and twentieth-century novels. Of particular interest is his description of modernist impulses to "manage" or "defuse" the historical elements issuing from the past, present, and future claims of time's linear progression. I too invoke a conception of "linear" history in my study, and though I employ the term with some hesitation, I concur with Jameson that an essential distinction must be made between a synchronic vision of history that emphasizes a pattern of developments within a specifically designated period, and a diachronic vision that views history "in some 'linear' way as the succession of . . . periods, stages, or moments." *The Political Unconscious* (Ithaca: Cornell University Press, 1981), 28. History may come to us only in the form of "prior textualizations" (35), but this is not to say that it is without a point of reference, nor to minimize the extent to which it is experienced, by characters, narrators, authors, and readers alike, as necessity. The designation of a "political unconscious" identifies the medium through which "the repressed and buried reality" of a "fundamental history . . . comes to vital articulation in narrative form" (20).

temporary literary theory and Marxist theory as well by developing analytical strategies that are at once alert to the requirements
of larger political concerns—emphasizing a collective dynamic—
and sensitive to the psychological terms embedded in nineteenth-
century cultural forms, and in our own post-Freudian analytical
climate. These issues are related to a major conundrum in contemporary theory, the problem of the individual subject.

Fredric Jameson is sensitive to this tension between a view of
history as a process of domination by specifically defined social
groups, and a view that emphasizes the actions of individual subjects. In his words, "the notion of 'class consciousness,' as it is central in a certain Marxist tradition, rests on an unrigorous and figurative assimilation of the consciousness of the individual subject
to the dynamics of groups." He goes on to argue the necessity of a
"whole new logic of collective dynamics, with categories that escape the taint of some mere application of terms drawn from individual experience (in that sense, even the concept of praxis remains
a suspect one)."[17]

This study does not meet the call for "a whole new logic of collective dynamics." Rather, I attempt to demonstrate how the fictional representation of individual experience can be translated
into a view of the collectivity that is not merely an enlargement of
individual experience. The recognition of the inseparability of
psychological and political factors in our literary analyses should
be distinguished from an oversimplified valuation of the categories
of individual psychology.

The problem remains that Marxist hermeneutical practice has
yet to offer an adequate method for squaring the focus on subjective experience inherited from the nineteenth century with its own
commitment to a praxis that emphasizes the collectivity. A cate-
gorical dismissal of the idea of individuality as "bourgeois" is
clearly inadequate. Jameson observes of history itself that "we
may be sure that its alienating necessities will not forget us, how-

[17] *The Political Unconscious*, 294–95.

ever much we might prefer to ignore them,"[18] an observation that seems to apply as well to the category of the subject, a similarly alien territory to Marxist practitioners. Most would admit the impossibility of a Marxian hermeneutic that proceeds without some notion of the subject, and apart from the tenuous terminologies of religion, or its modern equivalent, psychology. While we should bear in mind that notions of character are historically determinate and thus necessitate self-conscious analytical reflection, they are also potentially productive loci for our interpretive strategies. Moreover, if we are to be honest about our own historical conditioning, as well as sensitive to the texts we study, such categories are unavoidable.

Within our readings, these persistent psychological categories are most accurately regarded as *problematic* designations, acknowledged registers of the aspirations of characters and narrators. But by analyzing separate acts of domination and exploitation, my study shows how the growing entrenchment of the American capitalist system infiltrates every aspect of individual psychology. This is not a valorization of coherent selves, but an effort to reflect upon the struggles of the individual mind with the inevitability of its own fragmentation: to locate the impact of prevailing systems of domination where it is most fused. Novels provide an opportunity for witnessing in distilled form, through the fictional experiences of their subjects, the *actualities* of larger social and political processes.

The problems of textual reflexivity and individual subjectivity highlighted by Marxist theorists are of special importance to American novels. By elevating isolated figures such as Natty Bumpo, Ahab, and Hester Prynne, American novels appear to empower their characters beyond the constraints of civilization and the wilderness. And just as American novels have been seen to support an ideology of individualism, they have also been taken, as our opening survey shows, as particularly resistant to history,

[18] Ibid., 102.

in both its philosophical and its contextual forms. The political implications of such assumptions about American novels will be elaborated throughout my readings. Here it is essential to explain my choice of textual examples.

First, the range of my examples over a period of American history that included the rise of consumer capitalism and of the American novel allows me to see the convergence of key political and economic, as well as literary, developments. Second, it may occur to some that my selections seem only tangentially concerned with the problem of history, that other works by American authors appear much more readily engaged with the subject of historical knowledge. Hawthorne's *Seven Gables* is often seen as less historically serious than *The Scarlet Letter*. James's works are found to exemplify their author's own willed evasions of history. And Dreiser is regarded as a writer so unreflectively bound to the power of history as to nullify any historical interest. Yet it is precisely my argument that the works I have chosen, in their at once elusive and complex dramatizations of attitudes toward temporality and history, point to a distinctive, one might say especially anxious, cultural relationship to history.[19]

Finally, these works may also seem slightly unorthodox in their conception of "the hero," an issue that requires some elaboration. *The House of the Seven Gables*, with its array of valetudinarians, and *The Bostonians*, with its aggressively satirized reformers, seem to preclude from the outset any idealizing tendencies. Compared to *The Scarlet Letter*, its predecessor in the Hawthorne canon, or *The Blithedale Romance*, its successor, *Seven Gables* is noticeably lacking in strong-willed rebels. Its characters are for the most part timorous and vacillating, and even the rebelliousness of the novel's

[19] Jameson has observed that "a case could be made for the peculiar disappearance of the American past in general, which comes before us in unreal costumes and by way of the spurious images of nostalgia art. . . . This has something to do with the triumphant and systematic way in which the American past, and most particularly its great radical traditions, have been stamped out in almost every generation." See "Interview with Fredric Jameson," *Diacritics* (Fall 1982): 74.

ostensible rebel, Holgrave, takes a crucially equivocal form. Like the histories they narrate, and the narrow dreams they pursue, the personages of this novel are veritable fragments, whose depictions throw into question the very possibility of an integrated personality. The same may be said for the characters of *The Bostonians*. From the novel's opening, we know that we are in a different Jamesian universe from that which spawned the revered likes of Isabel Archer, or the strongly ambivalent Hyacinth Robinson. Figures such as Basil Ransom and Olive Chancellor are portrayed largely from the outside, obviating the usual Jamesian penetration into fine, discriminating minds. We see into these characters infrequently, and then our view is hampered by the biting sarcasm of the novel's narrator.

Unlike *The Bostonians*, *The Wings of the Dove* features characters capable of sustained reflection on their own mortal conditions. Apprised of her tragic destiny from her first appearance, the novel's doomed heroine appears to exemplify the possibilities of transcending loss and contingency through the sheer powers of imagination. Yet the ideals of heroism are undermined in the novel's view of how Milly's illness is manipulated by her community. Through this view, the novel provides a historically precise critique of nineteenth-century romanticizations of suffering and death. By showing how the characters themselves stage and exploit Milly's illness as a dramatic event, with her life and death becoming the province of a kind of aesthetic entrepreneurialism, the novel reveals how deadly an untempered and acquisitive aestheticism can be. This in turn aligns maneuverings for money and power in the novel's society with the exploitative potential of storytelling itself.

An American Tragedy provides the most pronounced case of the tension between romantic notions of the individual and a process of social fragmentation that radically undermines it. One of the novel's most important scenes pictures its main character's struggle to confirm or retrieve the remains of the tenuous romantic self of his childhood. Clyde's groping homage to a romantically constituted self near the novel's end involves an effort to replace the "miscellaneous threads of cloth" that have come metonymically to represent him. Yet the novel itself insists that his action is futile, that the experience of American society can only generate fragmentation.

All of these novels portray the decentering of the romantic subject in the expanding consumer-capitalist world of mid-nineteenth- to early-twentieth-century America. But the decentering process in these novels is more complicated and ambivalent than most current theories on the American novel would allow. For it seems as misguided to believe that any novelist could hope to escape the imprint of historical developments in his society as to argue that a writer like James, for example, was entirely apprised of the historical possibilities afforded by his society and how he might in turn reshape them. I am questioning, in other words, critical views that automatically assume that James's works register his aspiration to evade the historical demands of his contemporary world.

It may by now be apparent that my arguments rest on some degree of textual reflexivity.[20] I am not suggesting here that all literary narratives inevitably challenge or subvert existing social orders, including those constructed within their own bounds. It

---

[20] A good example of this reflexivity occurs in the Woody Allen movie, *Hannah and Her Sisters*. In one scene, the Woody Allen character returns to his apartment carrying the symbols of American Christianity in a grocery bag. The camera dwells on the jar of Hellman's mayonnaise and loaf of Wonder Bread after he sets them on the table. It is a moment in which the viewer perhaps feels some discomfort; for so obvious are these packaged emblems of White American culture that the movie reaches the point of parodying its character's "alienated Jewish" assumptions. The symbols seem mildly inappropriate since the faith the character wishes to embrace is Catholicism—a set of cultures not fully in sympathy with these American products. The imprecision suggests that to this "Jew," all "Christians" are alike. The fine line between laughing with the character and laughing cynically at him indicates a tension that pervades the film. Is the film a self-congratulatory romance for a young, ethnically savvy, professional, American elite, or is it a critique of this growing class and its aspirations? I would argue it is both: that the film both indulges and self-consciously criticizes the values of a new urban elite.

would be mistaken to assume that we can so easily penetrate the parameters of our own academic discussions to see into works that "subversively" undermine them. Yet the examples of my study afford particularly acute instances of an American narrative genius for suppressing historical facts. By illuminating a cultural tendency to evade historical and political conflict, these American novels provide a reflexive vision of the political stakes involved in the act of narration. They reveal how literary narratives are implicated in the power struggles of the societies that produce them. These struggles are figured in the works themselves, both as narrative strategies and as social phenomena. These novels, and by implication a wider range of American literary works than we might have imagined, reveal through patient, close analysis, significant patterns of sustained dialectical reflection upon the ways in which literary narratives incorporate historically pressing issues. Such patterns are of considerable importance, not only in modifying earlier predominant views of American literature, but also in challenging recent post-structuralist methods whose conclusions tend to obviate connections between literature and the society in which it is produced. I might add that they also call into question certain new historicist readings that treat American authors as unregenerate aspirants to a "world elsewhere."

But the real test for any historical narrative may be, as Hayden White poses it, "whether our transportation into this imagined world returns us to our own ready to do *political* battle for *its* transformation or rather deepens our alienation by adding the sadness of 'what might have been' to its dispiriting effects."[21] I distinguish between types of narratives that betray and facilitate a deep consciousness of characters' historical circumstances and those which perpetuate history's refusal or denial. Within the terms of my explorations, "consciousness" will be defined simply as the ability to act, whether this action leads to direct political involvement or takes the form of narrative assertion. While these two types of ac-

[21] See Hayden White, "Getting Out of History," *Diacritics* (Fall 1982): 6.

tion are hardly identical, it is important that we acknowledge not only literature's power to prepare the groundwork for political action, but also that political action may take forms other than the most obvious ones. It is possible, I shall argue, to see representation itself as a form of political engagement.

Each of my examples, *The House of the Seven Gables* (1851), *The Bostonians* (1886), *The Wings of the Dove* (1902), and *An American Tragedy* (1925), betrays the ambivalence toward historical engagement that typifies the novel in an era of capitalist expansion.[22] And the portrayed resistance to historical experience contained in these works serves to powerfully engage the whole problem of history's evasion. The denial of history, in other words, is revealed to be a pivotal political as well as psychological strategy of the characters and narrators who inhabit these novelistic societies. Indeed, these exposures of the tactical nature of history's evasion serve as implicit critiques of twentieth-century critical efforts to dehistoricize classic American literature.

From the characters' wholesale denial of the past at the close of *The House of the Seven Gables*, through the timeless agrarian myth of Basil Ransom in *The Bostonians*, to the relentless design of *An American Tragedy* (in which the world's possibilities at the novel's close monotonously replicate those at its beginning), American novels picture efforts by characters and narrators to deny historical

---

[22] The repression of history at the end of *Seven Gables* typifies Jameson's conception of literary modernism, whose roots are found in mid-nineteenth-century romance. Jameson's generic chronology encompasses the parallel developments of mercantile capitalism and middle-class ideology. The class antagonisms and contradictions of capitalist social life are first apprehended (Romanticism), then affirmed as the referent of an objectively envisioned world (Realism), and finally systematically repressed or sublimated through a fusion of metaphysics and melodrama (Naturalism). A similar attempt to locate the middle-class basis for blindness to historical change is made by Lukács. The middle-class aspect betrays "a motionless gaze, in a moment of time suspended." The middle class is unaware "of capitalism as an historical phenomenon, as being itself the result of historical forces, as having within itself also the possibility of change. . . . The ultimate question of purpose and origin" is to them inaccessible. See Jameson's discussion in *Marxism and Form* (Princeton: Princeton University Press, 1971), 185–86.

change, and their own capacity for action in altering their societies. And through these dramatizations, Hawthorne, James, and
Dreiser reveal a partial immunity to the ahistorical delusions that,
to greater and lesser degrees, govern their fictional subjects, a
point that will be taken up in this chapter's final section. For my
purposes, it is most essential to recognize how these novels register
the ideological underpinnings of all perceptions of time and history. The resistance to confronting one's historical circumstances
is always ultimately aligned with efforts to defuse the psychological and political conflicts inherent in those circumstances.

The Politics of Time-Telling and Historical Narration

The belief that our perceptions of time and formulations of historical knowledge are always bound by ideology is implicit in critical
theories that ascribe a particularity to middle-class attitudes toward time and history. Prominent among these is Roland
Barthes's specification of the grammatical underpinnings of a middle-class resistance to history. Barthes reveals how the most local
and precise manipulations of people's perceptions of time can deflate their feelings of control over the political processes that govern their lives. Barthes's naturalized myths follow from a particular view of historical causation, which minimizes the role of
human agency.[23] It is consonant with Raymond Williams's idea of

[23] Barthes's image of the lion in the Latin grammar, with the timeless, not to
mention tautological, justification of his reign—"because my name is lion" (101)—
provides a striking example of myth's powers of erasure. Suggesting the "abnormal
regression from meaning to form" (103), the lion as mythic signifier lacks the historical fullness it formerly possessed as a linguistic sign. In "a purely linguistic system," the lion has a history, existing within "a whole system of values" (103). As a
mythic requisition, the lion, like the displaced lion in the Pyncheon map of New
England, is without a historically specific and appropriate context. "There is no
doubt if we consulted a *real* lion," Barthes observes, "he would maintain that the
grammar example is a *strongly* depoliticized state, he would qualify as fully *political*
the jurisprudence which leads him to claim a prey because he is the strongest, unless we deal with a *bourgeois* lion who would not fail to mythify his strength by giving it the form of a duty." "Myth Today," in *A Barthes Reader*, 101–103, 133–34.

"abstract determinism," wherein "some power (God or Nature or History) controls or decides the outcome of an action or process beyond or irrespective of the will or desires of its agents." To this view, Williams opposes an "inherent determinism," wherein determination follows from knowable "conditions" or "laws," from "precise knowledge of the inherent characteristics of a process and its components." While human beings may be limited by ideological and circumstantial factors, still, historical events are perceived as the result of visible causes and subject to human intervention. Thus, determination involves an acknowledgment of limitation rather than an ironclad acceptance of human entrapment.[24]

The American novels of my study offer implicit critiques of the types of abstract determinism defined by Barthes and Williams. Within these works, the submergence of historical process is consistently identified with acts of domination, or with efforts to deny the human engagement in social arrangements. In the chapters that follow, this tendency will be discussed by way of examples such as the avoidance of their mercenary activities by Hepzibah Pyncheon and the narrator of *The House of the Seven Gables*, the evasions of "the real" by characters in *The Bostonians*, the guilt of complicity motivating the transcendent aspirations of Merton Densher in *The Wings of the Dove*, and the echoing denials of responsibility that form the sinister chorus of Dreiser's *An American Tragedy*.

Each work contains its own undermining of efforts to evade history: consider the irritating repetitions of *Seven Gables*'s shopbell, the ironic undertones of James's narratives, and the sardonic echoes that ridicule the deterministic structure of *An American Tragedy*. But the strongest critiques occur in scenes where the characters are directly confronted with their immersion in history. The protagonist of *An American Tragedy*, for example, is notoriously insensible of his relationship to history. Clyde Griffiths inhabits a timeless void as he pursues the rags-to-riches plot of his American success myth. Through much of the novel, the narrator

[24] Williams, *Marxism and Literature*, 84.

mocks Clyde's benightedness, his lack of historical insight. And the reader bears witness to Clyde's desperate vacillations between his American Dream on the one hand, and his self-incriminating actions on the other. But at one point, Clyde is made to confront the bonds of historical time. At Sondra Finchley's summer home, following Roberta's drowning, Clyde recalls the series of actions that comprise the history of that grim day. "Yet tying up in a single bundle, in order to have them laundered, other odds and ends he had worn that day. And, as he did so, terribly, sickeningly conscious of the mystery and drama as well as the pathos of his life— all he had contracted since his arrival in the east, how little he had in his youth. How little he had now, really."[25]

In a society where the self is defined by material trappings and possessions, Clyde has progressed from youth to manhood unchanged: his lack of possessions signals a powerful sense of lost time never to be renewed, a sense that grows increasingly desperate as he nears death. Brought to confront what Henry James called the "ragbag of memory," Clyde achieves a painful awareness of his own participation in historical events. But this exceptional moment of Clyde contemplating the present with reference to the past signals the fleeting recognitions afforded by such backward glances.[26] For Clyde's contemplation of his past actions dissolves into a rhetorical revery on the nature of time. And it is noteworthy that Clyde evinces in his return to the present a still-passive view of his experience. Unable to accept responsibility as an actor in history, to sustain the notion of responsibility that historical consciousness portends, Clyde continues to waver between a sense of the pacifying powers of eternal time and a desire to accommodate his past actions.

[25] *An American Tragedy* (New York: Signet, 1964), 564.
[26] Self-recognition is a process that is fundamentally historical—a restoring or rethinking. The *OED* defines "recognition" as "the action of reviewing or revising" (2:2442). This suggests that there is no possibility for confronting the self, that the self only exists in relation: reshaped in lieu of a fleeting past, or perhaps hopefully imagined in relation to an elusive future.

In contrast, through much of *The Bostonians* Olive Chancellor maintains an unrelenting vigilance over the powers of time, seeking to control her experience by anticipating every possible event in her life and by rewriting history. A late scene, however, pictures Olive confronting a past reality over which she has no control, re-experiencing its most bitter and profound messages. Crossing the beach at Marmion, Olive "relives" her past life with Verena and recognizes the real terms of their relationship. This tortuous vision brings with it an awareness of her own deep love for Verena, a love that goes beyond her hope of possessing Verena but is built upon the realization of her loss. Forced to acknowledge her connection to a past made of emotions that cannot be transcended, Olive comes to accept her historical experience. Olive's vision here can be seen as enabling her rush onto the stage at the novel's end. This need not be viewed as a self-destructive act. Formerly a character defined by her silence, basking vicariously in the eloquence of her pupil, Olive here replaces Verena at the rostrum. Though we do not hear her speak—the last we know of Olive, she is standing before a restless but hushed audience—this final action may be regarded as an assertion of her powers for political action in the novel's society.

To recall Hayden White's words, Olive has returned to the world "ready to do political battle."[27] Her reaction to a confrontation with her past seems less muddled than Clyde Griffiths's response. In James's works, historical consciousness often appears to further present action in a suggestion that the powers of imagination indeed have material consequences. Yet this leads us to the question of how precisely such historical recognitions are seen to function in the worlds of Hawthorne, James, and Dreiser.

Can narrative serve to foster a historical consciousness that leads to political action? Do the narrative histories of characters confer a sense of historical experience as a plane to be altered by human intervention, or do they instead contribute to a sense of the irrevers-

[27] From Hayden White, "Getting Out of History," 6.

ible powers of time? Most narrative theorists who are committed to ideological analysis resist such claims. Yet the issue of a text's ideological limits is complicated by the fact that an awareness of the double role of artistic narratives is built into each of my novelistic examples. This knowledge is partly the province of narrative personae who periodically betray a consciousness of their own ideological entrapment. In the duplicitous position of standing guard against the historical evasions of their characters while engaging wholeheartedly in their own, the narrative voices of Hawthorne, James, and Dreiser are reminiscent of Walter Benjamin's "angel of history," that temporally twisted figure whose "faith is turned toward the past" while a "storm irresistibly propels him into the future to which his back is turned. . . . This storm is what we call progress."[28] If the narrator figures I examine can be said to possess "personalities," they would be personalities founded in contradiction. These narrators are spectres, haunted equally as servants to the past and as harbingers of the future, anticipating their own deaths at the ends of their narratives. Their marginality is mirrored in their relation to ideology, as they point both into and out of their ideological binds.

The question of how history is repressed or defused but always in some way mediated through the processes of historical narration is central to this study, and it informs the organization of individual readings. I adopt a three-stage dialectical model in moving from analyses of history as seen from characters' perspectives, to the narrators' perspectives, and finally, to history as it is marginalized in the political vision of a textual unconscious. This typifies the ambivalent movement toward and away from historical consciousness in the novels of my study.[29] My model seeks to ex-

---

[28] Benjamin, *Illuminations*, 257–58.

[29] Georg Lukács describes the virtues of a dialectical method in *History and Class Consciousness* (Cambridge, Mass.: MIT Press, 1971). By "dialectical," Lukács means that the members of a relation are seen as fundamentally interactive, continually changing in relation to one another. "All social phenomena," he writes, "change constantly in the course of their ceaseless dialectical interactions with each other. The intelligibility of objects develops in proportion as we grasp their function in

pose the various levels of historical consciousness in each novel, set against one another as parts of a dialogue on the nature of time and history. The simplest stage involves the characters' attitudes toward time and history, which frequently waver between a sense of time's eternal powers and the painful view of a history for which they are responsible. The more complex second stage records the narrator's quarrel with his characters' quests for transcendence, his subversion of their mythic histories through various ironic or unsettling devices. The final stage, an unconscious that is inaccessible to the characters and narrator, discloses both underlying political conflicts and a self-reflexive awareness of the text's own politics of narration. This third level unravels both the characters' myths and the narrator's ironic overturnings of them. It reveals what cannot be evaded by characters or narrators: the claims of social ties, and the sense of collective responsibility, which oppose their rhetorical obsessions with time. Nor can this history as necessity be *narrated* and thereby defused or managed. It persists as a threatening, uncontainable cause.

The extent to which historical narratives can themselves be seen to thwart or to encourage political action is illuminated by a textual example that will serve as the paradigm for issues analyzed in all of the works. Midway through *The House of the Seven Gables*, an entire chapter is devoted to the narration of a historical tale by its author, the novel's protagonist, Holgrave. Holgrave's "Alice Pyncheon" offers the fullest narrative version of the Maule-Pyncheon land dispute sketched out in the novel's opening chapter, and at various points by other characters. This tale-within-a-tale represents a moment where the control over narrative sequence is given over to a fictional presence other than the narrator. It is not accidental that this conferral of singular narrative authority upon a character evokes a historical tale whose plot involves a power struggle between American "aristocrats" and "plebeians." The lit-

---

the totality to which they belong. This is why only the dialectical conception of totality can enable us to understand *reality* as a social process" (13).

eralization of narrative power through its exchange in "Alice Pyncheon" mirrors the larger power struggle between upper and lower class within the novel itself.

Told to a Pyncheon descendant by the offspring of a Maule, the storytelling process replicates the terms of the tale it recounts. The bewitchery exercised by Matthew Maule over Alice Pyncheon equals the narrative authority exercised by Holgrave over Phoebe; both contain the potential for seduction and exploitation. But Holgrave significantly resists the opportunity. This may suggest that Holgrave has learned from the past. Yet something more complicated is at stake in the tale's vivid conflation of narrative power and the potential for human domination. Holgrave's refusal to exploit Phoebe does not derive simply from his view of Matthew Maule. It seems to have a logic of its own built into the act of narration.

The story's ending is the key to the portrayal of narrative as a process that defuses its own quest for authority, and with it, an awareness of political conflict. Maule and Pyncheon may be bitter rivals for land and power, but by the narrative's end they unite in grief over the mystifying powers of nature. Maule can only regret his momentary sway over the Pyncheons; he has proven himself too "rude" to rule in the novel's world. Joining in the communal mourning for Alice Pyncheon, he bemoans his former actions. Thus, the picture of class antagonism is emptied out. All are united in sorrow against that common human enemy, death, as political polarization is replaced by natural harmony.[30]

The fact that a narrative repression of social conflict is actually depicted in Holgrave's tale suggests a reflexivity in the larger nar-

[30] My argument differs from Walter Michaels's view that there is no particular class division apparent in the story or in the larger narrative, but instead, "a conflict between two different modes of economic activity" ("Romance and Real Estate in *The House of the Seven Gables*," *Raritan* 2 [1983]: 69). I will not pursue the point here (it is the subject of Chapter Three), except to say that the signs of profound class antagonism, though often cloaked, are readily evident throughout the novel, and particularly in the tale of "Alice Pyncheon." The question of its reality is precisely what both narratives beg. Michaels's provocative reading is explored more fully below.

rative toward its own harmonizing and conciliatory impulses. *Seven Gables* offers an extended series of narrative levels. First, we have Holgrave as storyteller, a narrator who first highlights and then subsumes the political conflicts that pervade his fictional society. At the next level, we locate the novel's narrator, an ambivalent figure who often emphasizes the class antagonisms at large in the New England town of his setting, but equally often retreats into a perspective more eternal than historical. Whether read as harmonic or ironic, the novel's ending in its merging of aristocratic and consumeristic fantasy seems an undeniable evasion of the historical contingencies of its setting—a nineteenth-century American town in the era of capitalist expansion. From the narrator's perspective, the ending seems a retreat from the deepest problems raised by his narration. Finally, we consider some critical reconstruction of Hawthorne himself, which, whatever the biases of the critic, is always lurking somewhere within his procedural assumptions. The Hawthorne of *Seven Gables* seems convinced that narrative often functions to assuage or to repress apprehensions of social conflict. The question is, does his novel by this very portrayal point a way out of the deluded self-consciousness afforded by historical narration? I believe this question can be profitably explored, though perhaps not answered, by examining the author's role in his text's politics of narrativity. For it is my claim that theories about the political tenor of American narratives invariably come to focus around attempts to define the relationship of the author to his text.

The Place of the Author in the Politics of Narrativity

It seems inevitable that every critical reading, no matter how resistant to the problem of authorial personality, contains a working notion of the author's ideological views. Recent theoretical debates have been much concerned with efforts to articulate or eradicate the author's role in establishing the possible meanings of his work. E. D. Hirsch and Michel Foucault are helpful in this respect since they have maintained clear and opposite positions in the debate over authorial intention.

Hirsch believes that an author's intended meaning is always recoverable, indeed, that it is the primary obligation of responsible analyses to ascertain an objectifiable authorial purpose.[31] Meaning, he maintains, does not exist apart from individual consciousnesses. Texts have a priori significances that are put there by their authors, who draw upon a finite set of literary conventions and historical referents in creating their works. For Hirsch, the interpreter's task is to specify the text's horizon through study of the author's life and other writings, as well as the linguistic conventions and cultural practices of his day. From this range of historical sources, the interpreter sketches out a limited range of meanings for the text, which he calls "the author's intention." A thorough immersion in autobiographical, biographical, and historical texts pertinent to the author's work should ensure against the imposition of modern assumptions on past works.

But Hirsch's method is itself subject to historical criteria. Can the critic leave his own historical disposition behind to embrace the objectively reclaimable world of the properly historicized author? Hirsch's commitment to the alleviation or erasure of the puzzling or mystifying claims of literary texts is consistent with his reliance upon the fixity of historical texts. Hirsch's underestimation of the critic's time-boundedness also overestimates the objectivity of historical understanding, which itself never escapes the dilemmas and prejudices of the working historian. The "imaginative Americans" of my study resist such efforts to seize the intended meanings of their works, and through them a vision of the author's personality.[32]

Michel Foucault, in contrast, subordinates the thinking subject

---

[31] In an essay entitled, "Meaning and Significance Reinterpreted," Hirsch has qualified and extended his theory. *Critical Inquiry* 11 (December 1984): 202–225. See also *Validity in Interpretation* (New Haven: Yale University Press, 1967).

[32] Hawthorne resists such efforts most emphatically, I think, and James, most self-consciously.

CHAPTER ONE

to larger structures of thought, to account for "the tyranny that language exercises over human consciousness."[33] In his essay, "What Is an Author?" Foucault focuses on the functional aspects of literary language, separating the individual who writes from the discourse he produces. Dismissing critical notions of "the man and his work," Foucault offers the concept of "the author function." Rather than a fixed presence, the author is a process that serves to "characterize the existence, circulation, and operation of certain discourses within a society." And far from autonomous, the author is "tied to the legal and institutional systems that circumscribe, determine, and articulate the realm of discourses; [the author] does not operate in a uniform manner in all discourses, at all times, and in any given culture." Rather than authorial identity and purpose, Foucault posits a "variety of egos . . . a series of subjective positions" held by any given class. Indeed, he argues that the need for an author-subject must itself be seen historically, and he points to an era when "discourse would circulate without any need for an author," when readers will finally know the truth of Beckett's phrase, "What matter who's speaking?"[34]

Foucault's arguments represent a necessary check on what has been nearly a century of Anglo-American reifications of the literary author, but it is, as Foucault observes, precisely our historical burden to be absorbed with the minds behind texts. Historically conditioned as we are, it is probably preferable to confront rather than to reject the terms of our obsession. Hugh Kenner ponders the dilemma of authorial presence in *The Pound Era*. "Flaubert," he writes, "had wanted the artist, lonely as God, to be somewhere outside his work, which is impossible: impossible because words are said by somebody; because—at the furthest remove from the intimacies of breath—a bicycle saddle and handlebars, even when no sculpturing hand molests their shapes, denote by their power

[33] Hayden White, "Structuralism and Popular Culture," *Journal of Popular Culture* 7 (Spring 1974): 769.
[34] Foucault, "What Is an Author?" in *Language, Counter-Memory, Practice*, 115, 124, 130–31.

to combine into a bull's head a possibility some human eye has seen. Art does not 'happen.' The vision that made it is part of it."[35] The more inspiration one derives from a work of art, Kenner implies, the more avidly one pursues its originating consciousness. And though Wayne Booth and more recent theorists have understood the authorial vision to be more than the voice that narrates, we still desire a grasp of some human consciousness behind the literary work.[36]

Although the conflation of author and narrator has been cautioned against by literary theorists, it has persisted as the implicit assumption of most novel criticism. This may be because we have not adequately explored the problem of authorial perspectives in novelistic works, particularly from the angle of a politics of narrativity. Though most sophisticated analysts would agree that the author is not the narrator, few have ventured to propose other ways of considering the author's elusive presence within the text.

At this point, it is worth taking a moment to explain why I find it necessary to hold on to some notion of the author's presence within the ideological tensions generated by the text. My effort to delineate a politicized authorial consciousness within the text follows from my interest in the ideological role that authorship itself has played and continues to play in the nineteenth century and in our current critical debates.[37] The authors of my study take a radical view of the notion of authorial consciousness. They are involved

---

[35] Kenner, *The Pound Era* (Los Angeles: University of California Press, 1971), 33.

[36] Booth, *The Rhetoric of Fiction* (Chicago: University of Chicago Press, 1961). Catherine Belsey joins the chorus against "the tyranny of the author" in her fine summary of recent developments in critical theory. See *Critical Practice* (New York: Methuen, 1983), 29 and passim. Yet there are other tyrannies to beware, including the tyranny of the reader and the tyranny of the critic. As Walter Davis has argued, it is necessary that all critics subject their methods to regular "deconstruction." Though some methods are decidedly "blinder" than others, a self-consciousness about the blinders imposed by one's own critical method seems an essential step in the direction of critical insights. An illuminating debate between Stanley Fish and Walter Davis appears in *Critical Inquiry* 4 (June 1984): 695–718.

[37] A place to begin in exploring this vast topic is Lawrence Lipking's *The Life of the Poet* (Chicago: University of Chicago Press, 1981).

in a critique of Romantic conceptions of subjectivity and selfhood that includes a critique of their own authorial roles. Their criticism of the possibility of individuality, the erosion or decentering of the bourgeois subject in an emerging capitalist society, led them to dispense with the idea of the omniscient authorial consciousness. Just as selfhood in their view is socially constructed and dependent, so is the author. Undermining the deepest assumptions we hold about singular authorial identity, they redefine the authorial consciousness as social and collective rather than personal and individual. I shall have more to say on this issue below. For now, I want to look at what is lost when an author's vision in his text is overly defined.

Most Hawthorne scholarship rests upon some idea, whether consciously or unconsciously held, of the author's personality, as revealed by the authorized narrator of his works. John Franzosa stresses the historical rationale for such personalizing tendencies: Hawthorne's works invite intimacy in fulfillment of "the shifting expectations of his contemporary readership."[38] But Michael Colacurcio has lamented critical propensities to forsake the books in Hawthorne's library for the persona in the library armchair. "We may need to look again," Colacurcio warns, "at all those 'gestures' which not only invite 'intimacy' but tempt the creation of a criticism based on 'purpose' as opposed to the evident design of achieved meaning."[39]

The need for a more text-centered approach to authorial politics as a means of opening up our explorations of the political perspectives of American novels can be seen most clearly by examining three key re-interpretations of works by Hawthorne and James. These analyses all share a focus on ideological issues, and significantly, for our purposes, all betray the difficulties that arise when unquestioned biographical assumptions about an author form the basis for the interpretation of his work.

[38] Franzosa, "A Psychoanalysis of Hawthorne's Style," *Genre* 14 (Fall 1981): 402.
[39] Colacurcio, "The Sense of an Author: The Familiar Life and Strange Imaginings of Nathaniel Hawthorne," *ESQ* 27 (Fall 1981): 131.

The subtext for Walter Michaels's essay "Romance and Real Estate in *The House of the Seven Gables*" is Hawthorne as patrician. According to Michaels, Hawthorne treats the Pyncheons' land claims "somewhat nervously,"[40] indicating his personal investment in a title "based on neither labor nor wealth and hence free from the risk of appropriation" (70). He therefore needs to articulate "his own defense of property" (69). With Hawthorne on the side of the Pyncheon aristocracy, the novel, instead of portraying a conflict of power or class, reflects its author's disdain for the speculators of his era who were undermining individuality and social stability. Michaels's Hawthorne is an aesthete who fears an increasingly industrial and commercial present and offers in its place a compensatory world elsewhere. Hawthorne's ideal is expressed by the Pyncheons' "antimimetic map," which images "the security of romance's bare right" (72). Consonant with the sentiments of a displaced aristocracy, Hawthorne's resistance to mimesis reveals his larger fears of historical change.

Michaels's is a strong argument, but it overlooks the extent to which the novel itself dramatizes the evasions of their real historical circumstances by its characters and narrator. In context, the Pyncheon map is presented ironically, as the symbol of the family's tyrannical ahistoricism—of their attempts to wrest the specific world of Waldo County from its locality. And the novel throughout questions efforts to posit a realm safely sequestered from nineteenth-century mercantile capitalism. Indeed, *Seven Gables* can be seen as an allegory about the inability of Americans to confront the historical reality of past and present. Despite their attempts to deny it, the novel's narrator and characters are vividly *in* history, a point that will be treated at length in Chapter Three.[41]

Brook Thomas's "*The House of the Seven Gables*: Reading the Romance of America" posits a Hawthorne on the opposite side of the

[40] Michaels, "Romance and Real Estate," 71.
[41] And see Roy Harvey Pearce's discussion of the problem of history in Hawthorne, "Hawthorne and the Sense of the Past Or, The Immortality of Major Molineux," *ELH* 21 (1954): 327–49.

CHAPTER ONE

political spectrum from Michaels's, but Thomas's analysis is guided by a similar conflation of author and narrator. Thomas's Hawthorne etherealizes his aesthetic in order to dissociate it from "the conservatism of the novel" (196). By calling his work a romance, Hawthorne takes a stand against the Pyncheons; "in setting out to maintain his innocence by aligning himself with the Maules and writing a romance that does not establish false claims to authority, Hawthorne does not escape the sins he hopes he will. Instead, like Colonel Pyncheon, he constructs his own *House of the Seven Gables*, which through the metaphor of a spatial structure tries to combat the flow of time" (205).[42] Like Michaels, then, Thomas overlooks the novel's subtle undermining of the struggles of characters and the narrator to flee their historical entanglements.

Despite his reputation as an avid experimenter with different points of view, Henry James has also been frequently confused with his narrators. Mark Seltzer, in an impressive study, suggests that James denies the quest for power inherent in his narrative methods. In effect, he accuses James of a duplicitous concealment of strategies aligned with some of the most powerful and repressive institutional forces in his society. James's art, so construed, functions in a conciliatory role, mirroring and underlining the authority of these forms and thereby entrenching their power.[43]

Like Thomas and Michaels, then, Seltzer makes no distinction between James's vision and the acts of suppression he is representing. But such a reading denies one of the most powerful effects of James's description: its intricate exposure of power in London and Washington. Seltzer's conclusions are themselves achieved through a certain blindness to the aesthetic properties of James's narrative.

The analyses by Michaels, Thomas, and Seltzer share a concern

[42] Brook Thomas, "*The House of Seven Gables*: Reading the Romance of America," *PMLA* (May 1981).
[43] Seltzer, *Henry James and the Art of Power* (Ithaca, N.Y.: Cornell University Press, 1984).

34

for the relation between art and the prevailing social and political discourses of the historical milieu. But all insist that the author's view of the political conditions inscribed in his text is confined and coherent. I am interested in how a restraint from confining the authorial point of view at the outset of our readings, and, with it, the larger political perspective of a novel, can help us to formulate a politics of narrativity. As I argued above, whether or not we like to admit it, we base our interpretations of literary works in assumptions about their authors. What I am suggesting therefore is that rather than suppress or deny our propensity for such suppositions, we expand and develop our sense of how authorial consciousnesses might actually figure into the political visions registered in their texts. By focusing upon portraits of narrative action in novelistic works, rather than attempting to localize their authors' own sympathies, we come to view the author as the mediator among the text's various narrative voices and political points of view. In keeping with this, novelistic narrators can best be regarded as refractions rather than reflections of their authors. And this includes characters, who spend more time narrating tales in novels than has usually been acknowledged, as well as specifically authorized narrators.

The essential points include the importance of recognizing the author's responsibility for a variety of perspectives in his work, while not confining his own to any one, and the need for withholding external preconceptions about the author's political stance from the political views generated by the text. The text is ultimately seen to register an overall political vision that is attributed to the author, but the analytical process, especially in its initial stages, is not limited by notions about the biographical author.[44]

[44] Milan Kundera's essay "Man Thinks, God Laughs" offers a complementary view of the matter. "Not only is the novelist nobody's spokesman," Kundera writes, "but I would go so far as to claim that he is not even the spokesman for his own ideas . . . in the course of writing he listens to another voice than that of his personal moral conviction. He listens to what I would call 'the wisdom of the novel.' Every true novelist listens for that suprapersonal wisdom, which explains why great novels are always a little more intelligent than their authors. Novelists

CHAPTER ONE

The assumption that authors are somehow more accessible than
the texts they produce strikes me as chimerical.

I would ascribe a reflexivity to the text that goes beyond the biographical author, but is still in some way attributed to the authorial consciousness. This argument for an authorial perspective
that inheres in the literary text is consistent with an overall emphasis upon close reading. It also seems to me a profitable way of
conceptualizing the deepest political insights and aspirations of
my literary examples.[45]

Within the complex design of the text, the author's vision
emerges as the medium for a socially heterogeneous perspective.
Mikhail Bakhtin's view of novelistic discourse helps to articulate
this relationship. In *The Dialogic Imagination*, he argues that narrators and storytellers "recover . . . themselves as specific and limited verbal and ideological points of view, belief systems, opposed
to the literary expectations and points of view that constitute the
background needed to perceive them. . . . The speech of such narrators is always *another's speech* (as regards the real or potential direct discourse of the author). . . . The author manifests himself
and his point of view not only in his effect on the narrator, on his

---

who are more intelligent than their works should change jobs." *New York Review of
Books* (June 13, 1985), 11. As Kundera suggests, we limit our greatest literary works
by reducing their meanings to the message of a historical individual. The step from
biography to narrative design is a great one.

[45] This study is not without a working sense of the political perspective of each
author examined. My Hawthorne, for example, holds traditional, Burkean sympathies toward an inherited past, at the same time that he is imaginatively gripped
by the technological and commercial innovations of his nineteenth-century present. He is sufficiently immersed to see both the benefits and the insidiousness of
these new industrial forces. Politically, as well, Hawthorne is marginal, committed
to certain conservative values, but with little sympathy for authority for authority's
sake, and subversively aware of how rhetorical claims by contemporaries for democratic equality diverge from the deeper realities of their social and political arrangements. The best sources for Hawthorne biography include: James Mellow's
Nathaniel Hawthorne in His Times (Boston: Houghton Mifflin, 1980); and Michael
Colacurcio, *The Province of Piety* (Cambridge, Mass.: Harvard University Press,
1984). More is said on the political visions of Hawthorne, James, and Dreiser, afforded by their texts, in the readings that follow.

36

HISTORY IN AMERICAN LITERATURE

speech and his language (which are to one or another extent objectivized, objects of display) but also in his effect on the subject of the story—as a point of view that differs from the point of view of the narrator." The author is the medium for the polyphony of discourses. Bakhtin emphasizes incoherence: the author's point of view is never "unitary and consistent," but always to be seen in its "three-dimensionality, its profound speech diversity."[46]

In the examples of my study, authorial consciousness is social consciousness, in terms close to those provided by Bakhtin. This followed from their authors' recognition of how their own literary projects were implicated in the historical changes impinging on Romantic categories of selfhood. Perhaps the most complicated aspect of the author's predicament in my examples is that ultimately these authors are enacting the paradox of deconstruction itself. Although they undermine the idea of the individual authorial consciousness, they nevertheless retain the notion of a critical vision that stands apart from the society it is describing. They exist as individual authors who not only provide a critique of the idea of the individual author, but who also demonstrate that this idea is historically conditioned and therefore unavoidable. Like Theodor Adorno's critic, they could be *in* this world, and at the same time see to criticize it.[47]

Novelists work through a social context, addressing a historically specific audience whose concerns are replicated and deconstructed as the various political points of view in their fictional societies. Deriving his social portrait from a distillation of the various political ideas at large in his society, the novelist exposes their inevitably contesting claims. Novelists write, not for the pure mo-

[46] Bakhtin, *The Dialogic Imagination* (Austin: University of Texas Press, 1981), 313–15.
[47] Adorno, *Minima Moralia*, trans., E.F.N. Jephcott (London, 1978), 126–27. I am grateful to Victoria Kahn for drawing my attention to the connection between my view of these novelistic narrators and Adorno's critic. Kahn applies Adorno's example to Machiavelli's *Prince* in her essay "Virtu and the Example of Agathocles in Machiavelli's *Prince*," *Representations* 13 (Winter 1986): 63–83. See also Adorno's *The Dialectic of Enlightenment* (New York: Continuum, 1987).

tive of self-expression, nor as spokesmen for a class, but always as embodiments of the social vision. Yet if authors are not to be seen as fixed presences, but as mediators of the points of view of narrators and characters, the problem remains: how might we conceive of the author's relation to the narrative repressions of conflict?

In recognizing the authorial point of view as an expression of the collective vision, we not only reclaim the fundamentally social nature of narrative, but also create the possibility of locating within the authorial perspective the Utopian political energies that Jameson regards as endemic to any text. While any individual is always blindly positioned *within* the social totality, the authorial vision conceived as the collectivity harbors the potential for awareness of the impact of *larger* social and institutional beliefs and practices upon the lives of individuals. These authors can be identified with a Utopian consciousness implicit in their texts, which inscribes and criticizes the function of society's prevailing ideologies through exposing their effects.

The site of the authorial perspective in the works of my study can be seen as a consciousness of the contradictory nature of political and social life in America. Hawthorne, James, and Dreiser were well aware of the extent to which the pursuit of power in American democratic society was diffused and concealed, at once everywhere and nowhere. Yet Americans' fears of political polarization and conflict, these writers knew, in no way lessened the coercive impact of institutions upon the lives of individuals. If anything, this implementation of authority through evasion rendered the authority irrefutable. The most innocent and insidious aspect of American liberal ideology is the belief that America is somehow immune to the claims of any ideology: a society of free and open discourse where no factions are allowed to rule.[48]

---

[48] The classic statement on the place of power in an American democratic state is de Tocqueville's *Democracy in America*, trans. Henry Reeve, 2 vols. (New York: Vintage, 1945), see especially vol. 2, bk. 4 on "Influence of Democratic Ideas and Feelings on Political Society." Among recent analyses of American liberal politics,

Though these authors were clearly confined by the prevailing ideologies of their specific historical circumstances, their authorial roles conferred a consciousness of their entrapment. Their works offer this consciousness or conscience to their readers, supplying a means to recognize our engulfment by the contradictory terms of our social institutions.

Far from aesthetes with their heads in the sand, these authors were apprised of the political obligations incurred by their insights, their responsibilities as conscious members of American society. To this end, they portray characters and narrators immersed in history and their narrative efforts to evade or compromise the conflicts implicit in their circumstances.[49] They recognized the double-bind of their narrative projects. They knew that in some sense the tools of their craft bound them to the social institutions and ideologies they criticized.

That recognition provided a way out. Their depictions of con-

---

one of the most penetrating is Theodore J. Lowi's *The End of Liberalism*, 2nd ed. (New York: Norton, 1979). See as well Albert O. Hirschman, *The Passions and the Interests* (Princeton: Princeton University Press, 1977). Morton Horwitz's study, *The Transformation of American Law, 1780–1860* (Cambridge, Mass.: Harvard University Press, 1977), argues that a legal system was established in America that institutionalized a ruling elite while making it appear that the system was open and dynamic. And for the synthesis of political and literary rhetoric, see Bercovitch's *The American Jeremiad*. Also pertinent to this discussion is Jackson Lears's *No Place of Grace* (New York: Pantheon, 1981); see especially ch. 1 where Lears analyzes the "evasive banality" of "official" American culture.

[49] Mikhail Bakhtin's discussion of "represented" speech in *The Dialogic Imagination* is close to my notion that American novels portray their characters managing time and history. As Bakhtin writes, "The speaking person in the novel is always, to one degree or another, an *ideologue*, and his words are *ideologemes*. A particular language in a novel is always a particular way of viewing the world, one that strives for social significance." Thus, no ideological perspective remains unchallenged when set against the "dialogizing background" of a novel. Every position (in our case perhaps an antiquarian or a critical view of history) is "contested, contestable and contesting," and none can "forget or ignore, either through naivete or by design, the heteroglossia that surrounds it" 332–33. The contesting histories of *The House of the Seven Gables* offer a fine illustration of Bakhtin's dialogic babble. It is appropriate that Judge Pyncheon does attempt to ignore the chimney-corner legends, and that his effort is ironically overturned by the novel's narrator.

39

tradictory impulses to flee and transform historical entanglements in the societies of their novels led to the imagination of worlds in which such flights would be neither necessary nor desired. By exposing the operation of ideology in their societies through inscribing it within their works, they could bring their readers to reflect upon the duplicitous effects of narrative at large. Such insights are fleeting, but the novels themselves exist as possibility. Through their readers, they become politically active visions, giving voice to a disenchantment that is audible to all those disposed to listen.

The next chapter takes up the problem of historical narration from the perspective of nineteenth- and early-twentieth-century theorists of history. Like their literary counterparts, these theorists are concerned with the problem of the past's accessibility, in particular with the barriers to historical truth imposed by the interpreter. For them, too, the act of interpretation becomes as much an object of study as the past to which it supposedly provides access. None of them would be prepared to dismiss altogether the possibilities for historical "truths," but they would concur with Pierre Menard that there indeed exists a past to be forgotten.

TWO

The Problem of History in American Historiography

The idea of the perfect historian involves also some moral elements . . . that ready sympathy, namely, whereby he transforms himself, for the time being, into the character he is depicting.—George Marsh, 1847

The difference between an annalist and a historian is, that the mere facts of the first as used by the latter become correlated events, which illumine each other, and get their angles of reflection from many causes . . . the conditions of the time, which give rise to the facts; the views of the period in which they are studied; and the idiosyncracies of the person studying them.—Justin Winsor, 1890

If you are going to "go to history," you had better have a clear idea of which history you are going to, and you had better have a pretty good notion of whether the one you are going to is hospitable to the values you carry into it.—Hayden White, 1982

THE EPIGRAPHS that open this chapter represent a series of assumptions about history. Each emphasizes in some way the interpreter's role in framing historical narratives. Without some informing standpoint, there is no history, only a mass of detail. At the same time, these views reveal a movement in the philosophy of history toward a theory that goes beyond the acknowledgment of how the historian creates the past in narrating it—a theory that suggests the past's unyielding mysteriousness, its resistance to repetition or reformulation as a familiar requisition of the historian's imagination.[1] The need to formulate a philosophy of history

---

[1] Here I depend on R. G. Collingwood's conception of historical thinking, which can never be "a passive surrender to the spell of another's mind; it is a labour of active and therefore critical thinking. The historian not only re-enacts past thought, he re-enacts it in the context of his own knowledge and therefore, in re-enacting it, criticizes it, forms his own judgement of its value, corrects whatever errors he can discern in it." *The Idea of History* (New York: Oxford University Press,

of this kind—one aware of the inevitability of translating the terms of the past into those of the present, and at the same time of the radical difference of the past—absorbed the energies of the most serious historical theorists in America from the mid-nineteenth century on.

In the following pages I shall sketch historiographic landscapes for Hawthorne's *The House of the Seven Gables* (1851), James's *The Bostonians* (1886) and *The Wings of the Dove* (1902), and Dreiser's *An American Tragedy* (1925). My survey is meant to be suggestive rather than comprehensive; I am concerned less with historical trends than with particular developments within each period, but I shall suggest larger shifts, from an emphasis on the historian as spiritual guide, to a more positivist regard for "scientific" evidence, and then to an increasing disenchantment with claims for objectivity that accompanied the popularity of new social scientific methods. The extension of historiographic methods in this final period parallels a growing belief in the utility of historical knowledge for social engineering in the present.[2]

1946), 215; see 205–282. Yet Fredric Jameson's remarks on history serve as a useful qualification to Collingwood's privileging of the historian's imagination, particularly his assurance that the past can be relived. Jameson warns against historians' claims for "modernizing 'relevance' or projection" that ignore "the claims of monuments from distant and even archaic moments of the cultural past on a culturally different present." Jameson continues, "Only a genuine philosophy of history is capable of respecting the specificity and radical difference of the social and cultural past while disclosing the solidarity of its polemics and passions, its forms, structures, experiences, and struggles, with those of the present day." *The Political Unconscious* (Ithaca: Cornell University Press, 1981), 18 and passim. Of special relevance to this discussion is the collection of essays edited by Robert Canary and Henry Kozicki, *The Writing of History* (Madison: University of Wisconsin Press, 1978). See in particular essays by Lionel Gossman and Hayden White. Gossman notes that "the attack on historical realism [was] begun in the early nineteenth century. . . . For many who reflected on the problems of historical knowledge, the fact that the knower is himself involved in the historical process as a maker of history . . . was the very condition of historical knowledge" (24, 26).

[2] I use the terms "Romantic," "Scientific," and "Social Scientific" to group these historiographic changes. These terms are employed for the sake of convenience: what follows takes into account the often inconsistent and contradictory ideas about history contained in each period. More to the point, serious modifications

The historical figures presented in the following pages will for the most part be unfamiliar to literary scholars. Names like Hildreth, Winsor, Burgess, and Robinson have received no formal attention from literary scholars and little from American historians disinclined to study the lesser figures of American historiography. But we cannot really grasp Hawthorne without Hildreth and Marsh as well as Bancroft; James is incomplete without a view of the scientific historians; and Dreiser has to be considered in relation to the New Historians. In arguing this I risk the charge of positivism or contextualism. But I do not mean to argue for the predetermination of these authors' historical visions by their historiographic contexts. I would insist quite oppositely on the inseparability of my literary and historiographic examples—that "influence" works in both directions, and that these writers helped to shape the problem of history in their eras.

Let me be precise about the connections between the writers and historians in each period. In the mid-nineteenth century there was a prevailing concern with the instrumental, political uses of history writing. Many of the historians in this period were either politicians themselves or campaign biographers. Historiographic debates ranged from Democratic party romancers like Bancroft to historical debunkers like Hildreth. The prevailing theories of this time combined sympathetic responsiveness toward past subjects with rigorous antiquarianism. But overall, the tone was progressivist: one learned about the past in order to better know the future. In his book on American history writing during the first half of the nineteenth century, George Calcott shows that the study of the past was meant to reveal the true nature of the present. In citing the impact of German organicism, he describes how the recovery of the German past in ancient myths and legends facilitated the creation of a contemporary German state.[3] Although Hawthorne's

---

and reversals of predominant historiographic assumptions are frequently to be found in contemporary fiction.

[3] Calcott, *History in the United States: 1800–1860* (Baltimore: Johns Hopkins University Press, 1970), 16–18 and passim.

historical fictions might be seen as a similar effort to reveal America's origins, his work must finally be aligned with a more "critical" historiography. As his most theoretical historical fiction, *The House of the Seven Gables*, suggests, the deepest historical findings more often expose than glorify the present. The unrelenting irony in Hawthorne's readings of the Puritans casts doubtful rather than flattering shadows on the American present.

The historiographic period that comprises the background for the literary development of Henry James is usually characterized as the era of scientific history. The term "scientific" has multiple meanings, but for these historians it meant some human determination by uncontrollable forces, whether climatic, biological, social, or mechanistic. The consistent term is determinism, and though someone like Henry Adams flirts throughout his career with the more relativistic notions of a later scientific community, the mechanistic vision was predominant. In the same way that Hawthorne stood critically apart from the politically polarized debates of his day, Henry James can be seen as set against this determinist vision. Like Justin Winsor, he acknowledged the importance of making historical judgments, and viewed a sense of the past as a grave responsibility.

James believed that we make ourselves through our visions of history, and our judgments of the past limit our present possibility. In confronting our power to reconstruct the past, we embrace the power to change its course.[4]

The era of Dreiser's *An American Tragedy* (1925) saw the advent of a "New History," a movement known for its expansion of historiographic methodologies. Divisions between historians and social scientists in this period grew less and less clear, as historians like Robinson and Beard sought to integrate new social scientific techniques into their research, and economists like Thorstein Ve-

---

[4] This is consistent with the view of James's historical vision set forth in Chapter Five. For James, as I argue more extensively there, an emphasis on history as a fabrication or imaginative construction frees us to recognize our power in relation to its fashioning, both past and future.

blen wrote genealogies of their contemporary research subjects. Dreiser in part shares the belief in environmental determinism that characterizes the work of most New Historians. But I shall argue that he finally rejects this view, and that his works offer an anatomy and critique of an American culture ideologically committed to the naturalness of social systems. Like the most skeptical historiographers of his era, Dreiser emphasizes the benefits of confronting history aslant as a process more arbitrary and flexible than social elites would have it believed.

Romantic Historicism in America

Near the opening of James's *The Portrait of a Lady*, Lord Warburton proposes marriage to Isabel Archer with an eye to real estate. "Some people don't like a moat," he remarks, referring to the medieval splendor of his home. Isabel's response is unequivocal: "I adore a moat."[5] In considering the historical imagination in mid-nineteenth-century America, we might ask ourselves: to what extent did Americans "adore a moat," and what might this suggest about their attitudes toward history?

Commentators from Hawthorne's day to the present have complained that the American sense of history is superficial, a romancing of castles rather than a solid grounding in a religious, moral, and intellectual inheritance. Yet James's heroine eventually achieves a complicated sense of the past; and, in general, study of nineteenth-century periodicals and histories reveals the extent and intensity of debates on the subject of history writing. These debates suggest the century's profound confrontation with history's psychological and political uses.[6]

---

[5] Henry James, *The Portrait of a Lady* (New York: Penguin, 1979), 110.

[6] Even Michael Kammen, studying the formation of an American tradition through transformations in revolutionary iconography, takes for granted the essentially ahistorical terms of American attitudes toward the past. Referring to "the lack of shared historical interest in the U.S.," Kammen concurs with prevailing scholarly opinion, which ignores the complex and extensive theorizing about history going on in the period (*A Season of Youth* [New York: Knopf, 1978], 3). And Fred

CHAPTER TWO

The period that preceded Hawthorne's writing of *Seven Gables* (1850–1851) was a watershed in American historiography. Americans in the early part of the century were preoccupied with the need for a definitive national history.[7] Biographies of George Washington by Aaron Bancroft and Jared Sparks, both celebrational tracts, were typical. The founding of local and national historical societies facilitated widespread reverence toward the past. Writing history was a means of articulating individual and collective values. Fred Somkin (among others) has analyzed the connection between all this activity and belief in America's mission. Paradoxically, Somkin has observed, Americans' feelings of "unprecedentedness" encouraged their research of the past. Because American history revealed the nation's *original* destiny, it could be studied without the sense of oppression that characterized other national histories.

The American version of romantic historiography is best exemplified by the work of George Bancroft (1800–1891). Educated

Somkin, who intends to examine, in the spirit of Charles Pierce, "the belief men *betray* and not that which they *parade*" (*Unquiet Eagle* [Ithaca: Cornell University Press], 8), seems to spend much of his study on the testimonies to America's prosperous destiny ritually "parade[d]" out at political fundraisers and Fourth-of-July celebrations. American interests in history during this period were less polarized than a conception like "the party of Hope" and "the party of Memory" would lead us to believe. A complex meta-level of historiographic concerns is to be found in lectures, reviews, and essays of the time. Some of the best-known and persuasive analyses of nineteenth-century Americans' attitudes toward history remain: R.W.B. Lewis, *The American Adam* (Chicago: University of Chicago Press, 1955); David Levin, *The Romantic Historians* (Stanford: Stanford University Press, 1959); Roy Harvey Pearce, *Historicism Once More* (Princeton: Princeton University Press, 1969); Ann Douglas, *The Feminization of American Culture* (New York: Knopf, 1978), esp. 197–239; and Michael Colacurcio, *The Province of Piety* (Cambridge, Mass.: Harvard University Press, 1984).

[7] Scholars who have provided particularly useful discussions on the development of American historiography during this period are: Levin, *Romantic Historians*; David Van Tassell, *Recording America's Past* (Chicago: University of Chicago Press, 1960); Somkin, *Unquiet Eagle*; George Calcott, *History in the United States, 1800–1860*; Bert James Loewenberg, *American History in American Thought* (New York: Simon and Schuster, 1972); and Kammen, *Season of Youth*.

at Harvard and then in Germany, Bancroft found German idealism compatible with his democratic faith in the powers of human reason. His ten-volume *History of America* (1834–1874) combined an American providential design and German organicism. The past was the antitype of the future, and Bancroft's history assured Americans of their heroic destiny. As he wrote in the preface to volume one, he had dwelled "at considerable length in this first period [of the American past] because it contained the germs of our institutions . . . the maturity of the nation is but a continuation of its youth."[8] Like Hegel, who saw the modern Prussian state as the culmination of German history, Bancroft idealized the democratic administration of Andrew Jackson. The law of history was progress, and "the common judgment in taste, politics, and religion, the highest authority on earth."[9]

In an address delivered at Williams College in 1835, "The Office of the People in Art, Government, and Religion," Bancroft described the role of the historian in a democratic state. The historian unveils the triumphant evolution of the national spirit and places it within a universal framework. Historical events must be traced "not only to their authors and to their immediate causes, but to the place which they occupy in the progress of humanity." As part of the general progress of humanity, historiography had made great strides since Herodotus and Livy. Bancroft located historical truths "in the internal sense which places us in connexion with the world of intelligence and the decrees of God."[10] His history, which, according to one wry observer, "voted for Jackson on every page,"[11] embodied the sentiments of his age.

An editorial on "The Philosophy of History" in the *North American Review* of 1834 corroborates Bancroft's view of history as a tale

[8] Bancroft, *The History of the United States of America*, abr. and ed. Russell Nye (Chicago: University of Chicago Press, 1966), 6.
[9] Ibid., 249.
[10] Russell Nye, *George Bancroft* (New York: Knopf, 1945), 99–100.
[11] Ibid., 106.

of human progress, and an instrument for "self-improvement."[12] The essay is noteworthy for its confrontation of what Bancroft's history merely epitomizes—the link between politics and history. The essay begins with a rather innocent proposition: history tells the "truth" and predicts the future. Through rational understanding, the past affords humans awareness of their powers of Reason, and greater control over their destiny. By this standard, the author observes, the masses of Europe have been defrauded by their historians. They have not "been permitted to unfold the long scroll of the past, to learn their natural and inviolable rights; to be advised of the encroachments of power; to discover behind the scene the secrets of political management."[13] Americans must be more circumspect: though historiography may be revelatory, it inevitably serves political interests.

Debate over the purposes of historical inquiry during this period sometimes approached the intensity of direct political conflicts. This is exemplified by Richard Hildreth's *History of the United States* (1849–1852), a self-conscious rejoinder to Bancroft's democratic romance of America's past. Also Harvard-educated, Hildreth (1805–1865) turned to history writing following a career as a newspaper publisher and writer of biography, philosophy, and fiction. As historian, Hildreth consistently criticized "romantic" historiography. In the 1849 "Advertisement" for his *History*, he asserted, "Of centennial sermons and Fourth-of-July orations, whether professedly such or in the guise of history, there are more than enough. It is due to our fathers and ourselves, it is due to truth and philosophy, to present for once, on the historic stage, the founders of our American nation unbedaubed with patriotic rouge." The claims of an 1851 preface are even more confrontational, as Hildreth presents his history as "undistorted by prejudice, uncolored by sentiments, neither tricked out in the gaudy

---

[12] *North American Review* (July 1834): 36.
[13] Ibid., 49.

tinsel of a meretricious rhetoric, nor stretched nor shortened to suit the purposes of any political party."[14]

Influenced by French Utilitarianism, Hildreth criticized the religious emotionalism of the Great Awakening, and denounced the free-thinkers of the French Revolution for their similarly deluded "appeal to first principles."[15] But the most controversial part of Hildreth's history had less to do with philosophy than with narrative tone. Hildreth's history seemed to belie his own calls for "impartial" objectivity. The paradox was that it was more partisan than most. His denial of governing assumptions and biases made his work the *unconscious* register of his own prejudices. As a reviewer in the October 1851 *North American Review* explained, Hildreth's excessive detachment from his historical subjects resulted in a history devoid of any but present concerns. Because Hildreth never brings the past alive, the *only* energy in his history is derived from the historian's present obsessions.

Another reviewer characterized Hildreth's attitude as regrettably contemptuous: "The style even of 'centennial sermons and Fourth of July orations' is more creditable to the writer's feelings, and more conformable to the truth, than this bitter and sarcastic manner."[16] For this reviewer, a sympathetic antiquarianism is essential to "creditable" historical scholarship. "If Mr. Hildreth had pored over the records and memorials of the Puritan fathers of New England as long and as diligently as some of our antiquarian friends have done, he could not have written their history in the stern, sarcastic, and depreciating tone which now characterizes his work."[17] Hildreth's lack of sympathetic understanding betrays faulty research: had he immersed himself in the materials of his

[14] Loewenberg, *American History in American Thought*, 262, 269.
[15] Harvey Wish, *The American Historian* (New York: Oxford University Press, 1960), 61–63.
[16] *North American Review* 73 (October 1851), 411–47.
[17] Ibid., 444.

subject, he could not have maintained such a presentist "rationality."

Hildreth's history exposes one of the great truths of historical meaning, that events can never be exclusively conceived in the terms of their present—historical understanding inevitably absorbs the biases of succeeding generations. Therefore, any historian who refuses to consider a past event in light of the knowledge of its consequences not only engages in willful blindness, but denies his own historicity as well. The more self-conscious the interpreter is about his own historical conditioning, the less distorted his history is likely to be.

The Romantic historiography of Francis Parkman (1823–1893) offered another alternative to the works of Bancroft. Parkman, who graduated from Harvard in 1844, combined a passion for the classics with an interest in American Indian lore. Given Parkman's increasingly archaeological involvement with Indian culture, it is appropriate that he is responsible for introducing the native American past into the narrative of romantic historiography. Rather than challenging Bancroft's methods on his own territory, Parkman treated subjects that were muted in Bancroft's history. If Bancroft's history provided a genealogical romance for an American democracy, Parkman's history insisted on the cultures omitted from that view. In the preface to his *History of the Conspiracy of Pontiac* (1851), Parkman refers to the conquest of Canada as "an event of momentous consequence in American history. It changed the political aspect of the continent, prepared a way for the independence of the British colonies, rescued the vast tracts of the interior from the rule of military despotism. . . . Yet to the red natives of the soil its results were wholly disastrous." The final sentence here is the key to a history that serves as a romantic elegy on the stamping out of Indian culture. Parkman's relentless research into Indian archives and his firsthand acquaintance with the traditions of Indian tribes in the Rocky Mountains suggest his commitment to preserving a record of a vanished race.

Though the undertone of inevitability that pervades Parkman's history, especially in light of the charges of racism leveled against him by later historians, seems to preclude a serious critique, his closing description of the death of Pontiac reveals a profound view of the connection between political and narrative repression. "Tradition has but faintly preserved the memory of the event," he writes, "and its only annalists, men who held the intestine feuds of the savage tribes in no more account than the quarrels of panthers or wildcats, have left but a meagre record. . . . Neither mound nor tablet marked the burial place of Pontiac. For a mausoleum, a city has risen above the forest hero; and the race whom he hated with such burning rancor tramples with unceasing footsteps over his forgotten grave." Thus it appears that the deeper conspiracy of which Parkman writes is the conspiracy to *forget* the Indians' extinction. The destruction of a civilization symbolized by Pontiac's death is repeated on a narrative level, figured as the denial of inscription: "Neither mound nor tablet marked the burial place."[18] By linking the white man's progress ("a city has risen") with the repression of inscription ("neither mound nor tablet marked") and historical memory ("forgotten grave"), Parkman's closing image suggests a refusal to accommodate the national amnesia about the American Indian.[19] And Parkman's conclusion of his own narrative with this image of Pontiac's unmarked grave implies an alignment between the Indians' extinction and the end of historical meaning.

We find historical theorists in this period increasingly concerned with what is omitted from predominant or "official" histories, which they relate to the problem of interpretive bias. An 1855 editorial in *Harper's Magazine* emphasizes the poetical nature of history writing, celebrating the great descriptive powers found in the histories of Thierry. The great historian, it says, must be, above all, a great painter of "reality," rendering his subjects so that "we

[18] See Francis Parkman, *The Conspiracy of Pontiac and the Indian War after the Conquest of Canada*, 3 vols. (Boston: Little and Brown, 1898), I: ix-x, III: 187–89.

[19] My reading is indebted to Philip Fisher's section on Parkman in *Hard Facts* (New York: Oxford University Press, 1985), 22–26.

shall see the people, stand on the spots, be present at the scenes he depicts." Yet linked to this concern for the pictorial details of the past is an interest in formerly unrecorded common scenes, "how parsons lived, how weavers pursued their calling," which are seen in the editorial to modify the perspective of canonized historical works.[20] An 1862 *Harper's* editorial concurs in asserting that historical truths must be sought beneath the layers of "what purport to be true records." The editorial goes on to discuss the "constantly told" story of the uprisings in Saint Domingo, which provides a contemporary example of the unreliability of authorized testimonies. The "usual understanding" is that the slaves inexplicably rose against their masters in a savage blood bath. But the same set of circumstances retold by "indifferent French eye-witnesses" reveals the "cruelties that were too often inflicted upon the slaves."[21]

An 1856 review essay on "The Art of History-Making" in *Littell's Living Age* displays a similar distrust in the reporting of historical evidence. The author's critique of a set of recent histories suggests the era's rigorous historiographic standards. Focusing particularly on a newly published Hanoverian history by Dr. Doran, the reviewer disputes his translations and source quotations, denouncing Doran's general lack of "common pains and accuracy." Doran's excuse, that he is writing "lives" rather than formal history, is dismissed as irresponsible. "Truth is truth, alike in great matters and small. If a man chooses to write the history of courts and drawing-rooms, he ought to be as minutely accurate . . . as his betters ought to be about empires and common-wealths. . . . Dr. Doran *is* . . . writing history."[22]

The authors of these reviews picture an ideal history as combining an antiquarian's reverence for past details with a passion for truth. They suggest that if the historian is rigorous in his pursuit

[20] "Editor's Table," *Harper's Magazine* 10 (May 1855): 835, 836.
[21] "Editor's Easy Chair," *Harper's Magazine* 24 (May 1862): 846–47.
[22] "The Art of History-Marking," *Littell's Living Age* 48 (January 1856): 244–45, 247.

of data, he cannot fail to achieve the sympathetic immersion essential to a faithful portrait of the past. Yet these theorists are also deeply skeptical, accepting the inevitable distortions of any perspective, and recognizing a fair method to be an open admission of one's own prejudices. Finally, however, none of these theorists addresses the difficult question of how the historian actually encounters the past, a concern that dominates the thinking of George Marsh (1801–1882). Best known for his work in conservation, Marsh, a lawyer by training, seems far removed from the mainstream debates of American historiography. But his marginality perhaps accounts for the striking imaginativeness of his formulations, which are contained, so far as we know, in one very slim, and very neglected, volume. Marsh's lecture "The American Historical School," delivered at Union College in 1847 and published shortly thereafter, offers an eloquent synthesis of assumptions about history writing in this period, and provides an appropriate bridge to the subject of Hawthorne and history.

Marsh begins by linking his topic, "the temporal condition and prospects of man," to the idea of human progress. The story of history involves "the rules of practical wisdom, which the discipline of thousands of years has accumulated." The life of every individual tells the tale in miniature—the "perpetual sharpening and clearing of the intellectual vision . . . a constant elevation of the moral man."[23] Like Bancroft, Marsh sees history as moving toward a greater prosperity and happiness for all. Yet Marsh's philosophical emphasis affords a more complex vision of the problems underlying historical study. His subject is historical knowledge itself, its use and abuse, and he wishes to provide standards that would minimize the exploitation of history for political purposes, those which render the historian "the partial apologist of the errors and the crimes of his country or his party."[24]

Marsh urges instead that there are historical depths to be

[23] George Marsh, *The American Historical School* (Troy, N.Y.: Steam Press of J. C. Kneeland and Co., 1847), 5–6.
[24] Ibid., 7.

plumbed beneath the surfaces of histories now accessible in public archives. Anticipating the program of twentieth-century "annales" historians, he calls for a thorough exploration of "the actual condition of the masses" found in "judicial investigations of crime . . . statistics of the domestic workshop . . . the sanitary and economic condition of the people . . . the character and tendency of public amusements, the ephemeral popular literature of different periods." The historian must strive for "a familiar knowledge of the every-day life of a people . . . ," an underground view achieved through an immersion in the private and popular as well as the public and official past. [25]

Marsh's injunction to uncover the private histories of the fireside and the "secrets of their domestic economy" seems an uncanny preview of the chimney-corner legends in Hawthorne's *Seven Gables*. [26] The spirit of Hawthorne's work is also presaged in Marsh's warning against the expedient policies of American governments, which too often favor "the boundless field of enterprise that lies open before us . . . feeding that morbid appetite for novelty and change." The characters' closing dismissal of their pasts to enter the timeless domain of prosperity seems a step in the direction of an American "culture of consumption." Finally, the allusion to the manipulation of popular sentiments by democratic leaders, who mask the intentions of the "cabal" as the will of the people, anticipates the stirring indictment of Judge Pyncheon. [27]

But Marsh is closest to Hawthorne in a more subtle point: his insistence upon the essential "moral" ingredient in history writing. For in addition to possessing an antiquarian impulse, a commitment to the study of popular as well as elite experience, and a scientific regard for the rhythms of cause and effect, the historian must also harbor "some moral elements." And morality for the historian is a very specific property: the capacity "whereby he transforms himself, for the time being, into the character he is depict-

[25] Ibid., 9–10.
[26] Ibid., 10.
[27] Ibid., 15–16.

ing." This is not simply a method by which the historian gives life to history; it is the means of attaining "an intuitive perception of the possible and the true in historical portraiture." History without moral sympathy, Marsh concludes, is the tale of "unearthly, unsubstantial phantoms."[28]

It has been argued that Hawthorne's writings comprise a critical program designed to instruct his contemporaries in the moral and intellectual legacy of their Puritan past. Hawthorne's "major achievement," writes Michael Colacurcio, is as " 'moral historian'—his extraordinary power critically to discern and dramatically to recreate the moral conditions under which earlier generations of Americans had lived, and, in one way or another, sought salvation." Though Colacurcio's definition of "moral historian" is more complex than this brief description suggests, it is remarkably close to Marsh's 1847 conception. Immersed in the writings of his Puritan heritage, Colacurcio makes Hawthorne "our first significant intellectual historian," a characterization prefigured in Marsh's "perfect historian."[29] In both cases, the historian combines an antiquarian passion for the materials of the past with the critical sympathy achieved through its re-enactment.

Marsh and Hawthorne outline the most complicated aims of historical writing in mid-nineteenth-century America. Resisting the polemics of a Bancroft, they also eschew the objectivist claims of a Hildreth. Reliable history is based on a responsible antiquarianism, combined with a critical responsiveness that itself constitutes "historical morality." Like the majority of their era's theorists, Marsh and Hawthorne share Parkman's concern for the forgotten cultures of American history and a grass-roots approach to historical research, which points to an important difference between the middle and late nineteenth century. The popular emphasis in historiographic method saw a decline in the era of scientific and institutional history, reflecting the increasingly

[28] Ibid., 22.
[29] Colacurcio, *Province of Piety*, 13, 3.

conservative tenor of American society.[30] This trend is expressed
by what Michael Kammen observes is a late-nineteenth-century
interest in the constitutional over the revolutionary stage of America's beginnings. Thus the tale of American origins was defused of
much of its radical intonations. "The conservative view of our
Revolution," Kammen writes, "as being unique, comparatively
bloodless, completed and entirely fulfilled by 1789 grew steadily
stronger during the second half of the nineteenth century. . . .
The special virtue of our minutemen, apparently, was that they
respected Magna Carta and the Petition of Right more vigorously
than George III or Lord North."[31] The more popular and romantic concerns of an earlier generation of historians seem to have
given way to a more scientific interest in institutional development, and in material and technological advances. But just as the
previous period contained rumblings beneath the surface of more
prominent concerns, the era of Adams, Draper, and James offered
important exceptions to the mainstream debates among theorists
of history.

The Possibilities for a Science of History

The era from the 1860s to the closing decades of the nineteenth
century saw an increasing emphasis on scientific method in American history writing. Though the search for a science of history
was often tempered by skepticism toward the possibilities of his-

[30] On the growing conservatism of Americans bent on husbanding the fruits of
economic gains, and distinguishing themselves from vast numbers of immigrants,
see, among others, Jackson Lears, *No Place of Grace* (New York: Pantheon, 1981);
Lawrence J. Friedman, *Inventors of the Promised Land* (New York: Knopf, 1975); Eric
Hobsbawm, *The Invention of Tradition* (Cambridge: Cambridge University Press,
1983); John Higham, *History* (Englewood Cliffs: Prentice-Hall, 1965), *Writing
American History* (Bloomington: Indiana University Press, 1970), and "Hanging
Together: Divergent Unities in American History," *Journal of American History* 61
(1974): 5–28; David F. Noble, *America by Design* (New York: Oxford University
Press, 1980); and Alan Trachtenberg, *The Incorporation of America* (New York: Hill
and Wang, 1982).
[31] Kammen, *Season of Youth*, 73.

torical objectivity, the establishment of objective standards for the recovery of historical knowledge was considered to be the chief task before the founders of the American Historical Association in their inaugural convention of 1884. The overall agenda of scientific historiography can be seen as part of a general trend in late-nineteenth-century America: from romantic idealism toward more clear-eyed approaches to social facts. As John Higham has observed, scientific history emerged from a social climate that was "impersonal, collaborative, secular, impatient of mystery, and relentlessly concerned with the relation of things to one another instead of their relation to ultimate meaning."[32] Similar assumptions underlay applications of evolutionary theory that viewed events in strictly causal terms as links on a chain. Consistent with an increasingly mechanized and materialistic conception of experience, scientific historiography appealed to a society committed to "advancing the work of consolidation."[33]

The career of John William Draper (1811–1882) exemplifies the American search for a scientific historiography. A laboratory researcher and physician by training, Draper saw the study of history as the likely plane for extending his scientific principles to their logical social conclusions. Influenced by Comte and Darwin, like most social theorists of his day, Draper saw society as a natural organism. Yet in a way that suggested more immediate contemporaries such as Dewey and William James, Draper believed in the power of human will and rationality to effect human actions. Though "social advancement," Draper wrote, "is completely under the control of natural laws as is bodily growth," natural law only "limits our movements in a certain direction and guides them

---

[32] Higham, *History*, 94. Higham's analysis of the clipped historical horizon of the late nineteenth century is consistent with a study on the aesthetic features of realist literature by Harold Kolb. Realist metaphors, as Kolb points out, tend to be horizontal—more likely to exemplify interconnections between common objects in our world than to provide analogies with abstract or transcendent phenomena. Kolb, *The Illusion of Life* (Charlottesville: University Press of Virginia, 1981).

[33] Higham, *History*, 96.

in a certain way."[34] But Draper departs from this qualified determinism in his *History of the Civil War* (1867–1870), where he portrays climatic factors as irreversible determinants of southern destiny. By understanding how men's deeds "are determined by climate and their natural circumstances," we can explain the "immobility of southern society, its resistance to crop innovations, and adherence to an outmoded economic system founded on the feudal institution of slavery."[35]

John William Burgess and Herbert Baxter Adams were two other leading American historians who sought to develop links between science and history. Burgess (1844–1931), who became a founder of American graduate education and of the field of political science during his long tenure at Columbia University, had studied political science and history in Germany with scholars such as Mommsen, Ranke, and Droysen, and formulated a positivistic approach to the past, which "taught the student how to get hold of an historical fact." The essential first step in Burgess's method involved "distinguish[ing] fact from fiction . . . divest[ing] it as far as possible of coloring or exaggeration." Only then might the historian confront the vexing questions of cause and effect. Burgess's belief in the initial potential for objectivity reflected the ideas of his German mentors, whose historiographic practices were based on the process of amassing historical facts, which were then "synthesi[zed]."[36]

Burgess revised their claims, however, by offering a more subtle understanding of scientific method. From his readings of theoretical works by contemporary scientists, Burgess came to acknowledge the investigator's role in bringing into being the objects that he studies. Thus, Burgess demonstrates an awareness of the arbitrariness of scientific discovery, as articulated by fellow scientist Thomas H. Huxley. "It is a favourite popular delusion," Huxley asserts, "that the scientific inquirer is under a sort of moral obli-

[34] Loewenberg, *American History in American Thought*, 496.
[35] Ibid., 499.
[36] Ibid., 331.

gation to abstain from going beyond that generalization of observed facts which is absurdly called "Baconian" induction. But anyone who is practically acquainted with scientific work is aware that those who refuse to go beyond fact, rarely get as far as fact. . . ."[37] Burgess's own remarks serve as an appropriate conclusion: the concepts that order our apprehension of data are always "logically prior in terms of our understanding."[38] Moving one step beyond Draper, Burgess saw human reason as the activating force in history, substituting for Draper's predeterminate nature a rational force that acted as a motivating collective unconscious. This underlying power of reason guided human actors toward results "more advanced" than they had "consciously intended," a conception that followed from his Hegelian view of the modern state as embodying "the perfection of humanity."[39]

Like his contemporaries Draper and Burgess, Herbert Baxter Adams's (1850–1901) commitment to a fully scientific historiography was decidedly ambivalent. Yet the role he played in the institutionalization and specialization of historical study through the establishment of graduate education in history, and the founding of the American Historical Association, had a lasting impact in rendering history writing a less romantic enterprise. Adams was associated with Johns Hopkins University for most of his academic career, where his strong belief in scientific method was evident in his graduate seminars, which he characterized as "laboratories where books are treated like mineralogical specimens, passed from hand to hand, examined and tested."[40] Adams saw history as the study of institutional evolution, an interest kindled by his German schooling and kept alive by English and American colleagues, such as Sir Henry Maine and John Gorham Palfrey. These scholars were comparativists who studied the development of institutional forms from Italy to England to America, and Ad-

[37] Ibid., 352.
[38] Ibid., 348.
[39] Ibid., 352–56.
[40] Ibid., 367.

ams continued their explorations in his work on the German roots of New England town governments. Dubbed the "germ theory" of institutional history, Adams's method was criticized for stressing similarities over differences, the continuity of institutional patterns over crucial changes in time. For example, Frederick Jackson Turner's "frontier thesis," which sought to chart the endless expansion and change of America's frontier communities, as well as the frontier's unique impact upon American society, represented a self-conscious rejection of Adams's methods.

Other articulations of a scientific methodology for historiography during this period seem to vacillate between a commitment to scientific objectivity and an emphasis on the power of narrative design. An essay entitled "The Science of History" in the 1886 issue of *Hours at Home* concludes that poetry provides the most profound science of history, since "the greatness of the poet depends on his being true to nature, without insisting that nature shall theorize with him, without making her more just, more philosophical, more moral than reality." The historian is "successful . . . so far as he can let his story tell itself in the deeds and words of those who act it out. . . . His work is no longer the vapor of his own brain, which a breath will scatter; it is the thing itself."[41] Once the historian has lost himself sufficiently in the force of his narrative to allow his actual subjects to speak, his work has "reality."

The natural alignment seen here between the poetic sensibility and the aims of scientific objectivity form the basis for the work of the era's foremost historian, Henry Adams (1838–1918).[42] Born into one of America's most illustrious families, Adams was educated at Harvard and in Germany, and also served as an assistant

[41] "The Science of History," *Hours at Home* 2 (February 1866): 328–29.
[42] See William Jordy on Adams's dilemma as one "he never reconciled." My analysis of Adams is indebted to Jordy's comprehensive and illuminating book, *Henry Adams, Scientific Historian* (New York: Archon, 1970). Other critics who offer important insights into Adams's view of history include John Carlos Rowe, *Henry Adams and Henry James* (Ithaca: Cornell University Press, 1976); Lears, *No Place of Grace*; and less directly, Carolyn Porter, *Seeing and Being* (Middletown, Conn.: Wesleyan University Press, 1981).

to his father's ambassadorship to England during the Civil War, an experience recounted in ironic detail in his famous "autobiography," *The Education of Henry Adams*. Upon his return to America, Adams spent seven years teaching history at Harvard, but could not reconcile himself to academia, and devoted the remainder of his life to writing and travel. Adams's historiographic interests are usually described in terms of an arc, moving from faith in the essential order of history and the objectivity of historical knowledge, to despair over history's chaos and the relativity of historical meaning. Adams is thus the representative transitional figure who stands between the solid ground of nineteenth-century positivism and the uncertainties of twentieth-century modernism. But Adams's concerns are much less clearly divided than this arc suggests. In considering Adams's views, we need first to examine the convictions that he shared with other scientific historians of his era.

Like the histories of the Hopkins school, Adams's *History of the United States* features a "germ theory" of history.[43] The mature stages of national institutions are implicit in its first forms; earlier historical events foreshadow later ones. "Young as the nation was," Adams wrote in the opening volume, "it had already produced an American literature bulky and varied enough to furnish some idea of its probable qualities in the future."[44] In keeping with this, Adams presumes that the course of history is progressive and rational, a trend he sees replicated by the increasing precision of historiographic methods. The *History*, Adams wrote, "was intended only to serve the future historian with a fixed and documented starting-point. The real History that one would like to write, was to be built on it, and its merits or demerits, whatever they might be, could be seen only when the structure, of which it was to be the foundation, was raised."[45] The historian, in this view, is the humble specialist, engaged in a collective enterprise to which he contributes his nugget of knowledge. The "house of his-

---

[43] Adams, *History of the United States*, 9 vols. (New York: 1889–1891).
[44] Ibid., 1: 75.
[45] 1899 correspondence, in Jordy, *Henry Adams*, 16.

tory," like Henry James's "house of fiction," has many levels; each historian by way of "solid reasoning and thorough knowledge" supplies a "fixed and documented" brick from the past.[46] Perhaps the most ambitious of Adams's scientific aims in his *History* was the desire to chart "the evolution of a race." The uniquely isolated development of America provided the ideal test case for examining the growth of a national consciousness.

Just how closely the supposedly positivist claims of the *History* (1889–1891) approximate the skepticism of *Education* (1907, 1918) is seen when Adams's "objective" methods are compared to those of his more "literary" romantic predecessors. Though historians such as Parkman and Bancroft were committed to the importance of documentation, and Adams in turn was concerned with style, it is possible to outline fundamental differences. Seen in contrast to Bancroft's history, Adams's appeals to the reader's judgment and intellect over emotional response. He sees generalizations as implicit in sources instead of as superimposed by the historian and, perhaps most importantly, emphasizes large institutional patterns rather than specific personages or events.[47] Whereas formerly the meaning of historical events was discovered in the actions of individuals, now it was found in the impersonal effects of public institutions. This final distinction anticipates the crucial method of Adams's *Education*, where the manikin-narrator serves as the self-effacing vehicle for the drapery of larger social and political conventions. The *History*'s opening and closing frames, which both end in questions, typify Adams's prevailing vision of history. Adams's work is itself a sort of uncomprehending manikin, a mere object in the continual reinscriptions of historical understanding.

Thus, beneath his claims for an objective scientific method, a note of relativism was forever lurking. The effect of Adams's assertion that the "historian need only state facts in their sequence" was to diminish the historian's role and, consequently, to elevate

---

[46] 1873 correspondence, in Jordy, *Henry Adams*, 17.
[47] Jordy, *Henry Adams*, 6, 22.

that of the reader.[48] The reader of Adams's *History* relives the past as a participant observer: the moment of Jefferson's decision to leave politics, for example, is rendered as if the reader were present. By transforming his reader into a participant in the living history his work inscribes, Adams forces him to become a judge of the past as well, responsible for formulating his own "conclusions." In Adams's history, the historian is a medium who gives his reader an experience of the past, rather than an active, authoritative interpreter. Adams's shifting of the responsibility of historical interpretation from the historian to the reader was a radical maneuver that implied that there is no "fixed" view of the past to be handed over as the gift of experts.[49]

Adams's sweeping analysis of American democracy can therefore be seen to presume a democratic analytical strategy as well. And the process of historical narration in Adams's *History* seems for the most part to be consistent with that found in *Education*. His narrative wings shorn from the work's beginning, the manikin is the quintessential American democratic observer—self-effacing and obsessed with the "failure or success"[50] of a personal and national mission. It is also appropriate that this democratic narrative persona derives a powerful identity from a sobering awareness of his inconsequence.

But what is perhaps most exemplary about *Education*'s manikin-narrator is his ambivalent relationship to the past. On the one hand, his narrative actions suggest that the past is irrecoverable,

---

[48] Adams, *History*, III: 45.

[49] For my view of Adams's understanding of theories of relativism, I depend on Jordy's discussion. See Jordy, *Henry Adams*, 230–31 and passim. It should also be pointed out that such an emphasis on interpretive bias was no news to contemporary scientists. Lionel Gossman observes that the nineteenth-century scientist was well aware of the limits of objectivity and quotes Lucien Febvre's remark that in 1860 "Berthelot was already claiming that 'chemistry makes its object.' " "History and Literature," 26 and passim.

[50] On the vacillating American self-image of failure and success, see Sacvan Bercovitch, *The Puritan Origins of the American Self* (New Haven: Yale University Press, 1975); and Martha Banta, *Failure and Success* (Princeton: Princeton University Press, 1981).

and that any effort to forge a meaningful link between past and future can only indicate the disconnectedness of all history. On the other hand, his indefatigable pursuit of the past suggests that meaning may only be found in the cultivation of a past: that historical invention is the ultimate medium of human signification. Adams took the problem of the relativism of historical knowledge as far as it went in the late nineteenth century, but other theorists approached the radicalism of his beliefs. Some were more explicit in considering the political stakes that arise when the idea of historical knowledge is stripped of an objective basis.

Known primarily for his assiduous research work as a Boston librarian, a geographer, and most importantly, the editor of the ambitious eight-volume *Narrative and Critical History of America* (1884–1889), Justin Winsor (1837–1897) seems an unlikely source for a radical skepticism toward historical knowledge. But his essay "The Perils of Historical Narrative" (1891) may offer the most extreme and politically pointed questioning of positivism to be found in late-nineteenth-century writings on history. Taking up the assumptions of the "test tube" historians one by one, Winsor exposes their logical fallacies. He begins by distinguishing between the archivist and the historian, and he locates their chief difference in the latter's concern for causal factors. Attention to cause *makes* the historical point of view, with cause defined as "the conditions of the time, which gave rise to the facts; the views of the period in which they are studied; and the idiosyncracies of the person studying them."[51] For Winsor, historical knowledge is ongoing: the past is reviewed and rewritten by every generation.

But despite the subjectivity of historical understanding, there are truths to be discovered, and therefore there are barriers to truth. Among these barriers, Winsor cites the unreliability of past authorities moved by "national or local pride."[52] Distortions may be inevitable, but they are often politically motivated. "The polit-

[51] Justin Winsor, "The Perils of Historical Narrative," *Atlantic Monthly* (1890): 289.
[52] Ibid., 291.

ical prophecies that come true we remember; more that fail we forget."⁵³ The implication is that our amnesia is tactical: history is a record approached fitfully as much from fear as from inability, from the fear of knowing the unflattering details of our individual and collective pasts. "The historian must have the courage of the moth, and burn his wings to approach the light. Writers of a timid sort hold that to be a detective is to lower the dignity of history. Their art eschews what the camera sees, and trusts to the polite eye."⁵⁴ A history close to the truth, Winsor suggests, must forego such demands for politeness. His politic concern for the "ragged edges" of the past, regularly dismissed from more "timid" historical surveys, resonates strikingly with a work of fiction written (though not published) around the time of his essay—Melville's *Billy Budd*.⁵⁵ Earlier works by Melville, such as "Benito Cereno" and *Israel Potter*, highlight the process of historical narration. But *Billy Budd* is a special case in that the problem of narrative control over history is built into the way the story is told. The thematic concern with the repression of history is reproduced narratively in the story's stuttering, digressive plot.

In tones of ironic speculation close to Winsor's, *Billy Budd's* narrator questions the potential for achieving a truthful version of the past, given the inextricable ties between historical narration and political power. As the story implies, the ship's authorities are also the authors of its history. By offering us an "inside view," the narrator implies that more widely circulated versions of the ship's history approved by official chroniclers might be "missing the mark." The tale's subtext goes on to show how historical participants may intentionally obscure the details of past events. Like *Harper's Magazine's* Saint Domingo rulers, or Winsor's "timid" historians, those

⁵³ Ibid., 294.
⁵⁴ Ibid., 296.
⁵⁵ *Billy Budd*, in *Great Short Works of Herman Melville*, ed. Warner Berthoff (New York: Harper and Row, 1969). This contains the text of *Billy Budd* prepared by Harrison Hayford and Merton Sealts.

in *Billy Budd* empowered to tell "what happened" may have reasons to err in their recountings.

Captain Vere's manipulation of the perceptions of all on board the Bellipotent provides a blow-by-blow example of the subversion of historical information. From the immediate closeting of Billy to his insistence that his cabin boy let nothing seem amiss, Vere's actions typify a process of historical repression that has its haunting return at Vere's deathbed. As the numerous references to blurred vision and linguistic ambiguity suggest, there are as many cases of double-crossing as there are "double meanings." The story features a systematic blurring of historical information, which reaches the level of characters actively distorting one another's perceptions.[56] Significantly, all such maneuverings are missed by the literal-minded Billy Budd.[57] In a tale where the powers of speaking and silencing are pivotal, Vere is supremely adept at both. Though the marine soldier pointedly questions Vere's perspective at Billy's trial by inquiring as to a witness "who might shed *lateral* light" on past events,[58] the trial seems to repress rather than to uncover information, its outcome fixed from the outset by Vere. The mysterious homily that closes the scene, however, does shed light on the obscuring of historical information.

Beginning with its attribution to an author "whom few know," the passage revels in the subject of mystification. It is difficult, the narrator observes, to achieve a reasoned judgment under the "ob-

---

[56] Stanton Garner thoroughly analyzes Melville's alteration of historical information from the details of the story's eighteenth-century background. But he does not connect these observations to an understanding of how historical narration is portrayed in the story. See "Fact as Fraud in Herman Melville's 'Billy Budd,' " *San Jose Studies* (1977): 82–105. Other recent critics who provide insights into the matter of history in the story include Barbara Johnson, "Melville's Fist: The Execution of 'Billy Budd,' " in *The Critical Difference* (Baltimore: Johns Hopkins University Press, 1980); and Brook Thomas, " 'Billy Budd' and the Judgment of Silence," in *Literature and Ideology*, ed. Harry Garvin (East Brunswick, N.J.: Associated University Presses, 1982).

[57] *Billy Budd*, 435. Barbara Johnson offers a fine interpretation of the various characters of *Billy Budd* as different types of readers in "Melville's Fist."

[58] *Billy Budd*, 484 (emphasis added).

scuring smoke" of martial law. Having made this admission, the narrator goes on to suggest that those in power actually depend on the confusion of emergency situations to implement their will. "The greater the fog, the more it imperils the steamer, and speed is put on though at the hazard of running somebody down. Little ween the snug card players in the cabin of the responsibilities of the sleepless man on the bridge." This makes an ironic introduction to the all-too-clear addendum that follows: "In brief, Billy Budd was formally convicted and sentenced to be hung at the yardarm in the early morning watch, it being now night."[59] Yet Billy's conviction and sentencing in the dark is consistent with the obfuscations of the trial. The "imperil[ing]" of historical truths in *Billy Budd* offers a fictional register for the "perils of historical narrative" described by Winsor.

Melville's sense of the psychological and political ramifications of historical understanding affirms the views of another late-nineteenth-century American writer, Henry James. For James as well, manipulations of temporal perceptions and historical narratives serve as means of empowering the self and dominating others. Shaping and reshaping narratives of past experience, particularly in works of the major phase, is the modus operandi of James's characters. Figures like Kate Croy, Lord Mark, Maggie Verver, and Bob and Fanny Assingham derive their chief pleasure and necessary control in and over life by narrating their own and others' histories. Moreover, James's works contain ruthless caste systems of historical consciousness, privileging those who consult memory in awareness of history's effects over those who inhabit an ahistorical void.

Recognizing one's participation in the flow of past events is a way of acknowledging responsibility for their outcome, which is not merely a privilege but a necessity in James's worlds. In *The Golden Bowl* (1904), Maggie Verver gradually becomes aware of her own role in the affair of the Prince and Charlotte. "She found

[59] Ibid., 489.

67

CHAPTER TWO

time upstairs, even in her haste, as she had repeatedly found time
before, to let the wonderments involved in these recognitions flash
at her with their customary effect of making her blink. . . . Thus
she felt the whole weight of the case drop afresh upon her shoulders."[60] And in *The Wings of the Dove* as well, a sense of the past
involves a necessary recognition of responsibility. "We shall never
be again as we were!" Kate Croy proclaims, in response to Merton
Densher's closing effort to disavow the past in favor of an order of
time in which certain deeds can be erased and original selves reclaimed.[61] But in this novel there are no original selves; characters
are burdened from the start with the desires and conflicts of parents and relations.

James's preferred personae betray an implicit awareness of how
they are made by the past, and how they may in turn empower
themselves through its remaking. For James, one must know how
to use past materials for present judgment and action. His view of
historical consciousness is Nietzschian in a way few critics have
recognized.[62] For Nietzsche and James, creative forgetting is only
made possible by a confrontation with the past's essential terms.
Rather than repressed or submerged, the past is ideally "applied,"
as the soil for present action.[63]

[60] *The Golden Bowl*, (New York: Penguin, 1973), 355.
    [61] Henry James, *The Wings of the Dove* (New York: Norton, 1978), 403.
    [62] Stephen Donadio, who studies the intellectual links between Nietzsche and
James, underplays both of their views of history. Content with a James derived
from Quentin Anderson's transcendental lineage, Donadio argues that James's vision, like Nietzsche's, was essentially ahistorical, manifesting a concern for "inner"
culture as opposed to "historical" culture. Inner culture as Donadio defines it "involves no historical awareness, manifests no historical self-consciousness." Where
culture "for the European consists in bringing oneself into a proper relation to the
accumulations (both material and spiritual) of the past, for the American it consists
essentially in the cultivation of the self, the creation and rendering of personality as
a work of art." *Nietzsche, Henry James and the Artistic Will* (New York: Oxford University Press 1978), 18–19. My own sense is that both James and Nietzsche were
more apprised of the complicating necessity of links to the past than Donadio and
others allow.
    [63] My view of Nietzsche's historical ideas is based on his *The Use and Abuse of His-
tory*, trans. Adrian Collins (Indianapolis: Bobbs-Merrill, 1957).

This is in part the burden of James's *The Awkward Age* (1899), a work that appears provocatively at the turn of the twentieth century while picturing characters who refuse to step forward in history. The novel's closing portrayal of the retreat of Nanda Brookenham and Mr. Longdon to the ahistorical realm of Beccles suggests their inability to separate past from present, to recognize their possibilities as inhabitants of a new century. The novel's structural doubling of its opening in its closing scene highlights the characters' failure to embrace their historical circumstances.

The relativism of historical knowledge, and the psychological and political complications to which it gives rise, is a conviction shared by Melville and James, and it connects them to the concerns of many theorists of the late nineteenth century. The most serious authors and theorists of this period are apprised of the ways in which the past comes under the control of the most powerful interpreters of the present. The historical uncertainty that surfaces in *Billy Budd* as a vehicle of corruption and injustice serves in the worlds of Henry James as a source of freedom, provided one has the courage and imagination to view one's place in the unfolding of historical experience.

In summary, R. G. Collingwood's characterization of the late nineteenth century as a positivist age in historiography is only partially true. While Collingwood seems justified in ascribing a good deal of distrust in speculative theorizing, an overview of the major periodicals of the period reveals a good deal of debate over the role of historical inquiry in American life.[64] Moreover, it is important to keep in mind how a major historian of our next period described late-nineteenth-century historiography. In a 1935 essay entitled "That Noble Dream," Charles Beard wrote that Ranke's brand of

---

[64] See Collingwood, *The Idea of History*, 143–47. While Collingwood's discussion focuses on European developments, John Higham has made similar claims for the United States. Indeed, Collingwood's analysis of English and German thinkers disproves Higham's suggestion that a resistance to theoretical discourse was somehow unique to America, indicative of its pragmatic outlook. See Higham, *History*, 98.

positivism, though persuasive, hardly went unchallenged even in Germany, where such theorists as Schopenhauer, Droysen, Lorenz, Bernheim, and Lamprecht consistently betrayed a "penetrating skepticism" toward Ranke's views.[65]

History as a "Social" Science

The historical point of view that emerged from "the century of Comte, Darwin, Hegel, Marx, and Spencer" saw an enlarged role for the historical interpreter. Historians such as James Harvey Robinson, Charles Beard, Frederick Jackson Turner, and Thorstein Veblen unapologetically emphasized contemporary issues and problems in researching the past. Their particular brand of "historicism" has been defined as "the attempt to explain facts by reference to earlier facts . . . reach[ing] back in time in order to account for certain phenomena."[66] This evolutionary approach to present conditions by reference to earlier ones merged with a new interest in economic factors as primary motivating forces in history. Such concerns dominated the debates of the period that preceded Dreiser's writing of *An American Tragedy* (1925).

Early-twentieth-century historians were strongly influenced by developments in the social sciences to view their own research as useful for a greater understanding of their cultural present. Educated first at Harvard, and then in Germany like most of his predecessors in the field of political history, James Harvey Robinson (1863–1936) might have held to the relatively orthodox scholarship of his early career. Instead, as a historian at the University of Pennsylvania and at Columbia, Robinson became a leading proponent of the "New History." With his colleague Charles Beard, Robinson combined an interest in social and historical studies, and considered an understanding of the beginnings of contemporary

[65] In Fritz Stern, ed., *The Varieties of History* (New York: Meridian, 1956), 314–28.

[66] Morton White, *Social Thought in America: The Revolt against Formalism* (Boston: Beacon, 1947), 11–12.

institutions essential to their improvement. The historical present seemed most mystifying to these thinkers: whereas the past represented a fixed plane that allowed for a clear and detached perspective, the fluctuating present eluded comprehension. The major historians of this period seemed to agree that the past must be made to serve the present. As Robinson was fond of repeating, the historian's role was to help his reader understand the morning newspaper. In a 1912 tract on the "New History," Robinson took issue with a number of assumptions in previous historiographic methods. Qualifying the exclusive claims of political history by asserting that "Man is more than a warrior, a subject, or a princely ruler,"[67] he observes that earlier historians taught us "to view mankind as in a periodic state of turmoil . . . like geologist[s] who should have no use for anything smaller than an elephant or less romantic in its habits than a phoenix or a basilisk."[68] To remedy such distortions, Robinson advocates a more mundane approach, which he defines as a focus on "the ways in which people have thought and acted in the past, their tastes and their achievements in many fields besides the political." History is seen as the study of past institutions, now more broadly defined in social and economic as well as in "political" terms. Historical events are to be considered "expressions" of institutions, but not as ends to historical understanding in themselves.[69] So far this sounds like a vague democratization of Herbert Baxter Adams's "germ theory." A social instrument that develops alongside the "general progress of society and of the social sciences," history is a particularly powerful tool in American intellectual life.[70]

Robinson becomes more idiosyncratic and interesting when he describes the actual method by which historical understanding is achieved. Such a process, he informs us, is indistinguishable from the operations of memory. Robinson uses as his test case an ex-

---

[67] James Harvey Robinson, *The New History* (New York: Macmillan, 1912), 8–9.
[68] Ibid., 12, 49.
[69] Ibid., 15.
[70] Ibid., 25.

ample of the reader falling asleep while reading his history, and describes the reader's bewilderment upon waking. In struggling to discover where he is, and why he is seated before this open book, the reader must consult his memory. "The mind selects automatically," Robinson writes, "from the almost infinite mass of memories, just those things in our past which make us feel at home in the present . . . [supplying] what we need from the past in order to make the present intelligible."[71] From this example Robinson moves to a view of history itself as "an artificial extension and broadening of our memories . . . used to overcome the natural bewilderment of all unfamiliar situations."[72] History is thus seen as a bridge of consciousness that helps us to feel more at home in the present.

But this emphasis on the historian's present-oriented and even opportunistic pursuit of historical knowledge is balanced by another point in Robinson's discussion of methods. Arguing that the historian need not concern himself with entertaining his readers, Robinson claims that "the conscientious historian . . . cannot aspire to be a good story-teller for the simple reason that if he tells no more than he has good reason for believing to be true, his tale is usually very fragmentary and vague."[73] The first priority of history writing is to show how things come about; it must be confined to the hard facts, and to the "more or less permanent habits and environment of a particular people or person."[74]

In his summary statement on the "New History," Robinson considers the role of history in an era of increasing specialization. With each discipline claiming its own intellectual territory, the historian maintains the unique position of interdisciplinary seer who can grasp the whole picture. Whereas a theologian, a political scientist, or a sociologist each might view the Crusades in terms of his particular expertise, the historian is able "to retell the story,

---

[71] Ibid., 18–19.
[72] Ibid., 20.
[73] Ibid., 51.
[74] Ibid., 52.

utilizing all that they had accomplished, including what they had all omitted, and rectifying the errors into which each had fallen on account of his ignorance of the general situation."[75] Thus the historian is, "from a narrow, scientific point of view, a little higher than a man of letters and a good deal lower than an astronomer or a biologist." More importantly, he is "the critic and guide of the social sciences whose results he must synthesize and test by the actual life of mankind as it appears in the past."[76]

Robinson's theories, it must be pointed out, are hardly self-consistent. Historians on the one hand admit their incapacities as storytellers, presenting their knowledge accurately as fragments. Yet the historian is also a holistic weaver who can somehow integrate the threads of various specialities to achieve a unified vision of the past. Likewise, while the historian is dependent on the laws of contemporary social science for understanding the past, the social scientist is himself unable to devise these laws without some foreknowledge of "the actual life" of the past. Robinson's views seem to unravel as he moves from criticism of predecessors to formulations of his own. Yet this seems the dilemma of most of the era's theorists, who cite the centrality of present needs and knowledge for study of the past, but claim some essential and objective information to be derived from that past. Above all, these thinkers see history as a continuous process of reaction and change; the interpreter brings his sense of the present to bear on the past, and his sense of the past to bear on the present.

Such an assumption pervades the collaborative history by Robinson and Beard, *The Development of Modern Europe* (1907–1908). Dissatisfied with the static positivism of preceding historiographic practitioners, and skeptical about the literary uses of their enterprise, Robinson and Beard adopted a self-conscious stance toward their work, seeking to catch themselves in the very act of writing history. Their interest in the continuity of historical processes in-

[75] Ibid., 67.
[76] Ibid., 69.

fluenced their desire for an unmediated historiography, which involved a recognition of how the present was creating the past just as it was being created, at any given moment, by that past. Their aim was "historical explanation of the present," to see themselves as interpreters in the actual flow of historical experience.

Some historians were even more committed than Robinson to the idea of history as a tool of present inquiry. Thorstein Veblen and Charles Beard united a concern for contemporary problems with a complex grounding in economic theory. Though Robinson had also expressed an interest in economics by locating the roots of his theories in Marx's *The Holy Family*, it was Veblen and Beard who insisted on the pivotal causal role of economic factors in history. C. Wright Mills has nicely captured Veblen's aims as "a social thinker in the grand tradition": "To grasp the essentials of an entire society and epoch, To delineate the characters of the typical men within it, To determine its main drift."[77] Though Veblen (1857–1929) was by training an economist, his masterful *The Theory of the Leisure Class* (1899) was an early example of historiographic efforts to chart an economic genealogy of American life. Like its author, who remained a perpetual, though highly respected, outsider in the elite institutions of American academia, Veblen's work stands somewhere between the fields of sociology, history, economics, and cultural analysis.

Detailing the evolution of the leisure class as a biologist would a particular species of bird, Veblen described three stages of social development. The first stage was peaceful savagism, followed by militaristic barbarism, which grew into a type of predatory barbarism—the current state of American society. The predatory cast of modern life is seen in human labor, where only "arms are honorable," and "the handling of tools . . . falls beneath the dignity of able-bodied men," a situation that has a spiritual corollary. Indeed, the primary point for Veblen is "a spiritual . . . not a me-

[77] From Mills's introduction to Veblen's *The Theory of the Leisure Class* (New York: Mentor, 1953), x.

74

chanical one. . . . The change in spiritual attitude is the outgrowth of a change in the material facts of the life of the group, and it comes on gradually as the material circumstances favorable to a predatory attitude supervene."[78] Turn-of-the-century America amply supplies the requisites for a barbarism seen most vividly in the language of appropriation that governs the relations between men and women. Veblen compares earlier barbaric habits of "seizing women from the enemy as trophies" to modern conventions of "ownership-marriage. . . . Both arise from the desire of the successful men to put their prowess in evidence by exhibiting some durable result of their exploits."[79] Veblen sees individual ownership and surplus as the common enemies: in the example of present society, the possession of wealth "for the purpose of a commonplace decent standing in the community . . . ha[s] been replaced by the acquisition and accumulation of goods."[80]

Central to Veblen's argument, and what makes it such an important example of the "New History," is his view of the leisure class as an anachronism, exemplifying the present's servitude to outmoded forces set in motion by the past. Institutions, in Veblen's view, always run the risk of obsolescence: formed in the past, they can never be fully acclimated to present needs. The only spur to institutional change comes from the individuals who make up these institutions. Thus, the key to the growth and flexibility of institutions lies in the exposure of their members to the "intellectual and spiritual stress of modern organized industry, which requires a constant recognition of the undisguised phenomena of impersonal, matter-of-fact sequence and an unreserved conformity to the law of cause and effect."[81] The extent to which all social classes are forced to confront the realities of historical change, is the extent to which a given society can bring about productive changes in its institutions. And this is where Veblen's work be-

[78] Veblen, *Theory*, 31, 32.
[79] Ibid., 34.
[80] Ibid., 38.
[81] Ibid., 210.

comes radical in form as well as in content. For by attempting to bring "the leisure class" into confrontation with an unflattering genealogy, Veblen sought to elicit the shock of recognition essential to genuine social reform.

Though born into a wealthy midwestern family, Charles Beard's (1874–1948) taste of Chicago urban life in the 1890s led to a lifelong commitment to radical reform. During his term of study at Oxford, Beard was greatly influenced by the work of Ruskin, and he participated in the organization of Ruskin Hall and of the local labor reform movement. Beard's social activism continued as a faculty member in the department of history at Columbia. It is not surprising, given his political activities, that his historiographic methods betray strong revisionary aims.

In offering his famous economic interpretation of the Constitution's framing, Beard began by dissociating his work from previous schools of historiography. His monograph was not of the mystical Bancroft school, "which gives unity to the universe and order and connection to events." Nor was it aligned with the racial theories of the Teutonic school, or the positivism of "scientific historians."[82] The self-consciousness of Beard's challenge to previous historiographic practice is revealed by his disclosure of James Madison's *Federalist 10* as the inspiration for his economic historiography. Beard's location of an American ancestry for his methods was clearly tactical, and it suggests his awareness of his monograph's subversiveness. Modifying the hallowed status of America's founders to a nation anxiously assimilating growing numbers of foreign immigrants required a native methodology. Beard directly confronted the anticipated xenophobic reactions to his analysis: "Those who are inclined to repudiate the hypothesis of economic determinism as a European importation must, therefore, revise their views, on learning that one of the earliest, and certainly one of the clearest, statements of it came from a profound

[82] Charles Beard, *An Economic Interpretation of the Constitution of the United States* (New York: Macmillan, 1913), 1.

76

student of politics who sat in the Convention that framed our fundamental law."[83]

Employing hitherto unused source materials on the economic backgrounds of the participants at the Philadelphia Constitutional Convention, Beard's revisionary concerns were primarily methodological. Beard reopened a well-known chapter of the national past and brought new data to bear on his understanding of historical motivation: putting previous methods to the test, he found them wanting in depth and comprehensiveness. His exhaustive reexamination of this pivotal group in American history exemplified the New Historians' efforts to apply present advances in social scientific technique to the study of old problems. Beard's effort to analyze the political beliefs of convention members through the use of data on their class and economic standing was not an attempt to destroy the reputations of America's founders, but rather a means to bring them into sharper focus. When the methodological innovativeness of Beard's work is recognized, his study appears less patricidal, and more consistent with the historiographic theories of his contemporaries.[84] Like them, he was committed to the alignment of historiography and social science, and was dissatisfied with previous "romantic" and "positivistic" methods. He advocated a historiography that would be self-conscious about its governing assumptions, and modest about its capacities to render the past objectively.

It seems appropriate, in light of the foremost aims of the New Historians, to summarize their ideas by looking backward in time at a historian who can be seen as one of the harbingers of their movement. Frederick Jackson Turner (1861–1932) wrote one of the most important treatises to appear at the end of the nineteenth century: "The Significance of the Frontier in American History,"

[83] Ibid., 16.

[84] Just how radical Beard's monograph was has long been a source of historiographic debate. Richard Hofstader demonstrates that contemporary responses to Beard ranged from resounding approval to outrage. See *The Progressive Historians* (New York: Knopf, 1968), 212–15.

published in 1893. Turner, who was born in a Wisconsin territory on the edge of the frontier, was disposed toward the graduate education he received at the University of Wisconsin, which emphasized the role of western expansion in American history. But though he is best known as a theorist of the frontier, Turner wrote a more general theoretical essay in 1891 that is more directly relevant to the historiographic theories of the early twentieth century. "The Significance of History" espouses a cautious relativism. Every age, Turner argues, must rewrite the past, not because it changes but because "our comprehension of these facts change [sic]. . . . The historian strives to show the present to itself by revealing its origins from the past."[85] Turner's historiographic method is a catholic one; all disciplines, political, economic, and religious, are utilized in man's attempt to know himself historically. No history is ultimate, for every historian writes with the particular blinders of his own age. As Turner writes, "Each age must be studied in light of all the past; local history must be viewed in the light of world history . . . [which] enables us to behold our own time and place as part of the stupendous progress of the ages; to see primitive man; to recognize in our midst the undying ideas of Greece; to find Rome's majesty and power alive in present law and institutions, still living in our superstitions and our folklore."[86] Historical narration allows us to see ourselves in our human richness as inhabitants of time.

In a plea that harks back to a previous generation of democratic historians, Turner asserts that America's history not only comprises the Anglo-American past, but also includes the pasts of immigrants from various nations. Though they become "American," they do not give up their own pasts, but must be seen as "historical products . . . with deeply inrooted customs and ideas."[87] Turner's emphases—on the interconnectedness of past and present; the in-

[85] Frederick Jackson Turner, "The Significance of History," in Stern, ed., *Varieties of History*, 200–201.
[86] Ibid., 204.
[87] Ibid., 206.

separability of local, national, and international history; the need for liberality in historiographic methods; and the importance of recognizing the differences as well as the unifying similarities among Americans—typify the interests of the New Historians. Turner's most telling point is an elusive suggestion of the value to be derived from the act of thinking historically. In Turner's view, history writing is the essential medium for self-knowledge and change. History is only of use methodologically in what it aspires to, never as an object in itself. Turner ends appropriately with a quotation from Droysen: " 'History is not the truth and the light; but a striving for it, a sermon on it, a consecration to it.' "[88]

The link between Dreiser's conception of history in *An American Tragedy* (1925) and the theories of the New Historians lies in their shared concern for man's inescapable entrapment in time, and the accompanying awareness of the power to be derived from a flexible narrative relation to the past. Man is the product of his past, a fact that can serve as a source of freedom if recognized and put to work in the present. But consciousness is the key, and the past is only freeing to those aware of its pliability. Thus, individuals like Clyde Griffiths experience time exclusively as entrapment, while others, like Samuel Griffiths, are able to manipulate its effects. The differences among the relations of the characters to history are especially vivid in the novel's third book, which from its opening pages invokes the relativity of historical knowledge. Efforts to reconstruct the past of Clyde Griffiths, whose own eyes are beclouded by guilt over the past and fear of future retribution, are inseparable from the claims of present interests. More importantly, all these efforts suggest that human experience is made significant only through its retrospective interpretation.

In the novel's climactic boat scene, Clyde can be seen as tottering on the brink of historical signification. On the marginal waters of that "purely ideational lake," Clyde wavers between the anonymity of his timeless dreams and the notoriety of a historical ac-

[88] Ibid., 208.

tor whose life will become the province of interpretation. Landing on the side of history as meaning, his life becomes consequent, conceived by others to possess a coherent pattern. Clyde's fall, no less than Adam's, is a fall into the chaotic babble of historical interpreters, all striving for a singular knowledge of historical truth. And though they appear a babble, the various versions of Clyde's history told in Book 3 cohere sufficiently to ensure his condemnation. The novel's weary repetition of its opening in its closing scene suggests that no genuine historical understanding has been achieved in this world. Time, so far as the novel's characters are concerned, has stood still, and history will go on repeating itself to its end.

Historical knowledge as conceived in *An American Tragedy* is sufficient to kill, but inadequate to the task of self-knowledge posed by Turner. A view of the past here cannot be used to alter or invigorate the shape of the present. The novel points presciently to a major concern of historical theorists of the 1980s—the problem of what Hayden White has termed "getting out of history."[89] The "way out" of the trap of history for Dreiser is twofold. First one must recognize that history comes to us not as innocent or objectified facts, but always as part of someone else's scheme. This is the sense of the novel's opening sentences, which warn that soon this crumbling urban scene will be recoverable in fable alone. It is only by a recognition of how our sense of the past is mediated by the narrative frame of some other's point of view that we may begin to understand how to free ourselves from its chains. Clyde Griffiths's dilemma at the novel's end is that he is able to see the falsity of the versions of his past given by others, but is unable to move from this awareness to embrace the demands of his own historical narration. Apprised of the inadequacy of narratives of his past by others, he hopes for some objectively seizable past, failing to see that it is the *act* of narration alone that would

---

[89] See Hayden White's essay "Getting Out of History," a review of Fredric Jameson's *The Political Unconscious*, in *Diacritics* (Fall 1982): 2–13.

allow him to reclaim it. Clyde's consistent inability throughout the novel to embrace the possibilities of action is repeated in his failure to embrace the role of historian at its end. The novel closes on the "dazed eyes" of a protagonist incapable of confronting his necessary involvement in the recreation of his past.

The ending to *An American Tragedy* can be viewed in terms of Hayden White's distinction in his essay "Getting Out of History" between an ideological narrative that condemns human beings "to an eternal return of history's alienating necessities," and a narrative conducive "to the effort of liberating man from history."[90] Dreiser's novel pictures the triumph of the former. Yet White's essay ultimately undermines any liberating potential of historical narration. His closing question, "Is not all narrative an excuse for real political struggle?" leads him to interrogate the actual political consequences of common ideas of narrativity. "Is it not possible that the doctrine of 'History' so arduously cultivated by the Western tradition of thought since the Greeks as an instrument for releasing human consciousness from the constraints of the Archaic age, is ready for retirement along with the 'politics' that it helped to enable? And could not the death of History, politics, and narrative all be aspects of another great transformation, similar in scope and effect to that which marked the break with Archaism begun by the Greeks? The problem may not be how to get into history but how to get out of it."[91]

White's observations are provocative indeed, insisting that narrative represses and defuses the political contradictions we live by. In refuting its reparative or consciousness-raising claims, White exposes what I have called "the fallacy of historical self-consciousness." This fallacy may be defined as the hope that we can change our world simply by our awareness of how it has made us, and how we in turn have made it. White's is a troubling reminder of our own entrapment in the institutions that support our work, and

[90] Ibid., 6.
[91] Ibid., 13.

in the circumscribed discussions that energize those institutions.

In the following pages, we will encounter various fictional meditations on the possibilities offered by historical narration. Some of my examples will seem to take the more optimistic stance of the New Historians, representing the act of confronting the past narratively as a means for freeing present action. They will suggest that historical awareness is attainable, that it facilitates greater self-awareness and may even further political action. We will find other works less convinced of these propositions, and inclined to stress the danger of beliefs that the past can be confronted, understood, and applied. What all share are the questions themselves, the commitment to sustained reflection upon the psychological and political effects of historical narration. These are questions that our historians, far from having clarified, have more appropriately helped to complicate.

THREE

From History to Gingerbread:
Manufacturing a Republic in *The House*
of the Seven Gables

🦎

The reader must look for his local and national qualities between the lines of his writing and in the indirect *testimony of his tone, his temper, of his very omissions and suppressions.*—*Henry James*, Hawthorne[1]

THE HOUSE *of the Seven Gables* holds a precarious position in the canon of the American author commonly regarded as our foremost "historian." Less historically serious than its classic predecessor, *The Scarlet Letter*, it falls short of the contemporary relevance of its successor, *The Blithedale Romance*, which highlights the problems of nineteenth-century women and utopian reformers. On the whole, *Seven Gables* seems a more disengaged work, a rather loosely structured indulgence that Hawthorne wrote to appease his wife and contemporaries after the gloom of *The Scarlet Letter*. But if the novel feels inaccessible to us as a work of historical and political intensity, it may have to do with the fact that its very subject is the role of history in a democratic republic, and that its own dramatization of historical concerns reflects that role. One way to think about history's representation in *Seven Gables* is as a phenomenon continually evaded: history is most vividly evident as an absent cause.

This is especially true of the conclusion, where the characters' retreat into a realm of ahistorical harmony appears to absorb any lingering tensions generated by a sense of past or future historical developments. At the novel's close, the "evil genius" of the Pyn-

[1] (New York: Macmillan, 1966), 109–110.

cheon family is dead, Holgrave marries the last daughter of the
Pyncheon line to bury the hatchet of class antagonism, and all depart for their inherited country estate. Yet problems persist beneath the romantic haze that envelops the departure of the characters. For one, the ending is peculiar for a work that ridicules the
aristocratic pretensions of its characters, and whose preface criticizes the debilitating effects of inheritance. The contradictions of
the ending elaborate tensions that pervade the novel, and can be
profitably considered in terms of the novel's meta-historical approach to the problem of history. Our explorations in Chapter
Two, which demonstrate the extent of theorizing on history in this
period, allow us to see *Seven Gables* as part of a cultural dialogue on
the possibilities and limits of historical knowledge.

At its most basic level, *Seven Gables* explores the effects of the
"sins of the fathers" on the lives of the sons, an ancestral backdrop
from which another theme emerges: the social and economic development of nineteenth-century America, and the accompanying
cultural obsession with the making of a new republic. The idea of
the self-conscious creation of America is central to Sacvan Bercovitch's paradigm for the course of national history. He argues for
the special importance of ideology in the shaping of the American
nation, describing the persistent resolution of "antithetical cultural pressures" through the rhetoric of "the American way." For
Bercovitch, Hawthorne's narratives reveal a tension between the
hope in America's promise and the fear of its doom. But this view
may be too far from the claim that James makes for the elusiveness
of Hawthorne's national vision. In accepting the rhetoric of Hawthorne's narrators as the last word in his social and political perspective, Bercovitch forecloses what James foresaw: that Hawthorne's complicated narrative techniques may in fact betray his
social consciousness.[2]

[2] Sacvan Bercovitch, *The Puritan Origins of the American Self* (New Haven: Yale
University Press, 1975), 185 and 136–86. See also *The American Jeremiad* (Madison:
University of Wisconsin Press, 1978), esp. 205–210.

Like any cultural text, Hawthorne's *Seven Gables* is a vehicle of ideology. What is exceptional about this work is that it portrays the process of creating an ideology. Both narrator and characters are involved at some level in narrating a series of histories that picture a cohesive, harmonic American society in the face of social, political, and economic realities that it plainly contradicts. A key scene in the novel pinpoints the obsession with self-imaging that permeates its society. As Hepzibah prepares to open her cent shop, an eighteenth-century holdover which suggests the twilight aspect of the novel's sense of time, the narrator records the changes that have come about in nineteenth-century merchandising practices.[3]

Most striking among the differences between past and present is the aspect of the goods themselves, "of a description and outward form which could hardly have been known [in old shopkeeper Pyncheon's] day." The eighteenth-century items are practical and nondescript, "one containing flour, another apples," "square box[es]" of soap or "tallow candles." These raw and elemental goods are of a "low price . . . such as are constantly in demand."[4] Hepzibah's goods suggest the greater technological expertise and more aggressive salesmanship of the nineteenth-century producer. In the world of infant consumer capitalism, dealers are less concerned merely to supply necessities. Their aim is to entice customers through the appearance of goods on display, to activate human desires beyond the level of necessity toward those of material excess. Yet the exposure of contemporary culture contained in this scene runs deeper. Hepzibah Pyncheon, the would-be aristocrat turned bourgeois shopkeeper, is another agent of a new consumer

CHAPTER THREE

orientation that takes various images of cultural pride and turns them into saleable commodities in the American marketplace.

There was a glass pickle-jar, filled with fragments of Gibraltar-rock; not, indeed, splinters of the veritable stone foundation of the famous fortress, but bits of delectable candy, neatly done up in white paper. Jim Crow, moreover, was seen executing his world-renowned dance in gingerbread. A party of leaden dragoons were galloping along one of the shelves, in equipments and uniform of modern cut; and there were some sugar figures, with no strong resemblance to the humanity of any epoch, but less unsatisfactorily representing our own fashions than those of a hundred years ago. Another phenomenon, still more strikingly modern, was a package of lucifer-matches, which, in old times, would have been thought actually to borrow their instaneous flame from the nether fires of Tophet. (35–36)

As embodiments of cultural "mythologies," these modern goods reveal contemporary conceptions of self and nation.[5] The gingerbread Jim Crow perhaps best exemplifies Roland Barthes's notion of images that resolve collective anxieties and conflicts. This merry figure, "executing his world-renowned dance," defuses the specific historical conditions of blacks in mid-nineteenth-century America into one harmonious emblem. Via gingerbread, the complex and troubling black populace of 1851 is transformed into an eatable sweet doing an obliging "it's jes me folks" dance. Likewise, the lucifer matches represent the ancient source of fire now contained in a marketable commodity. The power of the wilderness

[5] Roland Barthes describes such middle-class myths as "constituted by the loss of the historical quality of things . . . the world enters language as a dialectical relation between activities, between human actions; it comes out of myth as a harmonious display of essences. A conjuring trick has taken place; it has turned reality inside out, it has emptied it of history and has filled it with nature, it has removed things from their human meaning so as to signify a human insignificance." For Barthes, the result of any "bourgeois" myth is to separate ordinary experience from its temporal hinges, from its place in historical time, removing it to an eternal order that serves to minimize or obscure "real" human existence. This description of Hepzibah's shopgoods paradoxically reveals the eternalized images of myth, and the conditions of commodity exchange that belie them. "Myth Today," in *A Barthes Reader*, ed. Susan Sontag (New York: Hill and Wang, 1982), 130–31.

emblemized in the Gibraltar-rock becomes a tourist's bauble, a monument now for sale in sweet shops across the country.

One could build upon the psychology of nineteenth-century economic life suggested by this scene of Hepzibah opening shop. Her obsession with the "public eye" (39), those who would have "the privilege of gazing" (46) into her shop window, exemplifies Marx's idea of the fetishism of commodities. Hepzibah's goods are personalized; they reflect her own self-image. In exposing her wares before "strange and unloving eyes," Hepzibah "is doubly tortured . . . with a sense of overwhelming shame . . . that the window was not arranged so skillfully, nor nearly to so much advantage, as it might have been." In light of Hepzibah's anguished "adornment of her person" (29) in the chapter's opening pages, it appears that the selling of goods has somehow become conflated with the selling of self, even for so unlikely a figure as Hepzibah.[6]

Any exploration of republic-making in *Seven Gables* must come to terms with the prominent personality of the novel's narrator, who provides a critique of his novel's society that goes beyond the polarities of celebrating and lamenting the prospective destiny of America. What is needed is a close reading of the narrative that presents the narrator as a highly idiosyncratic and strategic voice, and that speculates on the unconscious beliefs and anxieties that motivate social discourse. The narrator poses as his central subject the impact of the nation's past on its present. But attempts by him and by other characters to tell the story of a decrepit mansion and a fading lineage become, like psychoanalytic case studies, mirrors of their present psychological and political conditions. What is most striking for a novel whose governing idea is inheritance—in which the dilemma of historical determinism is seriously pon-

---

[6] This description seems to unite the excesses of Puritan self-involvement—what Bercovitch calls the Puritan "liebestod" of identity—with the objectification of human beings in capitalist society (*Puritan Origins*, 18–23). Richard Sennett provides a brief but interesting discussion on this point in *The Fall of Public Man* (New York: Vintage, 1978), 11–12.

dered—is that most of the characters seem unaware of historical changes, and appear strangely unaffected by their ancestors.

Hawthorne's characters and narrator, like Nietzsche's moderns, evade a present they are too ineffectual to meet by retreating into a mythic past. The novel suggests that history is only available to consciousness in reified form, which helps explain how the characters can be obsessed with theories of temporality and history, but deny their own relationships to their particular historical moment.[7] The contradiction is borne out in the wily argument of the novel's preface. Expressing a desire for latitude in the interpretation of history, the narrator refers to the past as a sort of garnish the reader is free to accept or disregard, "according to his pleasure." At the same time, however, the past is called a determining force, the "wrong-doing of one generation liv[ing] into the successive ones." This duplicitous vision brings us to the heart of the opposition traced through the pages of the novel, an opposition between two distinct attitudes toward time and history. The ahistorical or "mythic" view is concentrated in various contemporary images—products of the specific historical world from which they emerge that curiously deny that connection. The historical view found in the characters' (and narrator's) unconscious records the difference between the past and present, while establishing the roots of another historical reality, the advent of a new consumer world.

This chapter begins by exploring the characters' attitudes to-

---

[7] For a discussion of the term "reification" and its application to nineteenth-century American literature, see Carolyn Porter, *Seeing and Being* (Middletown, Conn.: Wesleyan University Press, 1981), ch. 2. Michael Colacurcio has described the sense of history in *Seven Gables* as "telescope[d] . . . from the other end. From the vantage of [Hawthorne's] own novelistic present . . . the impulse behind the historic romances of post-Puritan America led straight on, if not to the 'international novel,' then surely to the attempt to place America itself in historical (or perhaps in meta-historical) perspective." See *The Province of Piety* (Cambridge, Mass.: Harvard University Press, 1984), 32, 34. Colacurcio's work ranges brilliantly between close readings of Hawthorne's early tales to major theoretical arguments about the presence of history in Hawthorne.

ward history, focusing upon their denials of historical process. The analysis of history is then extended into a view of the narrator, his attempts to evade his perceptions of historical change by positing a realm of eternal and fixed meaning. Finally, there is an examination of the novel's confrontation with history, which, I argue, comprises the underlying political vision of the narrator and characters, and serves to contradict the eternal designs studied earlier in the chapter.

The Characters' Mirror of History

All of the characters in *Seven Gables* exhibit uncertainty about their place in history, which becomes for some an obsession with the past as a plane of time that can be imaginatively controlled. The characters' absorption with the past arises from their fears of "the very present that is flitting away from us" (preface). Yet it is also a realization of what that present contains. Their various uses of the past exemplify Walter Benjamin's idea of "commemoration," which expresses "the increasing alienation of human beings who take inventories of their past as of lifeless merchandise."[8] As Benjamin's notion implies, those who are alienated in the present replicate that alienation in their response to the past. The words "lifeless" and "merchandise" tell the story of human beings who do not see beyond the terms of commercial exchange and value, for whom the past can only bear the aura of a commodity. The escape to the past in *Seven Gables* is grounded in the very terms of the characters' commercial present, revealing how fully their contemporary alienation governs their past imaginings.

Hepzibah Pyncheon is the most obvious example of a character who uses the past to evade her present. The source of the narrator's sweeping claim, "In this republican country, amid the fluctuating waves of our social life, somebody is always at the drowning point" (38), Hepzibah's obsession with the family

[8] Walter Benjamin, *Werke*, 1 (Frankfurt, 1955), 487, quoted in Jameson, *Marxism and Form*, 73.

CHAPTER THREE

archives is a response to a contemporary sphere that threatens her submergence. One striking feature of the chapter that introduces Hepzibah's cent shop is the contiguity between the consciousnesses of Hepzibah and the narrator: both are reluctant to proceed with the respective tasks set out for them.[9] The narrator is a self-conscious procrastinator, loathe to begin a tale tainted by the profane details of commercial enterprise. Fashioning himself an aristocrat, unfamiliar with mercenary activities, he finds his forthcoming subject "disagreeably delicate to handle" and fears it may "damage any picturesque and romantic impression" (28) he had hoped his narrative might make. Chapter Two reveals the narrator still "loitering faintheartedly at the threshold of our story" (34); not until the middle of the chapter does he finally disclose Hepzibah's business venture. He hesitates and wavers before a historical reality he is unprepared to meet, just as Hepzibah, hoping to maintain her role as a surviving representative of the formerly well-endowed Pyncheon aristocracy, refuses Holgrave's payment for shopgoods, commenting, "Let me be a lady a moment longer" (46).

Hepzibah is "time-stricken," incompatible with the demands of the present, which leads her to fantasize a past over which her imaginative control might be complete. Her sense of the past is kindled by family ornaments that provide an overall view of Pyncheon attitudes toward history. Hanging on one wall is "a map of the Pyncheon territory . . . grotesquely illuminated with pictures of Indians and wild beasts, among which was seen a lion; the natural history of the region being as little known as its geography, which was put down most fantastically awry" (33). The other noteworthy item is a portrait of Colonel Pyncheon, standing and holding a bible in "one hand and in the other uplifting an iron sword-hilt. The latter object . . . stood out in far greater prominence than the sacred volume" (33). These ornaments reveal the

9 For an insightful parallel of Hepzibah and the narrator in different terms, see Michael Gilmore, "The Artist and the Marketplace in *The House of the Seven Gables*," *ELH* 48 (1981): 172–89.

Pyncheon view of history as a malleable plane of domination and plunder. The map suggests their indifference to the ecological and geographical details of the New England environment, exposing their isolation from the real world, and their inability to see that world from any but their own willful perspective. The portrait similarly depicts the Pyncheon method of operating in history— with God and the sword on one's side. The sword's visual domination over the sacred tome renders symbolically the Pyncheon conviction that if one wields the sword, spiritual sanction will follow.

Hepzibah's response to these historical emblems is superficially reverential, a feeling "of which only a far-descended and time-stricken virgin could be susceptible" (34). But it becomes apparent that Hepzibah's deeper response to the Pyncheon view of history is subversive in its own right. She has no sympathy for the modern embodiment of the old Colonel's creed, Judge Pyncheon; she is at odds with social law, the vehicle of past precedent; and the recurrent details of the family history that filter past her voluntary memories (through the agency of others, or sometimes despite herself) are often less than happily memorable (85, 127, 131, 243). What seems most compelling to her about these random images of family history is their suggestion that the past can be conceived apart from the processes of historical change, as an eternal fulfillment of human desire.

Another item in the family archives, the tea set with the Pyncheon crest, captures Hepzibah's desired view of time. Those pictured in the china setting "were odd humorists, in a world of their own; a world of vivid brilliancy, so far as color went, and still unfaded, although the tea-pot and small cups were as ancient as the custom itself of tea-drinking" (77). The family past that affords Hepzibah's imaginings is a realm without beginning or end, a world emptied of the details that would link it to a specific era or locale. The Pyncheon domination of their environment, once so complete that they need not concern themselves with any of its natural facts, is now mirrored in the remnants of that supremacy,

91

the tea service that seems to have waged a war against time and won, given its "vivid brilliancy," its "still unfaded" design. Hepzibah dwells in an imagined aristocratic domain that has conquered time itself. Yet the novel depicts a curious challenge to her reveries.

Whenever Hepzibah is immersed in her "aristocratic reminiscences," the shop bell rings to signal the demands of her present in the form of shop customers. In the first such scene, Hepzibah, seated in the oak elbowchair, literally stationed in the arms of the past, is "suddenly startled by the tinkling alarum—high, sharp, and irregular—of a little bell. The maiden lady arose upon her feet, as pale as a ghost at cockcrow; for she was an enslaved spirit, and this the talisman to which she owed obedience" (42). Hepzibah responds as if a spell wielded by a contemporary "talisman" is upon her. This scene calls to mind the experience of the Custom-House inspector, who, while poring over old documents, becomes entranced by a talisman in the form of a tattered letter from the past. But where Hepzibah's spirit is a shrill cry from the present, signaling the arrival of anonymous customers demanding service, the inspector's spirit is a haunting voice from the past, summoning its subject to filial and professional obligations. The personal entreaty of his talisman assumes the continuity of traditions between generations, and the dependence and loyalty of the subject. In *Seven Gables*, Hepzibah herself is the "ghost" being pulled into the present. Disconnected from a traditional past, she also is withdrawn from her effort to find some meaningful historical message.

The novel portrays characters so deprived of a connection to tradition that they cannot recognize how far their present has fallen from it. And no voices sound from the past to point up the difference. The past, contained in various wooden images, portraits, and territorial maps, is a field of "lifeless merchandise," reflecting a vision of history as an eternal plane for the playing out of human ambitions. Still, Hepzibah by necessity pursues some imaginative link to the past. And she is repeatedly called back from her imaginings as if to emphasize the impossibility of those connections.

The shop bell rings eleven times in the novel, intruding upon her communion with the "crested tea-spoons and antique China," just at those moments when she is lost in "ideas of gentility" (78).

By comparison, Clifford Pyncheon's relation to the past is one of complete immersion. He is introduced as so mentally fixed in the past that he is incapable of propelling himself forward: "paus[ing] at the head of the staircase; he paused again at the foot. Each time, the delay seemed to be without purpose, but rather from a forgetfulness of the purpose which had set him in motion" (103). Clifford comes to a standstill at each step because his lack of short-term memory leaves him without the idea of what "had set him in motion." Having erased all painful memories from his mind, his existence stationed in an unchanging youth, Clifford typifies the passivity that accompanies the lack of a discriminating historical vision.

Clifford's rapture over the scent of a flower in another scene further reveals his disorientation. "I used to prize this flower—long ago," he cries, "I supposed very long ago!—or was it only yesterday? It makes me feel young again! Am I young?" (110). Clifford's inability to distinguish among moments in time is inseparable from his self-alienation. Yet rather than an inevitable condition, Clifford's displaced memory suggests an unwillingness to accept responsibility for the necessity of action, a point that reemerges at the novel's end.

Significantly, in "The Flight of Two Owls" chapter, Clifford does take a concerted step, arising from the ancient mansion to enter his nineteenth-century present. As he and Hepzibah leave the family mansion, Clifford makes a point of directing her attention to the initials of his name carved into the doorpost years earlier (252). Clifford's gesture indicates the renewed identity that follows from his invigorated historical sense. Moments later, hurtling forward in the railroad car, Clifford posits his own theory of history, which views time as an "ascending spiral," the past giving way to an ever more promising future (277). At the center of Clifford's vision is the railroad, "the greatest blessing that the ages have wrought," a means of "spiritualiz[ing] travel" (277).

Clifford's admiration for the symbol of the new industry, indeed his entire discourse on history, is similar to that of Karl Marx, who in 1850 described the end of "all fixed, fast-frozen relations, with their train of ancient and venerable prejudices and opinions . . . [as] man is at last compelled to face with sober senses, his real conditions of life, and his relations with his kind."[10] Both Clifford and Marx place their hopes in the perpetual transformations brought about by industrial development; the key to social improvements is the acceptance of continual change. Hepzibah, with her mind like the railroad's "iron track" fastened upon Pyncheon Street and the house of the seven gables, personifies the nostalgic aristocrat's historical terror (258).

But Clifford's celebration of the new industrial age is short-lived, dissipating as the emblem of industrial force recedes from the horizon. He perceives that the railroad does not reflect some energy in himself, but is its own supreme power, leaving him torpid in its wake. Perhaps Clifford is freed from the delusion that technological innovation can be other than alienating to human beings; now aware, like Thoreau and Henry Adams, that progress takes us nowhere. Yet the scene also suggests that the powers of industrial change must be harnessed by individuals who are themselves sufficiently forceful to put those powers to good use. Moreover, Clifford's view fails to account for some crucial facts about his historical present, that inherited wealth, for example, still serves as a means to power in this new democratic industrial age—one of the chief ironies of the novel's ending.

The character with the most complex and confrontational view of history is Holgrave. A representative young man, seeking the prizes that in a new republic are "free to the hand that can grasp [them]" (181), Holgrave rails against the chains of the past, reject-

[10] Karl Marx, "The Communist Manifesto," in *The Marx-Engels Reader*, ed. Robert C. Tucker (New York: Norton, 1978), 476.

ing any forces that would minimize or confine the purposes of present ambition. Yet he also accepts an acquaintance with the past as a necessary check on more modern interests, inhabiting the ancient house of seven gables so as not to become "too much dazzled with my own trade" (91). He is Emerson's wandering youth, adopting one social vocation after another, but never "violat[ing] the innermost man" (177). His resilience is a direct outcome of his double historical sense. In comparison to the narrator, whose discussion of history seems continually to derail, and to the other characters, for whom the past is a realm of unconscious self-deception, he is the only one to self-consciously address the problems of his historical moment.

As the sole remaining heir to the legacy of "Maule's Curse," Holgrave carries the grievances of the old wizard into the nineteenth century, studying the past, so he says, to "know the better how to hate it" (184). But this sinister motive still allows him to resist past tyrannies, borne out in his refusal to take advantage of Phoebe after hypnotizing her. Holgrave also offers an important historical lesson to Hepzibah at the opening of her shop: actually "grappl[ing]" with contemporary forces is preferable to recoiling from them (44). Moments later, the terror of her imagination, working for a living, does vanish in her experience of it. As he suggests, working through the real world, confronting the demands of historical change, provides an edge of consciousness over threatening powers, whether they be autocratic individuals like Judge Pyncheon or the depersonalized processes of economic exchange.

Holgrave embodies the revolutionary potential of the lower classes in his bitter awareness of past wrongs and his ability to combine traditional powers with techniques of the modern age. This is most evident in his role as the novel's daguerreotypist. His claim for his mechanical pictures, that they reveal the soul behind the mask human beings present in public, does not differ fundamentally from the Maule legacy of "the family eye . . . said to possess strange powers" (26). The daguerreotype is a modern form of deep seeing, capable of penetrating the truths of its subjects.

Through its use of natural sunlight and scientific method, the daguerreotype can discern "the secret character with the truth that no painter could ever venture upon, could he detect it" (91). The daguerreotype is not only technically superior in its powers of detection, but more importantly, it allows its creator greater freedom to exhibit his results, protected as he is by the apparent objectivity of his mechanical techniques. While the portrait painter must muffle any untoward perceptions of his subject because his work of art is seen as a direct expression of his own convictions, the daguerreotypist is freed by the seemingly automatic processes of his reproductive methods. The mere agent of pictorial truth, Holgrave is not judged responsible for what his reproductions might reveal about a subject.

Nineteenth-century perceptions of the daguerreotype, "startling and cruel" in the words of one observer, accord with the mingled fascination and horror displayed toward Holgrave's work by some of the novel's characters.[11] Holgrave's continual interest in "seeing the original," his faith that close study can reveal what the general or public view misses, underlines the role of daguerreotypy in the novel as a technological aid to political insights. Like the earlier mesmeric powers of the Maules, daguerreotypes can reveal truths disguised by the viewing methods of established social hierarchies. It is significant that Holgrave consults the powers of mesmerism and the daguerreotype to exonerate Clifford from any misdeeds in the deaths of his uncle and Judge Pyncheon (303, 311).

The subversive element in Holgrave's daguerreotypes extends to his literary occupations. In parts, his history of "Alice Pyncheon" reads as a straight exposé of aristocratic pretensions and misdeeds, as seen in the first description of the family mansion where the derivativeness of its furnishings are detailed to humorous excess. The house is filled with random vestiges of European

---

[11] Charles Baudelaire, quoted by Walter Benjamin in "Some Motifs in Baudelaire," in *Illuminations*, ed. Hannah Arendt, trans. Harry Zohn (New York: Harcourt Brace, 1968), 186.

civilization, indicating the Pyncheons' attempts to replicate European manners in their native land. The furniture is "principally from Paris," the chimney tiles are "Dutch," and Maule enters to find Gervayse Pyncheon seated before "a fire of English sea-coal . . . sipping [what] had grown to be a favorite beverage with him, in France" (193). This lampoon of Pyncheon imitativeness is combined with a portrayal of the story's aristocrats as rapacious and insensitive. Alice, though hardly an attractive democratic heroine herself, with her "foreign" airs and dislike of New England, where "nothing beautiful had ever been established" (192), is clearly a pathetic sacrifice to her father's territorial greed. The narrator remarks disapprovingly that Gervayse Pyncheon "had martyred his poor child to an inordinate desire for measuring his land by miles, instead of acres" (208).

Yet, though more willing and able than the novel's other characters to accept the technological and political necessities of his historical era, Holgrave is just as fully bound up in its ahistorical mythologies. Thus the defusion of his radical potential at the novel's end is less alarming than it has seemed to many of the novel's critics.[12] Repeated allusions to Holgrave's unsettled nature undermine his reliability as a gauge for steadfast principles in the novel. As the typical American youth, he may have a strong streak of "self-reliance," but he seems to lack ideas. In regard to his radical ideals, the narrator observes that "he had that sense . . . which a young man had better never have been born, than not to have" (179). The listless, negative emphasis here is characteristic of the narrator's treatment of him. But Holgrave's own discourse, in the moments when we hear his thoughts, suggests an evasiveness that goes beyond the narrator's judgment.

[12] Among those who remark on Holgrave's change of faith are F. O. Matthiessen, *American Renaissance* (New York: Oxford University Press, 1941), 331–32; Marius Bewley, *The Eccentric Design* (New York: Columbia University Press, 1963), 163; Nina Baym, *The Shape of Hawthorne's Career* (Ithaca: Cornell University Press, 1976) 167–69; Michael Davitt Bell, *The Development of American Romance* (Chicago: University of Chicago Press, 1977), 182–84.

His much-discussed "conversion" speech recapitulates the narrator's qualified tone.

"It seems to me," he observed, "that I never felt anything so very much like happiness as at this moment. After all, what a good world we live in! How good, and beautiful! How young it is, too, with nothing really rotten, or age-worn in it! . . . Moonlight, and the sentiment in man's heart, responsive to it, is the greatest of renovators and reformers. And all other reform and renovation, I suppose, will prove to be no better than moonshine." (213–14)

Holgrave's transcendent optimism, as expressed here, seems curiously tentative; his phrases halt and hedge at every turn. One can take them for the instinctive distrust of the reality of happiness from a young man who has found little to hope for in history. But Holgrave is undeniably elated, and the cause of his joy is important to note. In refusing to take advantage of Phoebe as she sits captivated by his tale (211–12), Holgrave manages to avoid the ceaseless repetition of history. Holgrave here triumphs over the power of the past to dictate the deeds of the present; his self-conscious deviation from his ancestors' actions in similar circumstances liberates him from his inheritance.[13] Nevertheless, the distrustful tone of his monologue suggests the ephemeral nature of such victories. Holgrave is still an ambitious young man who must make his way in a shifty world. And the speech reveals the strain of scrupulosity in his character, his interest in what "is free to the hand that can grasp it."

We find Holgrave much more assertive in the novel's penultimate scene, where the death of Judge Pyncheon has resulted in the enrichment of Hepzibah, Clifford, and Phoebe. Phoebe notes how miraculously Holgrave's ideas have changed, to which he replies, "Little did I think ever to become [a conservative]. It is especially unpardonable in this dwelling of so much hereditary misfortune, and under the eye of yonder portrait of a model-conservative,

[13] This reading concurs with Michael Bell's discussion of the scene. See *Hawthorne and the Historical Romance of New England* (Princeton: Princeton University Press, 1966), 216.

who, in that very character, rendered himself so long the Evil Destiny of his race" (315). Perhaps Holgrave's liberation from his past in the previous scene with Phoebe justifies his literal turning of his back on history symbolized by the portrait of Colonel Pyncheon. Yet there are sinister touches in the novel's ending, which pictures the characters' withdrawal from the world of historical change. Holgrave's retirement (at the ripe old age of twenty-two) seems particularly ironic. Resolving to "set out trees, to make fences . . . to conform [him]self to laws" (307), Holgrave's new vocation sounds suspiciously like the program of suburban management overseen by the town's resourceful public servant, Uncle Venner. Uncle Venner too is involved in binding and circumscribing activities, "splitting up pineboard," "digging . . . gardens," "opening paths" (60–61). Fixer of public byways, domesticator of raw materials, consumer (via his pigs) of leftovers—Uncle Venner is a man who knows his place and is liked by others for that reason.

The exile of history at the novel's close is prepared for by the scene in the Pyncheon garden, where each of the characters constructs his respective mythical dream. All of the main characters, with the exception of the villainous Judge, are present at this "sober little festival," which takes place every Sabbath at the house of seven gables. The garden scene unearths a realm of self-deceptive fantasizing where everyone indulges his own characteristic "degenerate fiction."[14] Clifford's vision, appropriately, is "too indistinctly drawn to be followed by disappointment." Hepzibah enacts a role of "gentility . . . justifying a princesslike condescension." Phoebe's restrained sensibility yields a simple dream "for this short life of ours . . . [consisting] of a house and a moderate garden spot" (155–56). Holgrave alone is visionless, his countenance betraying only some mysterious "other interest" to explain his presence in this little knot of dreamers.

The "oddly composed" group assembles under "the ruinous ar-

---

[14] I borrow the term "degenerate fiction" from Frank Kermode's discussion of the differences between "myth" and "fiction" in ch. 3 of *The Sense of an Ending* (New York: Oxford University Press, 1966).

bor," which supplies a proper ceiling for their ineffectual schemes. For all their aspirations are dissolved in the chapter's ominous closure, which exposes their attempts to discover whole selves though projected dreams. The almost ruthless perspective, initially focused on Clifford, comes to implicate all the characters as "ruins" and "failures." Addressing Clifford, the narrator rails, "You are partly crazy and partly imbecile; a ruin, a failure, as almost everybody is. . . . Fate has no happiness in store for you; unless your quiet home . . . deserve[s] to be called happiness! Why not? If not the thing itself, it is marvellously like it" (158). The passage raises the question of what can make a human life meaningful. The impulse to dream is irrevocable, is even a source of dignity, the narrator seems to suggest. Yet the jeering tone here, a tone that pervades the chapter, undermines the characters' dreams. Clifford's "missing sense of power," described at the chapter's opening, seems emblematic of all the characters' dispositions. And Uncle Venner significantly compares the garden scene to what he expects to find at his retirement farm (155).

This brings us to the peculiar absence in *Seven Gables* of any forceful or heroic characters, such as Hester, Zenobia, or Hollingsworth, a Miriam or a darkened Donatello. Considered in terms of Coleridge's distinction between Fancy and Imagination, the novel's characters are all arrayed on the side of Fancy. None exhibit the transforming capacity to alter the world via the mind and its applications that constitutes the function of Imagination. Judge Pyncheon is powerful enough to make a world, but his is an entirely self-serving vision. Indeed, his characterization suggests that those capable of working through the materials of the historical present are ruthless and evil, plundering honest innocents in their wake. Holgrave's observations and actions are too ambivalent to prevent his eventual drowning in the reclusive dreams of the others. The characters in *Seven Gables* rely on the hope that their effortless personal fantasies can somehow be fulfilled. They cling to these mythic fragments, in their atomized modern world, until persistent fears of their own unreality subsume them all in the novel's fairy-tale ending. The novel's ending is a collective evasion of history: a series of forgettings that relieves the characters from the burden of historical action.

History seems to vanish in the love scene of Phoebe and Holgrave. And the community as a whole leaves the memory of Judge Pyncheon to future historians. His presence in the pages of American history is ensured, but he is banished from the novel's community, which "proceeded to forget that he had ever lived" (310). Likewise, information arising from the Judge's death, which provides the means of exonerating Clifford from any wrongdoing in the past or present, is shuffled away. Those "on whom the guardianship of his welfare had fallen, deemed it" unwise to expose Clifford to a "resuscitation of past ideas," consigning him instead to "the calm of forgetfulness" (313). Holgrave, perhaps most self-consciously of all, prepares to live without the bitter memories of his family's historical oppression. Even Uncle Venner, who "remembers [the town] with a mowing field on one side," is now fully graduated to the eternal world of romance, where he will inhabit "the sweetest-looking . . . gingerbread" house, in a haunting image of Hepzibah's mythical merchandise, now actualized (317). The departure of Hepzibah and Clifford from the family mansion, their emblem of the past, is effected "with hardly more emotion than if they had made it their arrangement to return thither at tea-time" (318). The novel's final image of Alice Pyncheon's ascension, leaving the weight of past sins behind in the ancient mansion, signifies the victory of myth over history. In collusion with the characters' aspirations, the narrator rewards their struggles, and his own, with this transcendent ending. Yet this vision is qualified by a small voice, which has persisted throughout the novel, bringing an awareness of historical conditions to the desires of the novel's characters.[15]

[15] The novel's ending might also be seen as a parody of popular nineteenth-century historical romances, which often pictured the heroine's final triumph in freeing the hero from the bonds of history. See Ann Douglas's discussion of the nineteenth-century "escape from history" in ch. 5 of *The Feminization of American*

The pair of comic relief figures who stand off to the side of the scene offer a merciless commentary on the miraculous fulfillment of the characters' dreams. "The sagacious Dixey" and his companion ponder, in the face of the Pyncheons' changed circumstances, whether their wealth is the work of accident or Providence. "If you choose to call it luck, it is all very well," the companion observes, "but if we are to take it as the will of Providence, why, I can't exactly fathom it!" To which the concise sage responds, "Pretty good business . . . pretty good business" (318–19). Clearly the order of visible sainthood is no longer operative, at least not for these two figures. The Pyncheons' enrichment has extricated them from the ordinary workings of causality governing the lives of these commoners. However, there is no obscurity about their especial virtue—their wealth is not the result of Providential favor but of luck.

This dialogue, abbreviated as it is, points the way to one of the foremost dilemmas in American democratic life. Why does one woman lose "five dollars on her outlay" (47), and another depart for a country estate in a barouche? One's "poor business, poor business" is another's "pretty good business." The scene's irony records the decisive difference: the practice of inheritance that prevails within the democratic system. But the myth of the American Republic is capable of resolving the contradictions. The novel

---

Culture (New York: Knopf, 1978). Also see Michael Colacurcio's view of the synchronic nature of time in a domestic tale like "The Wives of the Dead," as compared to the diachronic time sense of historical tales such as "Roger Malvin's Burial," and "The Gentle Boy." *Province of Piety*, 101. Michael Bell has drawn the most extensive comparisons between Hawthorne's romances and those of contemporary popular romancers in *Hawthorne and Historical Romance*, 162–73. My own sense of the novel's ending is closest to the spirit of D. H. Lawrence, who describes "the new generation" at the novel's close in blatantly antihistorical, consumer terms. "It is setting up in the photography line, and is just going to make a sound financial thing of it . . . old hates and old glooms are swept up in the vacuum cleaner, and the vendetta born young couple effect a perfect understanding under the black cloth of a camera and prosperity." *Studies in Classic American Literature* (New York: Penguin, 1978), 121.

closes upon the freshly endowed "aristocrats" departing for their inherited estate, with the happy newlyweds, symbolizing the rising middle classes, in tow. This brings us to the novel's narrator, the chief articulator, as well as deconstructor, of his society's myths. Despite his detachment, the narrator shares the characters' anxiety about historical change, and the novel's preface is an important forum for its expression.

The Narrator as Mythmaker

The preface of *Seven Gables* is best known for its distinction between the novel and the romance—a distinction, several commentators have recently noted, without a difference.[16] However idiosyncratic or deceptive, the argument of the preface is revealing for an exploration of the narrator's relationship to the past and present. In setting forth the radical freedom of the writer of romance, the narrator betrays his own designs on the subject of history.

From its opening, something seems disingenuous in the rhetoric of the preface, as if the narrator is dwelling upon distinctions between the novel and romance, and exploding them at every point, in order to convey a deeper message. The paradoxical resolve to "keep undeviatingly within his immunities," to remain firm and controlled within his radical gesture of freedom, typifies his mystifying aims. A marginal being, not fully at home in the imaginative realm of romance nor in realism, the narrator's attempt to "connect a bygone time with the very present that is flitting away from us" suggests a consciousness without a fixed place in history. His condition of artistic homelessness (seemingly self-inflicted, some suggest) mirrors an inescapable historical marginality; his position in regard to the genres of the novel and the romance re-

[16] See Nina Baym, *The Novel in Antebellum America* (Ithaca: Cornell University Press, 1984), and David Van Leer, "Moonlight and Moonshine: The Irrelevance of Hawthorne's Prefaces," MLA Special Session, December 27, 1983.

peat his relation to the elusive past, "now gray in the distance," and the fleeting present.

A ghostly navigator between the past and the present, the real and the fantastic, the narrator seems engaged in a struggle to transform his historical boundlessness into a form of aesthetic freedom. He can use the historical fragments available to him as materials for his alchemical artistic processes: the past as edging to fill out his tapestry, there for "picturesque effect," rather than a formidable thread in his novel's pattern. Likewise, the narrator would discourage overvaluing his novel's didactic aim, since moral truths "relentlessly" "impale[d]" on a story threaten its integrity as a work of art. Yet these two playfully voiced concerns clue us into even deeper issues: something more than a confession of generic and historical marginality seems to be on the mind of the preface's narrator. His absorption with rules and regulations, however ironic, implies that he is not as free as he supposes.[17]

The narrator's aim to detach his tale from the demands of momentary realities, inseparable from his didactic aim to discourage the adoption of obsolete practices from the past, expresses his fear of the past in its determining effects, and his even greater fear of the present, which, it seems, needs more strenuously to be denied. His method of legitimizing his project against the oppressive bonds of history, by paradoxically invoking a tradition of sources "long in use for constructing castles in the air," provides a key to his wily methods. Wishing to retain the idea of tradition, he eludes the historical obligations it entails by refusing to acknowledge any connection between his art and the real world. Yet his avowed aim to weave a tale having "more to do with the clouds overhead than with any portion of the actual soil of the county of Essex" is only one strain in a tale he does not control entirely.

Fredric Jameson's suggestion that every artist, in reacting to the

[17] The preface is fraught with legal language: the novel "must rigidly *subject itself to laws*"; the romance writer will "make a very moderate use of the *privileges* here stated"; "he can hardly be said, however, to *commit* a literary *crime*, even if he disregard this caution, though "it is not for him to *judge*" (emphasis added).

real, incorporates it somehow into his work of art, describes the way in which the narrator of *Seven Gables* inscribes past practices and present realities into his narrative in his struggle against their erosion of his imaginative power. And this reluctant vision is in fact the basis of the narrative's "political unconscious."[18] Before turning to that inescapable vision, let us first examine the carefully constructed world the narrator attempts to put in its place.

The narrator's ambivalence toward historical change is reflected in his attitude toward the unfolding of the novel's plot. Critics from Hawthorne's era to the present have remarked upon the novel's repetitive and even static quality, where descriptions seem not to forward the narrative's development but almost to impede it.[19] Devoid of a strong plot line, the narrative manifests a resistance to temporal process as progress, reading as a series of sketches and introductions of its various characters, a muddled consort of dra-

[18] By "political unconscious," Fredric Jameson means that "the production of aesthetic or narrative form is to be seen as an ideological act in its own right, with the function of inventing imaginary or formal 'solutions' to unresolvable social contradictions." For Jameson, the entire "modernist project" involves attempts to "manage historical and social, deeply political impulses." First, however, they must be "aroused." This ambivalent operation serves as the chief impulse of literary modernism: to alternately arouse and "recontain" a realist vision. Jameson's description seems to capture precisely the contradictory stance of the *Seven Gables* narrator, who flirts with history one moment only to flee its message the next. *The Political Unconscious* (Ithaca: Cornell University Press, 1981), 77–79, 266.

[19] Views of the novel's static narrative have rarely been joined to considerations of the novel's historical themes. Nevertheless, some of the commentary is noteworthy. One English contemporary of Hawthorne's complained about the narrator's habit of "overdescription," asking why "we are detained so long to so little purpose." Other contemporary reviews repeat this observation about the obsessive nature of Hawthorne's description, and the dilatory aspect of the narrative. See J. Donald Crowley, *Hawthorne: The Critical Heritage* (London: Routledge and Kegan Paul, 1970), 311–12. F. O. Matthiessen's remark that "the measure in which [Hawthorne] intended [*Seven Gables*] as a criticism of his own age is somewhat obscured by his treatment of time" is typical of twentieth-century views, which overlook possible connections between the narrative's distinctive features and its political and historical themes. *American Renaissance*, 322. See also Newton Arvin, *Hawthorne* (Boston: Little, Brown and Co., 1929), 212–13, and more recently, Kenneth Dauber, *Rediscovering Hawthorne* (Princeton: Princeton University Press, 1977), 139–42; Taylor Stoehr, *Hawthorne's Mad Scientists* (Hamden, Conn.: Archon Books, 1978), 93.

105

matic scenes that fail to cohere or develop. The novel's ending is often cited by critics as evidence of its overall lack of organization and purpose, especially in comparison to its taut predecessor, *The Scarlet Letter*.

The novel's diffuseness, rather than simply a function of Hawthorne's ineptitude, might be more accurately seen as an indication of the novel's growing opposition of different conceptions of history. The novel features a narrator and characters attempting to posit a mythic view of time as a stilled realm of eternal and unchanging significance, in the face of their unconscious historical sense of their experiences as part of an ongoing process of historical change. This is further complicated by the narrator's conventional belief in narration as a progress from beginning to end, which sets the task of narration itself on the side of the historical progress the narrator wishes to deny. The narrator's fear of the historical time of the novel's world is translated into his anxiety over the linear progress of his narrative.[20] This is most evident in the early scene where the narrator's reluctance to divulge the details of Hepzibah's shopkeeping venture repeats her own reluctance to confront her changed historical circumstances. This squeamishness about disclosing the evolving historical world of his subjects typifies the narrator's behavior throughout the novel.

The descriptions of the Pyncheon hencoop, introduced by the narrator as vain digressions, characterize well his habit of imagination. For the scenes that most appear to derail the narrative from its ostensible subject pinpoint his struggles against history. Like

[20] Gerard Genette's distinction between narrative time and story time is appropriate to this discussion. For Genette, narrative time is the duration of the recounting of the novel's events. Story time is the duration of the events themselves. This pair of durations can function on different levels in the same novel; e.g., the narrative time of Holgrave's "Alice Pyncheon" is congruent with the story time of the novel during Holgrave's telling of the tale, but different from the narrative time of the novel as a whole. However, the narrative time of the novel as a whole expands to include this story. In this way, the various stories that characters tell serve to impede the linear progress of the novel's narrative. See *Narrative Discourse* (Ithaca: Cornell University Press, 1980), chs. 2 and 3.

the earlier portrayal of Hepzibah's shop, their descriptive details read as casual efforts to offer local color.

The narrator begins by observing that the Pyncheon chickens ludicrously mirror the pretentious demeanor of their owner. Both function similarly as symbols of historical degeneracy: just as Hepzibah, the remaining representative of the noble Pyncheon line is "reduced . . . to be the huckstress of a cent shop," the chickens too are a "degenerated race" (38–39). Yet in a single image, these chickens are transformed from declining patricians suffering the effects of historical change to purveyors of the American Dream. The possibility for rejuvenation in the barnyard is embodied in the littlest chicken, described as possessing "the whole antiquity of its progenitors in miniature" (90). The second description of this chick extends its mythical significance.

It looked small enough to be still in the egg, and at the same time, sufficiently old, withered, wizened, and experienced, to have been the founder of the antiquated race. Instead of being the youngest of the family, it rather seemed to have aggregated into itself the ages, not only of these living specimens of the breed, but of all its forefathers and foremothers, whose united excellencies and oddities were squeezed into its little body. Its mother evidently regarded it as the one chicken of the world, and as necessary . . . to the world's continuance, or, at any rate, to the equilibrium of the present system of affairs, whether in church or state. No lesser sense of the infant fowl's importance could have justified, even in a mother's eyes, the perseverance with which she watched over its safety, ruffling her small person to twice its proper size, and flying in everybody's face that so much as looked towards her hopeful progeny. (151–52)

More than just a fond glance at the indulgencies of motherhood from the fowl's point of view, this passage exemplifies the mythical aspirations that pervade the world of *Seven Gables*. Through his imaginative conversion, the narrator, in league with the mother hen, transforms the destiny of this race of barnyard fowls from extinction to future promise. A symbol for the new American republic, the littlest chicken represents the hope of his historical era, standing among his fellow chickens as America stands among the

nations of the world. Youthful but aged, the chick is a new country formed by an "aggregate" of citizens from various older nations. Like the democratic land of opportunity, this biped is
looked upon as a sort of savior, "necessary to the world's continuance." Indeed, "the equilibrium of the present system of affairs"
depends upon the chick's well-being, a possible allusion to America's growing importance on the international scene. Even the
overwhelming anxiety of the mother hen suggests the national outlook of "failure and success"; she may harbor in her "hopeful progeny" an American president, or a notorious criminal.

   In its mythical connotations, the chicken resembles Holgrave,
who, prescient of "the harbingers abroad of a golden era, to be accomplished in his own lifetime," mistakenly supposes that "it mat-
tered anything to the great end in view, whether he himself should
contend for it or against it" (180). The narrator emphasizes that
Holgrave is hardly unique, that his self-important pursuit of the
American Dream is shared by innumerable American youths.
The chick, likewise, has counterparts in the hencoop. A less fortunate progeny becomes the "dainty" of Clifford Pyncheon's
breakfast (161). These depictions of the chick and Holgrave reveal
the profound ironic undercurrent in the narrator's vision. In such
passages, he presents the hoped-for transcendence and then a parallel set of circumstances that undercuts it.[21] Despite the grand
ambitions they or others hold for them, Holgrave and the chick are
limited by the realities of their specific historical moments. Both
are inhabitants of history, who might end up, or might have been,
respectively, a bitter old man with unfulfilled ambitions or a

   [21] Paul de Man's view of Romantic notions of time, particularly his description
of the ironist who "seals the ironic moments within the allegorical duration," sheds
light on the ambivalent temperament of the *Seven Gables* narrator. The narrative
consciousness also seems similar to the description of Schlegel, "isolated and alienated," deprived by his "consciousness of his ability to act. He nostalgically aspires
toward unity and infinity; the world appears to him divided and finite." Paul de
Man quoting Peter Szondi, in "The Rhetoric of Temporality," in *Interpretation:
Theory and Practice*, ed. Charles Singleton (Baltimore: Johns Hopkins University
Press, 1969), see esp., 193–94, 201–203.

boiled egg. Yet the narrator's transcendent designs often go un-qualified in passages that reveal his own mythic ambitions in all their eternal glory.

One such instance involves a characteristic Hawthornean scene—a view of a local processional, the masses on parade. Here, the narrator concedes his personal formula for prime viewing. He comments, "in order to become majestic, [the parade] should be viewed from some vantage-point, as it rolls its slow and long array through the centre of a wide plain . . . for then, by its remoteness, it melts all the petty personalities, of which it is made up, into one broad mass of existence" (165). Thus, the transforming aim of the mythical impulse is revealed: it makes the particular general, the human and physical abstract. The preferred image of humanity is an eternal and unchanging one, a point of view achieved only from a sufficiently "remote distance."

This description reasserts the desired "vantage-point" of the preface, where the narrator declares his freedom from the clam-oring demands of a contemporary world in bondage to history. His is to be a perspective detached and transcendent, of clouds rather than earth. From such a point of view, the distant world is amorphous, but beckoning in its mysteriousness. Significantly, the world is not left behind here, nor imaginatively dissolved. Rather, "the reality of the world [is converted] into an image of the world." As in the previous scenes in the cent shop and the hen-coop, this particular parade on a single day in a New England street becomes an abstract principle of humanity. As a specific sit-uation, with distinguishable human participants, the scene con-tains a provision for human action. But this eternalized perspec-tive offers a locked image. As all humanity, rather than a particular group, the scene is removed from the plane of action to one where human experience is unchanging and unchangeable.

The narrator's vision of eternity also encompasses Garden of Eden imagery. Recurrently, the characters' world is seen as a re-vived Eden. One of the first such allusions continues to emphasize the importance of narrative distance: Alice Pyncheon's rosebush looks "as if it had been brought from Eden." Yet the rose must be viewed "at a fair distance" if one is to achieve a sense of its original freshness. On closer inspection, one perceives "blight and mildew" (71). The illusion of the vegetation's purity, of its freedom from the particular effects of degeneration, depends upon the viewer's detachment. There is a note of almost scientific delicacy in these instructions; the observer must be cautious not to intrude upon the object of his scrutiny. And the greater one's removal from the world, the more it may accommodate one's desire. As with his pose of "disembodied listener" in Chapter Two, the narrator here equates satisfaction of desire with the denial of his time-bound self.

In one of the central Edenic scenes, the world of historical contingency is actively banished. Holgrave and Phoebe are a type of Adam and Eve in the romantic resolution that unites them. Amidst the sin and history of the seven-gabled house, Phoebe and Holgrave "were conscious of nothing sad nor old. They transfigured the earth, and made it Eden again, and themselves the two first dwellers in it" (307). Through their union, the descendants of the Maule-Pyncheon conflict replicate the purity of existence before the fall. Their union banishes all that is "sad" or "old," paving the way for the novel's romance ending—which harmonically resolves the bitter historical tale of class struggle. The novel's Garden of Eden motif, like Barthes's definition of myth, portrays human experience as eternal and unchanging, "characterized by an indefinite repetition of its identity." Captured within these purified images, the novel's world can exist forever unassailable by the sins of the past, or the threatening tides of the present.[22]

[22] Michael Colacurcio writes that in Hawthorne's view, "no one could be, outside the limits of myth, Adamic; the human world being a form of continuous existences, the sinful choices of the past created powerful influences of limitation on the moral freedom of the present." The portrayal of the Edenic myth in *Seven Gables* can thus be seen in ironic terms. Once outside the mythical haze of one's desired view, Alice Pyncheon's rosebush appears blemished, a reflection of its own, as well as the viewer's, historically conditioned self. See Barthes, *A Barthes Reader*, 130; and Colacurcio, *Province of Piety*, 57.

By far the most potent of the narrator's eternal designs are the characterizations of Phoebe and Judge Pyncheon, who are distinctive in their roles as mythic types. Unlike the other characters, whose inner thoughts are often rendered, Phoebe and Judge Pyncheon are presented largely through what Gerard Genette terms "external focalization." As registers of collective sentiments, Phoebe and the Judge are loci for the aspirations and fears of the other characters. And the narrator is especially unrestrained in his treatment of them. Presenting Phoebe as the personification of virtue, the narrator shares in the other characters' homage to her sacred qualities. By comparison, Judge Pyncheon is unremittingly evil, and is reviled by the narrator in one of the most excessive passages in all of Hawthorne's works, the "Governer Pyncheon" chapter. As is often the case with diametric opposites, Phoebe and Judge Pyncheon share some similar symbolic traits.

From her introduction, Phoebe is intimately related to the sun. Recognizing a sympathetic being, the sun steals in to "kiss . . . her brow" (70), as she awakens for the first time in the ancient mansion. She is a natural light, "as pleasant about the house as a gleam of sunshine falling on the floor" (80). Indeed, her own homely being appears at times to evaporate. Bending over to kiss her, Judge Pyncheon finds himself in "the absurd predicament of kissing the empty air." A similar sense of Phoebe's airiness is felt by Clifford, for whom Phoebe was "not an actual fact . . . but the interpretation of all that he had lacked on earth" (142). To Uncle Venner as well, Phoebe is "one of God's angels" in whose voice "we recognize [that] of the creator" (138).[23]

---

[23] Many critics have emphasized Phoebe's similarities to Hawthorne's own wife, who was nicknamed "Phoebe." But it seems more interesting to explore the character's wider symbolic significances. Phoebe, it appears, fits into any critical paradigm. With her "gifts as a shopkeeper" and "manufacturer"; "the stern old stuff of Puritanism with a gold thread in the web"; as "a religion in herself . . . with a substance that could walk on earth and a spirit that was capable of heaven"—Phoebe seems the image of Bercovitch's secular-sacred "Myth of America" (79, 76, 168). And she functions as a social safety valve, giving the other characters hope when the world is most drained of possibility. See *The American Jeremiad*, esp. 18–28. In

While Phoebe spontaneously incorporates various powers of spirit and nature, Judge Pyncheon is an ardent manipulator of sunbeams with the sun's processes at his command. Manifesting a remarkable range of expression, he changes from "arid and disagreeable" one moment to "the sunniest complacency" the next (57). As the narrator remarks ironically, at times the warmth of his kindly aspect is so excessive "that an extra passage of the water-carts [is] found necessary to lay the dust occasioned by so much extra sunshine" (130–31).

The frequency of sun imagery for both Judge Pyncheon and Phoebe is an ominous note suggesting that the same forces can be used for entirely different ends. Eternal images of good and evil, embodying the distinction between true and false lights, these two characters also differ significantly in their treatment of others. Whereas naturalness is the key to Phoebe's character, with the lack of "design" in her actions repeatedly stressed (72, 76, 82, 118, 136), Judge Pyncheon is an intent schemer. The narrator's second full-length description of him is so qualified that he appears as a picture of how he would have looked had he been a more honest representation of himself.

It was the portly, and, had it possessed the advantage of a little more height, would have been the stately figure of a man considerably in the decline of life, dressed in a black suit of some thin stuff, resembling broadcloth as closely as possible. . . . His dark, square countenance, with its almost shaggy depth of eyebrows, was naturally impressive, and would perhaps, have been rather stern, had not the gentleman considerately taken upon himself to mitigate the harsh effect by a look of exceeding

---

another sense, Phoebe, unlike the forbidding Calvinist Deity, is a personalized spirit akin to the religious models of nineteenth-century popular novels. On this point see Douglas, *Feminization*, 5–13, 126–30, 230–39. And Phoebe is the quintessential middle-class girl; described as "orderly, trim and limit-loving," she maintains her balance of soul by "occasionally" indulging "the impulse of Nature in New England girls" through such moderate pastimes as listening to a concert or a lecture, observing a sunset, or "shopping about the city, ransacking entire depots of splendid merchandize, and bringing home a ribbon" (68, 131, 174). It is difficult to imagine Hester Prynne or Zenobia appeased by such circumscribed activities, which appear to be the ritualized leisure of a developing middle class.

good-humor and benevolence. . . . A susceptible observer, at any rate, might have regarded it as affording very little evidence of the general benignity of soul, whereof it purported to be the outward reflection. And if the observer chanced to be ill-natured, as well as acute and susceptible, he would probably suspect, that the smile on the gentleman's face was a good deal akin to the shine on his boots, and that each must have cost him and his boot-black respectively, a good deal of hard labor to bring out and preserve them. (116–17)

The repetition of the word "susceptible" in the above passage is hardly necessary for the reader to suspect that subterfuge is at the heart of Judge Pyncheon's character. The Judge's machinations, his literal and figural bootblack methods, yield a beneficent aspect that contradicts his true character. Yet the narrator cannot help acknowledging the genius of the Judge's appearance. The capitalist entrepreneur par excellence, Judge Pyncheon uses the physical facts of his makeup to create a desired image. And though the narrator abhors Judge Pyncheon's dishonesty, and the Judge himself would scoff at the narrator's rarefied disavowals of the profane world, the two are equally engaged in efforts to manage the limiting conditions of their particular historical circumstances. They differ in that the Judge exploits those "realities" which the narrator seeks to transcend. But the deepest implications of Judge Pyncheon's characterization are revealed by the narrator's response to him.

The narrator appears genuinely fearful of Judge Pyncheon, as a figure his mythic rhetoric is incapable of transcending. In this passage, the sheer fact of the Judge's skill in manipulating appearances seems to trouble the basis of the narrator's reality, his reliance upon his own powers of description. For the terms that reveal the Judge's contrivances in the first half of the description—"had it possessed the advantage of," "would have been"—become those used to describe the narrator's own perceptions in the second half. In other words, the "susceptible observer" has adopted the wavering terms of the Judge's subterfuge—"at any rate, might have," "would probably suspect"—to convey his own response to the

Judge. Thus the tenuous language that closes the description of Judge Pyncheon, however parodic, affirms his ultimate power, his ability to legislate the terms of discourse, and hence, the reality of the novel's community. The narrator's equivocal description of Judge Pyncheon is a concession to a character he cannot control, a persona so tied to the material world that he remains solidly resistant to the narrator's mythic designs.[24]

The narrator wages ideological war with Judge Pyncheon, a struggle typified by the paradoxical phrase the narrator employs in his attempt to dismiss him: "the big, heavy, solid, unrealities." As "the sadly gifted" seer for whom the whole structure of the Judge's vast possessions and benevolent deeds "melt into thin air," the narrator insists upon the unreality of the Judge's public reputation. Yet anyone doubting his moral uprightness need only recall his acts as judge, bible society president, treasurer of a widows and orphans fund, and devoted politician (228–31). Louis Althusser's discussion of state ideological apparatuses offers insights into Judge Pyncheon's characterization in precisely the area where the information seems most contradictory: the narrator's insistence on the insubstantiality of the Judge's integrity, versus its obvious solidity in the eyes of his fellow townspeople.

In defining state ideological apparatuses as social institutions that function by ideology rather than by violence, Althusser moves one step beyond the question of why individuals mask the real conditions of their existence in ideology. Asserting ideology's claims to "material" existence, Althusser locates that materiality in

---

[24] My view of the narrator's treatment of Judge Pyncheon is consistent with Frederick Crews's analysis; however, I would deny the attribution of patricidal anger on Hawthorne's part and what that implies. See *Sins of the Fathers* (New York: Oxford University Press, 1966), 174–77. Where Crews conceives the narrator's struggle in psychoanalytic terms, I would stress its political import, though the two are far from mutually exclusive. As the narrator describes him in a famous passage, Judge Pyncheon is a public institution, the closest a human being can come to the condition of an architectural edifice. He *is* his material possessions and public deeds, made up of all the things he has "grasp[ed]," "arrang[ed]," and "appropriat[ed]" to himself.

the practices of institutions and in the actions of individuals who are inevitably bound by ideology. Central to Althusser's conception is the inseparability of ideological beliefs and public actions. In Althusser's terms, Judge Pyncheon consists of the public actions that reflect benevolence upon him. Althusser's discussion is especially relevant to a work like *Seven Gables*, which is concerned with the problem of the increasingly public orientation of private self-reflection.[25] Indeed, the narrator emphasizes the Judge's belief in his own benevolence, never denying that "ultimately in his own view" Judge Pyncheon is a public benefactor (229).[26] Most of the novel's other characters lack sufficiently framed ideologies to spur them to action, residing instead in a passive stupor that offers little alternative to the Judge's dominion. Although the narrator establishes himself as a lonely railer who must in some way contend with the powers he represents, his verbal assault on the Judge does not occur until the Judge is safely dead in the ancestral armchair. Most importantly, the gleeful dismissal of the Judge's benevolent acts as "solid unrealities" fails to conceal the price paid for his secular supremacy: he has destroyed the greater part of Hepzibah's and Clifford's lives.

The Novel's American Republic

Having discussed various individual strategies for evading history, it remains for us to consider how a view of history as a collective dynamic makes its way into the narrative. The most vivid details of larger nineteenth-century social and economic patterns in *Seven Gables* are visible in the products of Hepzibah's shop; the demands of buyers, symbolized by Hepzibah's shopbell; the music of the Italian organ grinder; and Holgrave's daguerreotypes. All of these harbingers of the era of mechanical reproduction voice inescapable

[25] On this issue see Richard Sennett's *The Fall of Public Man*, especially chs. 8 and 9.

[26] See Louis Althusser, "Ideology and Ideological State Apparatuses," in *Lenin and Philosophy*, trans. Ben Brewster (London: New Left Books, 1971), 123–73.

changes in the characters' historical present. American society is pictured as a spiritual wasteland with the superimposed effects of consumerism and technology.

At the same time, at the level of political structure, the novel portrays a society of perpetual class struggle, waged through the mechanisms of public communication. The question of whose point of view is dominant, and in what ways it might be undermined by less prominent forms of social consciousness, arises again and again. A number of circumstances in the novel oppose public or official perspectives to the underground truths of the chimney-corner legends. Though, for example, no one openly questions the way in which Colonel Pyncheon usurps Matthew Maule's land, the "whisperings" among the storytellers of the hearth attest to the "invidious acrimony" of Pyncheon's actions (8). Moreover, the plebeian waters of Maule's Well are said to be forever after the cause of "intestinal mischief" (10). The clandestine nature of these oppositional views suggests a way of reading the novel's deepest vision of its contemporary society as a series of politicized returns of the repressed that repeatedly emerge to haunt the illusion of harmony in the official American republic. Given the novel's relatively cohesive little community, in which reformist impulses are easily accepted as rites of passage (88), what could be wrong with the possible exception of a bit of distress over land, or the unhappy separation of a morbidly attached brother and sister? The question of what could be wrong may be precisely the point of the novel's preface.

The issue of perceptual control is very much on the mind of the preface's narrator. His use of legal terminology, his voicing of intentions to control his readers' perceptions through various technical measures—"mellow[ing] the lights," "deepen[ing] . . . the shadows"—and most significantly, his argument against the past's domination of the present, suggest an obsession with the manipulation of the perspectives of others. But this interest in controlling his readers' senses of reality parallels the striking fact that each of his testimonies of artistic freedom is undercut by its ultimate referral to the audience's taste. The novel's historical connections may be received by the reader "according to his pleasure," either "disregard[ed]" or "allow[ed] . . . to float almost imperceptibly about the characters and events." The narrator has provided his tale with a moral not because he desires to; indeed, he voices a distrust of morality in fiction. His novel provides a moral so as not to be deficient in "moral purpose," or in other words, audience instruction.

By the preface's closing paragraph, the artistic prerogatives that began with the author have now become almost exclusively the province of the reader. The reader may "choose to assign an actual locality" to the novel's events, despite the sentiments of the author who would "very willingly have avoided anything of this nature." The author hopes "not to be considered as unpardonably offending." "He would be glad" if his work were to be taken "strictly as a Romance." Such fears of alienating contemporaries suggest an author out to sell books at any price. But the ending is a strange reversal for a preface that seemed initially radical in its statement of artistic freedom. The solicitude for audience reception, which appears to overtake and eventually drown the preface's original aim, raises an issue important to the novel as a whole. In addition to its ostensible function as "a denial of any resemblance to persons living or dead,"[27] the preface reveals an artist struggling to break free from the prevailing ideology of his contemporary society.

Of greatest interest to the narrator, who is concerned with the actual operation of ideology in his society, are the issues precluded from the range of acceptable social discourse. The term "ideological hegemony" is pertinent here, by which Raymond Williams refers to "the relations of domination and subordination, in their forms as practical consciousness, as in effect a saturation of the whole process of living—not only of political and economic activity, nor only of manifest social activity, but of the whole substance of lived identities and relationships, to such a depth that the pres-

[27] David Van Leer, "Moonlight and Moonshine."

117

sures and limits of what can ultimately be seen as a specific economic, political, and cultural system seem to most of us the pressures and limits of simple experience and common sense."[28] The
preface reveals the process by which certain perceptions are elim-
inated from what might be considered the bounds of "common
sense," a dynamic exemplified by the qualifications and eventual
submergence of the narrator's arguments.

The narrator's stance is important as a symbolic gesture. Since
it is the recognition of differences between ideologies that affords
their penetration, his marginal position between novel and romance, past and present, may signify an aspiration (albeit unconscious) to see beyond the predominant reality of his novel's world.
Throughout the novel, situations arise in which social differences
are de-emphasized in an effort to achieve the semblance of harmony. The preferred view is a sunny one; conflict and evil are confined to the character of Judge Pyncheon, or seep in through occasional cracks in the social veil. Yet continual allusions to the
antithetical truths of public authorities and the deeper truths of a
social underground lead us to question the cost of perceptual comfort.

Perhaps the distinction between the novel and the romance in
the preface is a meaningfully false one: the narrator's attempt to
convey a sense of differences to a society incapable of coming to
terms with class conflict. His references to the reader's desire and
right to choose may suggest that the novel can be read "as you like
it." One may rise from a reading of the novel with a conviction of
the ultimate harmony of the new American republic, as Holgrave-
Maule enters the American fold. Or one may close the novel with
a gnawing sense that all is not quite right here—that the novel has
all along pictured a social reality that contradicts such a harmonic

---

[28] Replacing the static "hegemony" with the idea of "the hegemonic," Williams
points out that "a lived hegemony is always a process . . . it has continually to be
renewed, recreated, defended, and modified. It is also continually resisted, limited, altered, challenged by pressures not at all its own." *Marxism and Literature*
(New York: Oxford University Press, 1977), 108–114.

conclusion. In portraying the difficulties of penetrating the ideological umbrella of American society, the preface paves the way for a narrative very much concerned with the problem of ideological hegemony, and the political components of the proverbial Hawthornean riddle: what is reality, what illusion?

The recognition of history as a process of change is one fact of life denied by the governing assumptions of the novel's characters, most of whom resist the challenges of their contemporary era. The fatalistic insistence by the narrator and the characters that history repeats itself flies in the face of stronger indications that history may repeat in outline, but moves forward with a difference that is irreversible.[29] The novel's underlying political vision offers a picture of modernity that recognizes that ancestral power is no longer the sole basis for authority in the contemporary world. Inherited power must now be combined with a commitment to movement and action, to the possibilities of social and economic change. The perspectives of most of the novel's characters seem various attempts to still and sanctify a world that increasingly eludes their grasp. Only the aristocratic prime mover, Judge Pyncheon, seems fully apprised of the dynamic potential of his age. Thus the subjects of political power and historical consciousness are aligned: given the remaining descendants of a "noble" family, the one who survives empowered is the one capable of transforming that supremacy into the terms of his age.[30]

[29] Other views on Hawthorne's vision of history that have been helpful in formulating my argument are Bell, *Hawthorne and Historical Romance*, and *The Development of American Romance*; Roy Harvey Pearce, *Historicism Once More* (Princeton: Princeton University Press, 1969); R.W.B. Lewis, *The American Adam* (Chicago: University of Chicago Press, 1955); Q. D. Leavis, "Hawthorne as Poet," in *Hawthorne*, ed. A. N. Kaul (Englewood Cliffs, N.J.: Prentice-Hall, 1966), 25–63; Gretchen Jordan, "Hawthorne's Bell: Historical Evolution Through Symbol," *Nineteenth Century Fiction* 19 (1964): 106–124; and John Gatta, "Progress and Providence in *The House of the Seven Gables*," *American Literature* 50 (1978): 37–48.

[30] While Holgrave is capable of uniting ancient and modern techniques, his sources—mystical and artistic—seem destined for eternal marginality, at least in the kind of society the novel portrays. As Roy Harvey Pearce has suggested, *Seven Gables* may represent Hawthorne's coming to terms with "the doctrine that material

The narrator's own persistent fears of modernity are exemplified by the novel's one extended description of its titular subject,
the house of the seven gables, where the changes from an earlier
era to "its more recent aspect" are suggestive. No longer majesti-
cally isolated from other town structures, the nineteenth-century
house is now part of a neighborhood that has "long ceased to be a
fashionable quarter of the town." The mansion is surrounded by
houses "mostly small, built entirely of wood, and typical of the
most plodding uniformity of common life." Lacking "picturesque-
ness," these homes fail to attract "imagination or sympathy."
Though the Pyncheon mansion retains its own graces despite the
presence of these unremarkable plebeian neighbors, it is compromised by its new surroundings—the house garden in particular,
"infringed upon," and "shut in" by adjacent structures. The narrator, however, points out that Nature has "adopted to herself this
. . . rusty, old house," as if to insist that no matter how historical
circumstances inveigh against the mansion (and its inhabitants), it
will be protected by the eternal forces of Nature, basking in the
sun of its "ever-returning Summer" (27–28).

The description of the house does not end on this hopeful note,
however, for the narrator must proceed with the task of describing
the mansion's parasite, the shop door. Pictured as "cutting . . .
through the side of [the] ancestral residence," this symbol of commercial enterprise appears to do violence to the sacred dwelling.
However heavy-handed, the portrayal of Hepzibah's commercial
venture signals profound changes in the novel's world, accompanied by a deep sense of loss. "Rich and heavy festoons of cob-
web, which it had cost a long ancestral succession of spiders their
life's labor to spin and weave," now "brushed away," provide a
metaphor for the departure of tradition (35).

---

things were primary instruments of political and moral progress." One might add,
"if placed in the right hands." See "Hawthorne and the Sense of the Past Or, The
Immortality of Major Molineux," *ELH* 21 (1954): 327–49. Also see Jonathan Arac,
Commissioned Spirits (New Brunswick, N.J.: Rutgers University Press, 1979), 94–
113.

This sense of nostalgia underlies much of the narrator's recording of historical change. Consider, for example, the necessity for expediency expressed in the narrator's intention to "make short work with . . . traditionary lore." The historical details are referred to almost lovingly. A faithful recounting of the house's past would provide "no small interest and instruction." His decision to forego such documentation arises from a desire to conform to the tastes of an age impatient with the historical details that would "fill a bigger folio volume." The overall concern voiced in the preface for audience approval is evident in this similar solicitude to provide "the freshest novelty" for contemporary readers (5–6). The narrator seems to fear that a past world he finds meaningful in all of its rich details may appear tedious to his readers. Nevertheless, he insists on confronting the reader with continual comparisons between past and present. And his sense of the differences, in fact a form of nostalgia as social criticism, comprises a significant part of the novel's political insights. For the narrator's view of historical change reveals some important shifts in the operation of power in the nineteenth century.

The greatest virtue of Puritan society from the narrator's point of view seems to lie in the visibility of class boundaries and the clarity of public images. Adjectives used to describe Puritan personages suggest an age of stability and honesty. Old Colonel Pyncheon betrays a "common-sense, as massive and hard as blocks of granite." The great ceremony christening the house of the seven gables is "made acceptable to the grosser sense by ale, cider, wine, and brandy, in copious effusion . . . and by the weight and substance of an ox."

Ushers stand at the house entrance apprising the high and low degrees of the celebrants and directing them to appropriate rooms. Class boundaries in this society are "easy to distinguish": seventeenth-century America denotes a highly stratified, paternalistic society in which public appearances reflect social truths. This is compared to the novel's nineteenth-century era, where social differences are masked or subtly conveyed; it seems that the caste system has not disappeared but gone underground.

The transformation in social appearances between the novel's Puritan past and its present is captured in the characterizations of the late Colonel Pyncheon and his descendant, the modern Judge.[31] Physical attributes, formerly expressive of the innermost man, are now tools for controlling the impressions of others. The portrayal of Judge Pyncheon suggests that there is nothing at the center of his soul, that any part of him may be sacrificed for the sake of an opportunity. His countenance features "a quicker mobility . . . at the expense of a sturdier something, on which [it] seemed to act like dissolving acids" (121). In contrast to the "original" Pyncheon's ruffs and collars of social supremacy, the modern Pyncheon's clothes do not appear "to differ in any tangible way from other people's clothes, [though] there was yet a wide and rich gravity about them" (56).

The description of Judge Pyncheon making his way down a public street illustrates that self-presentation has become a matter of manipulating images. "As is customary with the rich, when they aim at the honors of a republic, he apologized, as it were, to the people for his wealth" (130). Powerful men like Judge Pyncheon act deferential in public so as to obfuscate the class differences so out of keeping with the principles of a democracy. And the illusiveness of social appearances is extended to political practice, where politicians "steal from the people, without its knowledge, the power of choosing its own rulers" (274). In place of an older system of open elite rule is a new system where elite rule masquerades as popular government.

The details of Judge Pyncheon's hegemony could not be more

[31] My view of the comparisons between the Puritan Colonel and the modern Judge is largely congruent with Michael Bell's. See his discussion of Hawthorne's opposition between immateriality and materiality on the one hand, and past and present on the other, in *Hawthorne and Historical Romance*, 223–24. But my view stresses the *functional* distortedness of Judge Pyncheon's public appearance. Judge Pyncheon maintains political power in great part by keeping others off balance, continually mystifying and subverting their perceptions.

explicit. As he warns Hepzibah at one point, "with a quietude which he had the power of making more formidable than any violence, 'since your brother's return, I have taken the precaution . . . to have his deportment and habits constantly overlooked. Your neighbors have been eye-witnesses to whatever has passed in the garden. The butcher, the baker, the fishmonger, some of the customers of your shop, and many a prying old woman, have told me several of the secrets of your interior' " (235–36). The low tones that veil Judge Pyncheon's speech suggest his awareness that subdued methods are more effective than violence. And this description of his neighborhood network demonstrates how power can be wielded through perceptual and discursive channels alone.

The nineteenth-century society of *Seven Gables* is one in which human beings are disconnected from a past world of meaningful traditions, and isolated in their present as well. This is a world of puppet figures set against a cramped horizon without historical depth. The pervading sense of spiritual desolation is most evident in scenes with Hepzibah and Clifford, but it is present also in many contemporary street scenes. *Seven Gables* features a young society without firmly entrenched traditions, beginning to incorporate the processes of industrial capitalism. Fredric Jameson's analysis of a later stage of American consumer society illuminates the crucial beginnings of such a world in Hawthorne's novel.

Jameson bases his understanding of consumerism on the idea of the simulacrum: "The reproduction of copies which have no original characterizes the commodity production of consumer capitalism and marks our object world with an unreality and a free-floating absence of the 'referent'—e.g., the place hitherto taken by nature, by raw materials and primary production, or by the 'originals' of artisanal production or handicraft." The pertinence of such an analysis to Hawthorne's novel is borne out by a description of one of Hepzibah's shop customers. This "very ancient woman . . . the very last person in town who still kept the time-honored spinning-wheel in constant revolution" (78) ushers in an age with a different conception of time, an age having less to do with the intricate designs of handicraft. The novel pictures a new order of production in "constant revolution" contrived to meet the demands of a growing market of American consumers.[32]

Hepzibah launches into a competitive sphere with her reluctant business venture. Her obsolescent gentility, the narrator indicates, is no isolated case; he could "point to several little shops of a similar description . . . where a decayed gentlewoman stands behind the counter" (39). Hepzibah is apprised of her modern competition, envisioning "the great thoroughfare of a city, all astir with customers. So many and so magnificent shops as there were . . . and those noble mirrors at the farther end of each establishment, doubling all this wealth by a brightly burnished vista of unrealities" (48). Hepzibah's exaggerated vision images a consumer world more appropriate to *Sister Carrie* than to *Seven Gables*.[33] Yet the form of her imaginings is instructive. The most threatening aspect of new mercantile practices is its power of distortion. The doubling effect of the shop mirrors exemplifies the intentional enlargement of human desires by modern retailers. Consumers are as slaves to the sleights of hand of the merchandisers, who seek to convey an aura of limitlessness in their commodity displays, instilling in turn a sense of the insatiability of human appetites. To Hepzibah, such a picture affirms the impossibility of her venture, and her fears of an uncontrollable modern world, of endless copies with "no original."

In the new republic, individuals may pursue ever greater promises of wealth and satisfaction; yet the image of their desire, as in the mirrors above, will always elude their grasp. This may explain the frustration and rage of the novel's American buyer. In her first day of shopkeeping, Hepzibah encounters a barrage of belligerent and dissatisfied customers. One "brutal customer," on failing to

[32] Fredric Jameson, "Reification and Utopia in Mass Culture," *Social Text* 1 (1979): 135.

[33] For a "Darwinian" view of the novel's society that is also applied to *Sister Carrie*, see Roy P. Male, *Hawthorne's Tragic Vision* (Austin: University of Texas Press, 1957), 127.

obtain tobacco, "dashe[s] down his newly-bought pipe" and leaves
the shop muttering curses. Others, seeking beverages "and obtain-
ing nothing of the kind, [go] off in an exceedingly bad humor" (53).
In a much later scene, another potential buyer, Mrs. Gubbins,
will not "hear reason" as she demands that "Old Maid Pyncheon
get up and serve me" (289). These descriptions characterize the
new consumer as egoistic and irrational. There are enough allusions to modern industry as a potentially positive force to dispel a
view of the narrative unconscious as simply antiquarian. Yet there
is no subtlety in the depiction of the consumer mentality on the
rise in the novel. Hepzibah's shopkeeping enterprise puts her at
the behest of the often ferocious demands of American buyers,
symbolized in the repetitions of her shop bell. But her hermetic
brother, Clifford, also registers a significant nineteenth-century
response to modernity.

Newly emerged from a living tomb at the point of his introduction in the novel, this man without memory is an imaginative in-
habitant of the past, troubled by the discrepancies between his
mental images and his sense perceptions.[34] Deprived of the faculty
of immediate memory, Clifford cannot remember an event taking
place earlier in the same day. Thus, he is peculiarly vulnerable to
the sounds of technological advances, which he is forced to experience anew at each reappearance. For Clifford, the rounds of
modern life can never become an acknowledged background hum,
for they are not repetitive but rather a continual fresh assault upon
his senses. There is something "terrible" about the railroad, whose
"energy . . . was new at every recurrence . . . and seemed to affect
him as disagreeably . . . the hundreth time as the first" (161). Clifford, moreover, resents the utilitarian emphasis of modern living,
where the water cart is "like a summer-shower, which the city-au-
thorities had caught and tamed, and compelled . . . into the com-
monest routine of their convenience" (160). Given the natural dis-

---

[34] Oliver Sacks offers a fascinating description of a form of amnesia much like
Clifford's discovered at the turn of the century in "The Lost Mariner," *New York
Review of Books*, February 16, 1984, 14–19.

junctiveness of his mind, modern practices appear to him in their most fundamental character as an unending series of stops and starts. Unable to connect the distant past of his youth to the world that has developed in the years he has spent in prison, Clifford feels adrift in a new world of endlessly repeating sequences. His experience is representative of the antiquarian's response to modernization.

One of the few sights that Clifford tolerates is the Italian organ grinder, whose portrayal reveals the status of art in the novel's contemporary world. A "modern feature of our streets," the organ grinder makes his rounds accompanied by a covetous little monkey and by a mechanical puppet show that he carries in his mahogany organ case. The performance features a community of manikins, a "fortunate little society," in which each member— scholar, milkmaid, cobbler, blacksmith—has a particular function to perform. The lone drawback to this harmonic cast of figures is that with the cessation of the organ music, the puppets fall into a state of complete torpor, leading the narrator to attribute the play to a "cynic" whose moral is that "we mortals . . . dance to one identical tune . . . and bring nothing finally to pass" (163). The scene does not close with this dismal maxim but returns to the image of the monkey, whose "small black palm . . . signifying his excessive desire for . . . filthy lucre" illustrates the moral condition of "more than one New Englander." Indeed, the creature is so hideous that Clifford, described as a "being of another order," is moved to a state of tears.

The passage mirrors the process of reading the novel. The ostensibly innocuous street scene, Hawthorne's attempt to bring a bit of common sunlight into his work, the cynical moral, which the narrator flippantly rejects as "too acrid," and the repulsive actuality embodied in the monkey, comprise the various narrative levels of *Seven Gables*. First, an image of harmony and sunshine, pleasing to a being like Clifford; next, a sorrowful moral, which clouds our view, but leaves us unimpeachable in its reference to the inconsequentiality of human efforts; finally, an image ("the moral condition of more than one New Englander") that forces us to confront our own role in a world we would prefer to observe from a perch of detachment. It is noteworthy that the scene ends with the gesture that draws the reader into the text, and consequently, perhaps into an examination of his responsibility for the condition of his own world.

The reappearance of the organ grinder near the novel's end, to dance around the corpse of Judge Pyncheon concealed within the house of the seven gables, raises additional questions about the terms of art in the novel's present. A homeless wanderer, originator of the "little enchantments" that, like "soap bubbles," "build up a home about them," the organ grinder is Hawthorne's alienated artist figure. The turning of his crank can make his windup community look happy or sad, reflecting an image of human harmony or torpor upon his living audience. But the artist must walk a tightrope between pleasing his audience and maintaining his artistic integrity. With his "quick professional eye," ever alert to the potential for accumulating capital, this artist is well aware of the monetary exigencies of his craft. Nor is artistic technique itself immune to the terms of modern life, for the depiction of the organ grinder also suggests certain connections between the repetitive whirl of modernity and artistic form.

The approaching sound of the organ grinder's music is one of repeated stops and starts, "several intervals of silence and then a renewed and nearer outbreak of brisk melody." His music, described as "dry and mechanical," is repeated "over and over again," despite his listener's boredom. Yet for those who know what is concealed within the Pyncheon mansion, there is "a ghastly effect in this repetition of light popular tunes at the doorstep" (292–95). In its juxtaposition of a human corpse and "dry, mechanical" music, the scene forecasts the possibilities for vibrant art in the modern world. But the most telling impact of modernity is to be found in the novel's portrayal of historical narration itself.

From its opening pages, the novel takes a theoretical approach to the problem of narrating a tale of the past. The narrator refers to the kind of tale he *could* tell, filled with historical details and betraying "a certain remarkable unity"; but he also refers to the more impressionistic tale he will in fact write, of "manners, feelings, and opinions" (5–6). Grounded in the terms of the present, his narrative is more revealing of the present in its uses of the past than of the past itself. In *Seven Gables*, the circumstances under view are always twice removed; there are no remaining participants as in *The Scarlet Letter*. Thus, the act of retelling the past, either individually or collectively, is more easily separated from the concern over what may actually have happened. The novel depicts the members of a new democratic republic coping with the pressures of their contemporary world through their manipulation of personal and national histories.

It appears doubly ironic then, that the absence of one agreed-upon version of the past in the community of *Seven Gables* is itself indicative of the impact of modernity—the characters' separation from traditional sources of meaning, and their alienation from one another. The proliferating versions of the Maule's Curse and Alice Pyncheon tales suggest that no one historical narrative is privileged and that the possibility for authoritative narration in the novel's society is questionable.[35] Narrating history in *Seven Gables* seems continually to degenerate into personal fantasy or political myth, with all the characters relating their separate and necessary versions of historical truth.

An examination of the narratives offered by the novel's parade of historians exposes their own psychological struggles as well as the larger political conflicts of their society. Hepzibah Pyncheon is a historian who lacks control over her narratives, using them as a substitute for life in the present. She loses herself in the "impalp-

---

[35] The emphasis on monotonous repetition in the society of *Seven Gables*, from the work of manufacturers to storytellers, signals what Edward Said terms the nineteenth-century "loss of the origin . . . the authority of a privileged Origin that commands, guarantees, and perpetuates meaning has been removed." Said explores the implications for narrative authority in the nineteenth-century novel in *Beginnings* (New York: Basic Books, 1975), 311 and passim, and especially ch. 1.

able" tales of the Pyncheon land claims, her fantasy compensating for her sense of reduced stature in the novel's society. Her imagination builds for her "a palace from whose highest tower she might look down" after the family fortune, the whereabouts of which is concealed in an "ancient map," is properly restored (64–65, 83–84). Though Hepzibah's historical fictions allow her to rise above the threatening tides of her present, her self-mesmerizing narrations are repeatedly drowned out by the peals of the novel's symbol of nineteenth-century commerce, the shop bell. For Hepzibah, tales of the past are an imaginative life preserver that vanishes and reappears in a ghostly fashion, that she seems at once to control and to be at the mercy of.

Judge Pyncheon's manipulation of past tales reveals his mercenary interests; for him, historical narratives have utility value—the potential material result of enhancing his estate. Like his ancestor, who built the house of the seven gables "over an unquiet grave," the Judge is impatient with irrational superstitious details. His response to Hepzibah's insistence that Clifford's stories about the Pyncheon territory are fantasy is consistent with his opportunistic disposition. Because he is not, as he tells Hepzibah, of "the dreaming class of men," Judge Pyncheon translates Clifford's dream vision into his own substantial terms, detecting "a backbone of solid meaning within the mystery of its expression" (235). Pyncheon's narrative thrice removed, his plot of a plot of a plot, is an effort to turn the work of imagination into the substance of earth. If there is a hint of materiality in any phenomenon, it appears that the novel's empiricist, Judge Pyncheon, will discover it. Moreover, as we shall see, his own and his ancestors' disdain for the chimney-corner legends has much to do with their maintenance of social power.

Holgrave's story, "Alice Pyncheon," suggests his own marginality as a young man both obsessed with the past and drawn to the future in his commitment to Progressivist Jeffersonian ideals. And the story demonstrates that Holgrave's historical marginality is inseparable from his ideological marginality. For as much as it betrays the subversive aim of exposing a prevalent class conflict, there seems to be an almost opposite sentiment at large in his tale: Holgrave's desire to exonerate himself through the characterization of Matthew Maule. Maule's social demeanor, the public perceptions of his "reserve" and the "suspicions of his holding heretical tenets in matters of religion and polity," are similar to Holgrave's position in his community (84–85, 190). The story's close, which pictures Maule now penitent, marching woefully behind the funeral procession, provides the strongest clue to its author's self-repressive tendencies. The message is clear: ungoverned passion in the morally upright world of the tale is an unqualified evil; the intertwined energies of class struggle and sexual desire must be denounced in the name of social harmony. "Alice Pyncheon" reflects a young writer attempting to vindicate his own radical impulses in picturing his main character's remorse for his overzealousness. Through his tale, Holgrave establishes himself as an author with a moral vision, an author who is not as eager to destroy the prevailing social system as he may at times appear.

The historical narratives of all the characters serve to reveal present narrators more than past truths. And the implicit struggle to instill one's own version of the past suggests a world in which no single authoritative story exists that could meaningfully tell all. It would be premature, however, to conclude that the novel entirely dismisses the possibility of historical fact. As much as it questions the potential for fully recovering historical truths, it nevertheless intimates that none of the versions of the past given by the characters adequately accounts for certain underlying details. At the novel's close, we find the characters enriched by the death of Judge Pyncheon, not by their recovery of some shadowy fortune. Indeed, the territorial map of their fantasized pasts is revealed as a worthless parchment. Yet is does contain an important disclosure about the usurpation of the original land claim from the Indians, a bitter fact that, like other painful bits of history in the novel, is easily shuffled away.[36]

[36] An ironic view of America's collective amnesia over the fate of the American

The characters' versions of the past are each exposed as evasions of history, but there is a form of storytelling that is more capable than others of penetrating the deeper historical truths of the novel's society—the chimney-corner legends.[37] These persistent rumblings of the "popular imagination" comprise the lone opposition to the powerful hegemony of the Pyncheon rule, which is underwritten by all printed matter and formal speeches referred to in the novel. The chimney-corner legends also constitute a view of history that consistently portrays it as a process of conflict and change. They persist through the generations because they are dialectical narratives, adaptable to the circumstances of each era. Passed on via the instrument of human voice, the legends represent an inside view that penetrates the self-serving truths of particular social hierarchies. Perhaps the essential feature of the chimney-corner legends is that all of the novel's characters believe in them, with the exception of the Judge.

The novel's first allusion to this underground point of view figures importantly in recounting the origin of the Maule-Pyncheon conflict. This historical dispute yields no "written record," but is reconstructed for the most part from traditional legends. These legendary details are viewed with suspicion by the narrator, who treads cautiously on the potentially irrational ground of communal hearsay. He is likewise distrustful of legendary views detailing the

---

Indians is found in other works by Hawthorne. See Colacurcio on "Roger Malvin's Burial," a tale that hints similarly at the "tragical farce" of America's Indian removal policy. *Province of Piety*, 116.

[37] Most critics of the novel have overlooked the significance of the chimney-corner legends. Notable exceptions are Edgar Dryden and Richard Poirier. Dryden sees the legends as forms of discourse that "allow involvement with others while minimizing the usual dangers associated with that activity." See "Hawthorne's Castles in the Air: Form and Theme in *The House of the Seven Gables*," *ELH* 38 (1971): 294–317, and Poirier, *A World Elsewhere* (New York: Oxford University Press, 1966), 106–109. In my view, the chimney-corner legends exemplify what Raymond Williams calls an "oppositional or alternative" cultural formation, which signifies the always incomplete hegemony of any dominant group. Yet the sporadic and fragmented nature of these legends suggests "the relatively mixed, confused, incomplete, or inarticulate consciousness of actual men." *Marxism and Literature*, 81–82.

CHAPTER THREE

circumstances of the late Colonel's death, citing them, so he says, "only to lend a tinge of superstitious awe" to his tale. As he rationally insists, "It were folly to lay any stress on stories of this kind which are sure to spring up around such an event" (7, 16). Such superstitious whisperings, he suggests, are vulnerable attempts of simple folk to cope with the mysteries of death. The narrator sets himself above these emotional outpourings, speaking from his tower of reason. But his disdain for legend, perhaps ironic even at this early point in the narrative, is short-lived. As if the novel's events are too much for him to cope with on his own, the narrator comes to depend increasingly on the chimney-corner legends.

One hundred pages into the novel, the formerly suspicious tales have become the "chimney corner tradition which often preserves traits of character with marvelous fidelity." And this legendary view is opposed to the "cold, formal, and empty words of the chisel that inscribes, the voice that speaks, and the pen that writes, for the public eye and for far distant time" (122–23). The legends offer a more vibrant vision, truer to what they describe than the deductive view arising from rigid principle or design that is often associated with the novel's rulers. The narrator's acquaintance, as it were, with Judge Pyncheon, his confrontation with a power to make individuals disavow their own deepest insights, may have increased his sympathies for the chimney-corner legends.

The "Governer Pyncheon" chapter, the narrator's most cynical diatribe against the Judge, centers upon his disdain for legend. In the middle of haranguing Judge Pyncheon's corpse, he details ironically all the reasons why the Judge is not afraid of superstitions. Adopting the mock persona of the dead Judge, the narrator scoffs at irrational beliefs, while at the same time constructing a fictional scene that will ultimately overturn the Judge's point of view. "Ghosts stories," he states in the Judge's voice, "are hardly to be treated seriously." He then proceeds to describe a parade of Pyncheon ghosts that will turn out to be mercilessly real. Thus, the scene repudiates Judge Pyncheon's unyielding rationality by authorizing the dictates of superstitious phantoms. One Pyncheon phantom, the old Colonel, irritably shakes his portrait in an inexplicable gesture that will be disclosed, three chapters later, to reveal the location of the precious Pyncheon land deed. And the appearance of the Judge and his son in this dim parade of ghosts will also be fully authorized in the novel's final chapter. The narrator's concluding apology for this "fantastic scene [which] must by no means be considered as forming an actual portion of our story" may be understood as undoubtedly ironic (278–81).

Legend also plays a crucial part in the story of "Alice Pyncheon." If we consider this tale-within-a-tale as a distillation of the novel's central themes and techniques, then the pivotal role accorded the legends by its narrator is revealing. The story blatantly articulates the acceptance or rejection of popular legends in terms of class warfare. There is gleeful irony in the description of the respect paid "popular beliefs" by Gervayse Pyncheon's sober lawyers, who dutifully order the search of Matthew Maule's grave on the advice of a superstitious old hag (196). And it is crucial that Pyncheon "did not see fit to inform the carpenter" of the search, which is carried out clandestinely. Mr. Pyncheon cannot disclose such trust in these legends, for any admission of his valuing of lower-class beliefs would imperil his standing in the eyes of the community. His social supremacy is founded in part on the perceived distance between his own rational perspective and the homely superstitions of the populace. As we have seen, "Alice Pyncheon" overturns some of its most subversive insights in its closing pages, Holgrave's critique of Pyncheon hypocrisy ultimately undermining the force of its own rebelliousness.

But the story's reliance upon legend as the truest source for historical narration suggests a conflict in the larger narrative between the underlying truths of these collective histories and the concern of rationalists to repress such "irrational" versions of the community's history. The repression of troublesome perceptions seems to operate in *Seven Gables* for the sake of establishing a nation. And the narrator's gradual recognition of the viability of legend does not minimize his own difficulties in reconciling the preservation of social harmony on the one hand with the truths of history on the other.

The chimney-corner legends provide an essential key to the political insights of *Seven Gables*. As a collective vision, these popular perceptions comprise a significant oral tradition in the novel, based on underground responses to experience, "truths of the hearth" attuned to the specific circumstances of each generation of speakers and listeners. By providing a point of view that continually undercuts the hypocrisies of society's powerful, and creating stories meaningful to all, the legends symbolize a collective means for coping with the fear and alienation engendered by the novel's greedy landowners, and arising from the social atomization of the characters' developing capitalist world. The fragmentariness of the chimney-corner legends suggests both the strategy and the limit of their effectiveness; yet in the novel's world, they represent a persistently daring perspective.

FOUR

The Politics of Temporality in
The Bostonians

HENRY JAMES'S *The Bostonians* is often viewed as his most extensive portrait of social conditions, his great effort to "do" Boston in the way that his French master Balzac had "done" Saumaur and Limoges. Critics have devoted much attention to the novel's rendering of the American context. Yet interconnections between its socio-political and artistic themes remain largely unexplored. Criticism of *The Bostonians* has stressed the task of evaluation, and has ranged from those who locate it among James's finest works to those who find it somehow "alien" to his most subtle talents.[1]

Though judgments of its quality differ, most critics see no interplay between the novel's socio-political and aesthetic properties, and share the twin assumptions that James's art is divorced

---

[1] Lionel Trilling points to the vision of America's thin and disconnected social life, and the "threatening sordidness" of the novel's cast of sexual misfits, in "The Bostonians," in *The Opposing Self* (New York: Viking, 1955), 106, 114–15. And in Irving Howe's words, James's portrait of America "as it stumbles into the factory age" is the work of an author "on the margin of American society, estranged from its dominant powers, helpless before the drift toward a world of industry and finance, money and impersonality . . . who finds a kind of solace . . . in the practice of his art." "The Politics of Isolation," in *Politics and the Novel* (New York: Horizon, 1957), 184. Quentin Anderson categorizes the novel as an inferior member of the Jamesian canon, featuring a fixed social atmosphere and a cast of characters who never grow or change. In this work, Anderson argues, "the struggle with the reader lapses," as the reader is no longer compelled to acknowledge, as he is in James's best works, "that values are recreated in individual consciousness at every moment." Instead of "inner conflict," we have "conflicting cultural assumptions." *The American Henry James* (New Brunswick, N.J.: Rutgers University Press, 1957), 42–47. Also see Peter Buitenhuis, *The Grasping Imagination* (Toronto: Toronto University Press, 1970), 158; and Charles Anderson, "Introduction," *The Bostonians* (New York: Penguin English Library, 1984), 22.

from political concerns and that the social world of the artist is simply reproduced in the literary work. The celebrators see the novel's social and historical world as inertly mimetic, and applaud the "accuracy" of James's American portrait. The detractors also assume that James merely reproduced the givens of his American context, although they question the suitability of this context to James's genius. Rarely does either sort of analysis consider the impact of the novel's narrator, a mystifying and often self-contradictory voice.[2]

This chapter explores the connections between the novel's social vision and its artistic features, and suggests the ways in which power and politics, rather than having been dismissed from James's artistic universe, are implicated in the very processes of talk and narration. In *The Bostonians*, power is conceived as the ability to establish one's own sense of time and one's own version of history.

The key characters' relations to time have important social and political significance. Miss Birdseye's chronic forgetfulness and penchant for tales of the past represent the self-glorifying aims of history writing in a democratic republic. In the case of Mrs. Farrinder, the consensual framing of mythic time becomes a blatant

---

[2] Sallie Hall has made an illuminating attempt to characterize the narrator of *The Bostonians* in her essay "Henry James and the Bluestockings," in *Aeolian Harps: Essays in Literature* ed. Donna Fricke and Douglas Fricke (Bowling Green, Ohio: Bowling Green University Press, 1976). I would, however, qualify and extend her view of the narrator. Rather than the "vir bonus: the man of plain living, high thinking, and lasting friendships" Hall describes, the narrator is more akin to Northrop Frye's "eiron figure," "the ironic fiction writer . . . [who] deprecates himself and, like Socrates, pretends to know nothing, even that he is ironic." *Anatomy of Criticism* (Princeton: Princeton University Press, 1957), 40. And a way of conceiving the narrator's experience of time is as Walter Benjamin's "angel of history . . . [whose] face is turned toward the past. Where we perceive a chain of events, he sees one single catastrophe. . . . The angel would like to stay, awaken the dead, and make whole what has been smashed. But a storm is blowing from Paradise; it has got caught in his wings with such violence that the angel can no longer close them. This storm irresistibly propels him into the future to which his back is turned, while the pile of debris before him grows skyward. This storm is what we call progress." *Illuminations*, 257–58.

attempt to gain power over others by controlling their temporal experience. Mrs. Burrage and her son Henry combine the manipulation of others' experiences of time with an insidious talent for managing human beings as commodities. And Selah Tarrant's ability to square spiritual disinterest with business interests, effecting a merger of sacred and profane time, typifies his American society's sanction of capitalist expansion through its rhetoric of divine mission. The novel's three central characters, Olive Chancellor, Basil Ransom, and Verena Tarrant, provide examples of how self-definition and power are pursued through the manipulation of historical narratives and temporal perceptions. Finally, the narrator's ambivalence toward the authority of his narrative role is revealed in assertions and denials of his own power to dictate the pace of the plot and the opinions of the reader.

From beginning to end, the novel highlights efforts to assert authority through imposing delays on others. In the opening scene, Olive exercises power by making her visitor wait. Her tortuously precise message, seemingly a gesture of politeness, in fact serves to increase the expectant visitor's anxiety over the moment of her arrival. The belabored explanation of Olive's delay merely heightens it, affording her attendants (Basil and the reader) little insight into her intentions. Olive here controls Basil by withholding herself indefinitely and springing on him when he least expects it. Indeed, throughout these opening scenes, the amount of time the ingenuous Basil spends waiting for others signifies his manipulation by the wily Northerners he meets.[3]

The entire party of Miss Birdseye's guests also suffers Mrs. Farrinder's delay (30). While being held in suspense is a circumstance at the heart of storytelling, it functions in this novel as a strategy in the power struggles of the characters. The ability to make another wait is pivotal in the novel's American culture, which is bent on progress and the pursuit of gain. The varying degrees of con-

3 Henry James, *The Bostonians* (New York: Penguin Modern Classics, 1966), 5, 9, 20. Parenthetical references in this text are to this edition.

cealment or ambivalence evident in characters' seizures of temporal control disclose a general distrust of authority in the novel's democratic society.

The novel reveals a tension between characters insisting on patience, as a means of marshalling their own and others' experiences of time, and their uncontrolled efforts to embrace the future, to pursue their desires in a headlong race against time. Both impulses exemplify resistance to historical process: the first, as a conscious imposition of delay; the second, by denying temporal constraints in rushing pursuit of some future satisfaction of desire. The narrator himself seems least sympathetic to the second impulse, appearing to erect a wall against the striving ambitions of the characters. This wall can function in two ways: it can force the characters and the reader to wait, delaying the revelation of some point expectantly anticipated; or it can force the characters themselves to review their pasts, to confront their places in history as a process of change that cannot be transcended.

The novel's final scenes betray an assertion of temporal authority through their dramatic suspension of Basil and Verena's climactic departure. This collective act of waiting can be seen as the narrator's method of educating (through the aid of his most historically sensitized character, Verena) the characters and the reader into awareness of a historical time beyond their control. And the narrator's withholding of the ending replicates Olive's intricately staged entrance at the novel's opening.

As in the previous chapter, I shall explore the attitudes of the narrator and characters toward time and history, analyzing the covert and overt "politics of temporality" as it emerges in the novel's society. I begin with the characters, examining especially the two central historical myths offered by Basil Ransom and Olive Chancellor. I then consider the narrator, looking at his frequent narrative anachronies, references to the past and anticipations of the future, as attempts to control the pace of his narrative, and thereby his own and the reader's experience of time.[4] Finally, I

---

[4] I borrow these definitions from Gerard Genette's discussion of narrative order

treat the manipulations of perceptions and historical tales by the narrator and the characters as avenues for suppressing and fomenting the sexual battles that prevail in the novel's democratic society. Though the characters all insist on the universality or naturalness of their own versions of time and history, their constructions invariably expose the specific conflicts of their world. In *The Bostonians*, the marginalized "reality" of the characters' society is located in the details of sexual politics, which disclose the subtle manipulations and uneven balances of power inherent in all of the novel's love relationships.

The Characters as Historians

Miss Birdseye is the novel's exemplary democratic personage, whose experience of time suggests the potential for historical consciousness in a popular state. As described in her introduction, her face

looked as if it had been soaked, blurred, and made vague by exposure to some slow dissolvent. The long practice of philanthropy had not given accent to her features; it had rubbed out their transitions, their meanings. The waves of sympathy . . . had wrought upon them in the same way in which the waves of time finally modify the surface of old marble busts, gradually washing away their sharpness, their details. In her large countenance her dim little smile scarcely showed . . . it seemed to say that she would smile more if she had time. (25–26)

The emphasis on "blurring" and "dissolving," the "washing away" of "details," suggests the delirium of Miss Birdseye's vision. Like a marble bust, she absorbs time as a process of erosion, rather than experiencing it as a course of significant accretions. Without meaningful lines to indicate a long life thoughtfully lived, Miss Birdseye's aspect repeats her amorphous consciousness: she rarely acknowledges time except to note that she doesn't have enough. Likewise, Miss Birdseye lacks a discriminating sense of history, which is linked to the impartiality of her democratic ideals. In the

---

in *Narrative Discourse*, trans. Jane E. Lewin (Ithaca: Cornell University Press, 1980), see especially chs. 1 and 2 on order and duration, 33–86.

narrator's words, "all her history had been that of her sympathies" (27), which "began at home and ended nowhere" (25).

Perhaps the telling irony of Miss Birdseye's relationship to history past and present is that though she suffers perpetually from memory loss, she harbors a fund of mythical memories. "A small battered brooch," for example, given by "one of her refugees in the old time" (34), betokens a legendary age of slave emancipations and "European despotisms" (26). Miss Birdseye's sense of the past is captured by the "wandering amiable tale" she delivers in her introduction of Verena Tarrant. Her narrative conveys a "universal familiarity," mentioning "Dr. Tarrant's miraculous cures . . . with all the facts wanting," and Verena's tour as a series of "accepted and recognized wonders, natural in an age of new revelations." Throughout, the figure of Abraham Greenstreet "kept reappearing" (48). Miss Birdseye's tale contains the properties of myth in Roland Barthes's terms: illustrative without "facts," and highly repetitive, its images are offered as "natural" "revelations." A vision of the past with little historical foundation, it represents the political intentions of its professor.[5]

The tale Miss Birdseye tells here is reminiscent of her jumbled thoughts aroused by the arrival of the Tarrants at the scene's beginning: "Selah Tarrant had effected wonderful cures. . . . His

[5] Roland Barthes's discussion of cultural myths that function as "kinds of arrests," depriving the subject of its history, is pertinent here. As Barthes writes, "Myth is constituted by the loss of the historical quality of things: in it, things lose the memory that they once were made." What is "particular, historical" now becomes "universal, eternal." "Myth does not deny things, on the contrary, its function is to talk about them; simply, it purifies them, it makes them innocent." And one of the chief powers of myth is derived from its recurrence, its ability to convince is founded in part on the "indefinite repetition of its identity." "Myth Today," in *A Barthes Reader*, ed. Susan Sontag (New York: Hill and Wang, 1982), 93–149. Among studies that examine the mythologizing of history in mid-nineteenth-century America, as engaged in by such authors as George Bancroft, Francis Parkman, and John Motley, are Michael Kammen, *A Season of Youth* (New York: Knopf, 1978); Fred Somkin, *Unquiet Eagle* (Ithaca: Cornell University Press, 1967); and David Levin, *The Romantic Historians* (Stanford, Calif.: Stanford University Press, 1959).

wife was a daughter of Abraham Greenstreet" (30). But the difference between the two passages is critical. From inner ruminations to narrated speech, Miss Birdseye's ideas have taken on "universal" significance, and are now offered to the assembly "as accepted and recognized wonders." Miss Birdseye is the novel's grand assumer, who signals the potential for historical consciousness in a democratic nation where history may exclusively equal myth. The product of a "hospitable soul," that "needed but a moment to swallow and assimilate" (48) details, her "monumental" histories serve the needs of her contemporaries.[6]

Moreover, in an era of developing media technology, in which human behavior increasingly takes its cues from sources of public information, Miss Birdseye plays an important role as a processor of collective self-images. It is precisely her capacity to represent her own life to others that makes her so important to the women's movement. Olive has her "relate her battles," hanging on every mythologized recollection. And Verena, having met innumerable martyrs, has "seen none with so many reminiscences as Miss Birdseye" (155–56). Miss Birdseye gives Verena and Olive a sense of the past that convinces them of the heroic destiny of women. As the narrator asserts, "these modern maidens" manifest a "contagion" for the "perennial freshness of Miss Birdseye's faith." Her vision deprives the present of any but interim status, portraying it as a profane waiting-station between an epic age they feel they have lost and a future that promises its rebirth. But though Miss

[6] Nietzsche's model for different types of historical consciousness can be used to classify its forms in *The Bostonians*. The "antiquarian" response, in Nietzsche's words, is a "raking over all the dust heaps of the past"; history is "mummified," no longer an "inspiration to the fresh life of the present." "Monumental" history is history in the service of the future, a depiction of "effects at the expense of causes," in the delusive "knowledge that the great thing existed . . . and so may be possible again." "Critical" history represents Nietzsche's privileged historical perspective. In "the service of life," this point of view can "break up the past, and apply it, too." *The Bostonians* provides examples of each of these forms of historical consciousness: Miss Birdseye represents the monumental view; Basil Ransom, the antiquarian; and Olive (arguably near the end), Verena, and the narrator, the potential for a critical perspective. See *The Use and Abuse of History* trans. Adrian Collins (Indianapolis: Bobbs-Merrill, 1957).

Birdseye may appear as the "unquenched flame of her Transcendentalism" that persists through the "changing fashions of reform" (157), the taste for her repetitive fund of tales suggests the growing consumer world of her present.[7]

Miss Birdseye's consensual invocation of mythic time contrasts with Mrs. Farrinder's autocratic methods of time-keeping. The latter's aggressive majesty is conveyed in terms of her conscious efforts to direct the tempo of dialogues. Her talk is striking in its "great slowness and distinctness. . . . If, in conversation with her, you attempted to take anything for granted, or to jump two or three steps at a time, she paused, looking at you with a cold patience, as if she knew that trick, and then went on at her own measured pace" (28). Mrs. Farrinder's grand manner is based upon her ability to establish the pace of her interactions. Ever alert to attempts to subvert her temporal authority, she recognizes every "trick." Even the narrator is at the behest of her power, describing the "placid mask" she presents as one that "seemed to face you with a question of which the answer was preordained." Her aspect, which is apparently beyond the satirical aim of the narrator's descriptive powers, anticipates and forecloses whatever "question" or "answer" her features might arouse. She is "preordained," and thus the narrator can "contest neither the measurements or the nobleness" of her character (27).

Mrs. Farrinder's manipulativeness is also evident in her treatment of the crowd at Miss Birdseye's. In condescending acknowledgment of their claim to hear her speak, she offers a "smile which asked that a temporary lapse of promptness might not be too

[7] As Fredric Jameson writes, mass culture gives rise to "the historical reappropriation and displacement of older structures in the service of a qualitatively very different situation of repetition. The atomized or serial public of mass culture wants to see the same thing over and over again, hence the urgency of the generic structure and the generic signal." "Reification and Utopia in Mass Culture," *Social Text* 1 (1979): 130–48. For an interesting essay on James's relation to a developing consumer culture, see Jean-Christophe Agnew, "The Consuming Vision of Henry James," in *The Culture of Consumption*, ed. Richard Fox and Jackson Lears (New York: Pantheon, 1983), 65–100.

harshly judged" (30). Yet the prolongation of her delay reveals that her reluctance is less nervousness than a passive aggressive testing of her power over her public. The comparison of her delay to the figure of Achilles "remain[ing] within her tent" (42) extends the militaristic cast of her temporizing. Mrs. Farrinder can be prompt when she chooses. In encouraging Olive Chancellor to speak, she displays "a punctuality which revealed the faculty of presiding" (33). And her tyranny is even foisted upon the reader, who, the narrator remarks apologetically, "may find it difficult to keep pace with her variations" (48).

It seems appropriate that later mention of the struggle between Mrs. Farrinder and Olive over the reigns of their movement involves a debate over the importance of history. Mrs. Farrinder, "the commander-in-chief," is concerned only with the immediate character of their work in her tyrannical resolve "to keep the movement in her own hands." In contrast to the more consensual efforts of Olive and Verena to frame a vision of "the historic unhappiness of woman," Mrs. Farrinder does not "care" or "know much about history at all." Dispensing with the subtler mechanisms of historical narration in favor of immediate coercion, she is concerned "to begin just today" demanding women's rights for them, "whether they were unhappy or not" (142). Mrs. Farrinder's dictatorial plan is based on a defiance of the idea of process altogether. It is not surprising that she is the first to override Verena's delay at the novel's close. Refusing to abide another's time, Mrs. Farrinder "passes rapidly" through the backstage exit to reaffirm her temporal authority.

Mrs. Farrinder's counterpart in the realm of time publicly manipulated is Mrs. Burrage, who is also introduced on the battleground of dialogue. She is described as "looking as if she ought to be slow and rather heavy, but disappointing this expectation by a quick, amused utterance, a short, bright, summary laugh . . . and an air of recognizing on the instant everything she saw and heard. She was evidently accustomed to talk, and even to listen, if not kept waiting too long for details and parentheses; she was not continuous, but frequent, as it were" (132). Mrs. Burrage is another wealthy American matron whose power lies in her ability to make her own time. She pulls others along in her "quick" utterances and "short" laughs, which jar rather than reassure. The responses of others are subsumed on the instant by her dismissive hilarity.

Mrs. Burrage's methods are more overtly entrepreneurial than Mrs. Farrinder's. In detailing for Olive the advantages of a possible "alliance with the house of Burrage" (265), she alludes pointedly to her commanding financial position. Her businesslike air in "taking all sorts of sentiments and views for granted between them" is consistent with the way she "travers[es] an immense distance with a very few words" (263). What most impresses Olive about her dealings with Mrs. Burrage is her claim that time can be erased—bought, as it were—with everything seen "in a new and original light."

Olive resents the ease with which Mrs. Burrage subsumes questions of belief and commitment, especially her air of "taking up" their movement (a purchasable novelty) as one would respond to fashion changes. But though Olive abhors the way in which "people like Mrs. Burrage lived and fattened on abuses, prejudices, privileges, on the petrified cruel fashions of the past" (264), she must concede the "brilliant" artistry of her maneuvers. Indeed, Mrs. Burrage is careful to implicate Olive fully, by remarking upon her departure, "I am sure you won't feel that you have wasted your hour" (271). The dominance of her entrepreneurial vision is reflected in her son Henry's passion for consumption.

Like the wives of wealthy husbands who "consume conspicuously" to display their spouses' power, Henry's leisurely self-indulgence testifies to his mother's patronage. A cultivated dilettante, at Harvard on the pretense of pursuing a law career, Henry is principally a collector of rare items—"intaglios," "antiques," and "drawings by the old masters." Another pale version of Gilbert Osmond, Burrage is interested in Verena Tarrant as an inimitable item. His own genius lies in his talent for arrangement, for transforming human beings into still-life objects. At the party in his rooms his guests appear in assorted postures, withdrawn from the aggressively paced world of their American present. They become part of Burrage's atmosphere, melting into the tasteful pattern of his possessions:

His guests sat scattered in the red firelight, listening, silent, in comfortable attitudes . . . the covered lamps made a glow here and there, and the cabinets and brackets produced brown shadows, out of which some precious object gleamed—some ivory carving or cinquecento cup . . . the relations between men and women, in that picturesque grouping, had not the air of being internecine. (134)

Arrayed like bibelots among his own, Burrage's guests forget their conflicts; even Olive finds herself without her striving impulse, fading into the tranquil world of exquisite items and the piano music of Schubert and Mendelssohn (courtesy of the house of Burrage). Burrage's seductive atmosphere relieves all from the burden of history as they merge with his "precious" objects.

But Olive's immersion is only temporary, for she recognizes the threat posed by the Burrages. Burrage is himself merely another of his mother's possessions, though one she is concerned to keep happy. And the ease of their commodity world, with its amorphous engulfing action, seems to pose an even greater threat than that posed by Basil Ransom. Flexible liberals, the Burrages insist on their ability to accommodate the struggles of Olive and Verena. The Burrages' luxurious co-optation of political struggle ensures the relentless immobility of their world.

Selah Tarrant offers another example of the way in which power is conceived in the novel's society as the ability to erase a sense of historical process. Tarrant is as lacking in an internal life as Miss Birdseye; his "eternal waterproof" (88) provides an image of a man who lives entirely on surfaces. Tarrant is another impersonal democrat, his disposition a "waterproof" against the impact of experience. His talent for "conspicuous disinterest" provides a model for the reconciliation of materialist greed and spiritual idealism. Worldly success, as he explains to Olive, is best achieved by not pursuing it, the result of a process imperceptible even to the subject (99). Those chosen for high station will know who they are soon enough. The satirical portrait of Tarrant receiving Olive's payment for his daughter reveals the passive "spiritual" side of the American pursuit of gain. Confronted with the check, Tarrant looks furtively at it, then all around it, speechless, until it magically "disappear[s] beneath the folds of his waterproof . . . while his hands [continue] to fumble, out of sight" (144).

Consistent with this scene, Verena's purchase by Olive is concealed from Verena herself—money and its transactions are consigned to the periphery of polite society. But the terms of religious disinterest and business interest are shown to complement each other ominously. The attainment of wealth, the scene implies, is a miraculous phenomenon that "just happens" to the worthy who wait. Indeed, the road to success is mapped out after the fact. One denies the dirty dealings while they are going on, gazing anywhere but directly at them, and retrospectively any explanation can be offered. The scene underlines the strong commitment to the idea of divine intervention in the American ideology of success.

Verena's ignorance of a precedent for such transactions, of "what was done and what was not done," because she has "no worldly pride, no traditions of independence" (150), allows her to accept the actions of Olive and her parents. Without a vision of traditional propriety to challenge their opportunistic business deal, Verena perceives it as a standard in itself. It would not be far-fetched to take this episode as a parable of the absorption of business practices by the novel's developing nineteenth-century world. As some have argued, the apparent "lack of historic traditions" in American society ensured that "bourgeois relations of production . . . together with their representatives" would "sprout rapidly." Capitalism is released in nineteenth-century American society with exceptional force.[8] For Olive and Basil,

[8] Karl Marx, "On America and Civil War," *The Karl Marx Library*, ed. Saul K. Padover, 2 (New York: McGraw-Hill 1972), 1-77. Also see Alexis de Tocqueville, *Democracy in America*, trans. Henry Reeve (New York: Vintage, 1945); Louis Hartz, *The Liberal Tradition in America* (New York: Harcourt Brace, 1955), 50-86;

Verena's great attraction inheres in her "originality"; her historical innocence indicates that she can be shaped according to their wills. For almost all of the novel's characters, the possibility for erasing the real historical past and present and replacing it with one's own version of history provides the possibility for controlling and inventing oneself, and others.

Olive has depended on the Tarrants' easy surrender of the reform legacy embodied in their daughter, but she is herself more circumspect in manipulating her experience of time and reconstructing history. A complicated figure whose most private ruminations seem inseparable from her devotion to the cause of women's reform, Olive manages herself like a public proclamation or tract. She conducts her life according to theories "devotedly nursed," her convoluted reasoning sometimes trying even the narrator's powers of description. In attempting to render her deliberations over her method of traveling to Miss Birdseye's, the narrator finally admits that her "logic . . . was none of the clearest" (21). Olive's linguistic scrupulosity, the way in which thoughts and speech are contained within intertwisted strands of significant qualification, is inseparable from her fear of time. She cannot give to anyone or to any experience; everything is too strenuously qualified to be. Holding the world up before her as an image framed and reframed, she keeps experience at bay. Her face, in which "white skin had a singular look of being drawn tightly across her face," reflects her taxing control.

But Olive is engaged even more directly in controlling time. She experiences repeated prophetic forebodings, dim glimpses of the future that make her fearful and cautious in the present (20). Also prone to excessive reviewing of her past, Olive incriminates herself in gazes backward that disclose missed hints of some future ca-

---

and Carolyn Porter, *Seeing and Being* (Middletown, Conn.; Wesleyan University Press, 1981), 18-22. For an analysis of the literary rhetoric that united spiritual concerns and business practices from the Puritan era to the present, see Sacvan Bercovitch, *The American Jeremiad* (Madison: University of Wisconsin Press, 1978), especially 205-210.

tastrophe that might have been averted. One of these forebodings arises in her spontaneous decision to invite Basil to accompany her to Miss Birdseye's soiree. As their moment of departure nears, Olive experiences "an unreasoned terror of the effect of his presence" (21). Olive tries to downplay her dread, but the peculiar glimmers persist (77, 118, 102, 150, 246). And though the narrator initially attributes them to a supernatural source, these forebodings are psychologically appropriate to a character who so fears her own passion.

Possessed of a nature "like a skiff in a stormy sea" (10), Olive dreads being exposed to her own spontaneous feelings. By prearranging and anticipating events, Olive can superintend her emotions. In tortuous "watches of the night," during which she reprimands herself for every "lapse" of appropriate behavior, Olive establishes her control. When occasionally she relaxes her self-surveillance, the awkward energy of her disposition becomes apparent. Like a windup toy that stops suddenly without warning, Olive creates feelings of nervous expectancy in others. At Verena's first visit, Olive overflows with wild and contradictory emotions.

"You are so simple—so much like a child," Olive Chancellor said. That was the truth, and she wanted to say it because, quickly, without forms or circumlocutions, it made them familiar. She wished to arrive at this; her impatience was such that before the girl had been five minutes in the room she jumped to her point—inquired of her, interrupting herself, interrupting everything: "Will you be my friend, my friend of friends, beyond everyone, and everything, forever and forever?" Yet a few seconds later, Olive is already cautioning, "We must wait—we must wait. When I care for anything I can be patient." (70–71)

Foreclosing any sense of development in their friendship, Olive presumes intimacy from the outset. Yet her refusal to allow events to unfold in time in fact suggests a fear of her excessive intensity. By engulfing time, Olive can live beyond it, in a state similar to that achieved by Selah Tarrant and Miss Birdseye.

Her strategies also serve as means for controlling others. An unusual instance of Verena analyzing Olive reveals the potency of Olive's temporal manipulations. "Olive," Verena felt, "had taken

her up, in the literal sense of the phrase, like a bird of the air. . . .
Verena liked it, for the most part; liked to shoot upward without
an effort of her own and look down upon all creation, upon all history from such a height" (69). Under Olive's spell, Verena is no
longer conditioned by history, but incarnates it.

Olive's exclusive possession of Verena depends on the erasure of
historical constraints. Thus Olive emphasizes Verena's "purity,"
eradicating Verena's connection to her own origins. Verena's past
is valued atmospherically, for "having initiated Verena (and her
patroness, through her agency) into the miseries and mysteries of
the People." Olive aims to effect Verena's "rupture with her past"
(96), and to replace it with a mythical history that affirms the pair's
shared sacred mission and their archetypal link. Their relationship, Olive tells Verena, is based on eternal time; it has always
been and will always be: "I am a thousand years old; I have lived
through generations—through centuries. I know what I know by
experience; you know it by imagination" (119). Each of them sep-
arately "lack[s] an important group of facets," but together they
make "an organic whole" (137). Olive transcends time through
continual exertion, Verena, by the instantaneous power of imagination.

A description of the pair "muffled" within the snowbound silence of a Boston winter night, their reform vision "enlarged and
intensified" by the lamplit room, reveals the crucial medium for
their union. On isolated evenings, with the doorbell "foredoomed
to silence," they participate in the mythical reconstruction of the
past:

They read a great deal of history together, and read it ever with the same
thought—that of finding confirmation in it for this idea that their sex had
suffered inexpressibly, and that at any moment in the course of human
affairs the state of the world would have been so much less horrible (history seemed to them in every way horrible), if women had been able to
press down the scale. (153)

Examples of women empowered in the past, who "had not always
used it amiably . . . were easily disposed of between the two"
(153). The most telling image is of Olive "presenting" these truths

"again and again, and there was no light in which they did not seem to palpitate with truth" (159). Olive's repetitive presentation seems to ensure that her ideas "will palpitate with truth." It is through repetition that myths become obvious and natural. The ritualized readings of women's history by Olive and Verena affirm the sacredness of their mission, a conviction undermined by the narrator's reference to this "possibly infatuated pair" (137).

But the portrayal of Olive reviewing her past on the beach at Marmion is distinguished from these mythical encounters. Confronting a past "reality" over which she has no control, Olive recognizes that "Verena had been more to her than she ever was to Verena" (354). Olive's retracing of the past lacks the air of inspiration that characterizes her reviewing of history with Verena, That "mastered" past contrasts with this unsolicited past, as Olive is overcome with nausea at the disintegration of everything on which she had based her life.

Olive lived over, in her miserable musings, her life for the last two years; she knew, again, how noble and beautiful her scheme had been, but how it had all rested on an illusion of which the very thought made her feel faint and sick. What was before her now was the reality, with the beautiful, indifferent sky pouring down its complacent rays upon it. The reality was simply that Verena had been more to her than she ever was to Verena, and that, with her exquisite natural art, the girl had cared for their cause only because, for the time, no interest, no fascination, was greater. . . . Positive it is that she spared herself none of the inductions of a reverie that seemed to dry up the mists and ambiguities of life. These hours of backward clearness come to all men and women, once at least, when they read the past in the light of the present, with the reasons of things, like unobserved finger-posts, protruding where they never saw them before. . . . They understand as Olive understood, but it is probable that they rarely suffer as she suffered the sense of regret for her baffled calculations burned within her like a fire, and the splendour of the vision over which the curtain of mourning now was dropped brought to her eyes slow, still tears, tears that came one by one, neither easing her nerves nor lightening her load of pain. (354–55)

Here the character of prophetic glimmers and millennial hopes struggles to recontain the past in a vision that will propel her forward once more. Yet this is a process of review that Olive is finally unable to superintend. Rather than a conscious reshaping of the past, this is a "liv[ing] over."

Freud's distinction between repetition based on a contrived re-call of the past versus repetition that brings back "the repressed material as a contemporary experience" is relevant.[9] Though the scene contains traces of controlled recall, as evidenced by the met-aphor of the curtain (where the past is a purgative stage drama for Olive's personal benefit), there is a singular intensity to Olive's "pain." The fact that Olive is in motion implies that she is reen-acting her past, and the mention that her ramble is unconscious, "unnoticed" by her, furthers the contrast between this review and her magnified "watches of the night." Olive may be attempting to "read the past in the light of the present," to rationally learn from it, but her "rare" suffering and "tears" seem to drown the "splen-dour" of her tragic curtain call. This past seems beyond use. More-over, the narrator's distancing efforts, seen in descriptions of her musings as "mysteries into which I shall not attempt to enter, speculations with which I have no concern" (354), are revealing. His apparent fear of getting too close indicates the intensity of Ol-ive's experience.

Significantly, the passage that follows Olive's ramble highlights a consciousness incapable of making any assertions. The scene fea-tures Olive's violent imaginative negation of Verena in a staged drowning of her boat at sea. Envisioning the "nameless horror . . . the body of an unknown young woman, defaced . . . so that their tremendous trouble might never be" (356), Olive attempts to erase her painful love. But Olive's emotions cannot be so easily dis-solved; her "heart . . . gallop[s]" before the possibility that such a view of Verena's death might be real. She achieves her deepest vi-sion in this scene of a self that exists beyond strenuousness in the full awareness of her love for another. It is a vision gained in her

---

[9] Sigmund Freud, *Beyond the Pleasure Principle*, vol. 18 of *The Standard Edition of the Complete Psychological Works of Sigmund Freud*, trans. James Strachey, 24 vols. (London: Hogarth Press, 1953–1974), 18.

recapturing and recognition, on the beach and after, of a love for Verena that is not bound by Verena's response to her.

Perhaps the most controversial aspect of the novel's conclusion is the significance of Olive's final rush onto the stage. While many have read this Roman gesture as suicidal, Olive throwing herself to the lions, the scene may be viewed in terms of Olive's pivotal recognition. Following Marmion, Olive can be seen as a critical historian; having criticized her past, she can apply it in an assertion of her powers for social action. While Basil, with Verena, enters the sphere of domestic bliss to write his anachronistic denunciations of the modern age, Olive embraces the demands of "critical history" in her move to promote social and political change.[10]

Basil Ransom seems to possess a more peaceful and receptive sense of time than his earnest New England cousin. His preferred self-image is a man respectfully linked to tradition in an age grown overconfident of its forward-moving potential. A reactionary classicist, he is steeped in the rigorous reason of the ancients amidst a "womanized" generation overrun with "hollow phrases and false delicacy" (290). Like Olive's identification with the poor or Mrs. Luna's antiquated conservative ideology, Basil's intellectual life affords a unique or oppositional self-conception. Like these others, Basil defines himself as displaced and mystifying. Thus, he is certain that "[Olive] would never understand him," an assurance based on his conviction of his own intellectual superiority (18).

Basil's sense of distinctness is invariably cast in historical terms: his native South is caught in time, his sense of the past the treasured inheritance of his southern legacy. Yet Basil is also decidedly ambitious, and it appears that his departure from the South had

---

[10] This moment might be seen in the terms Hayden White offers in his essay "Getting Out of History." Distinguishing between historical narratives that liberate us from history and those which condemn us to the eternal return of the past, White observes that the real test may be "whether our transportation into this imagined world returns us to our own ready to do *political battle* for *its* transformation or rather deepens our alienation by adding the sadness of 'what might have been' to its dispiriting effects." *Diacritics* (Fall 1982); 6. For further discussion of White's essay, see Chapters One and Two above.

much to do with its destructive slowness, recollected in the "long, empty, deadly summer on the plantation" that he spent studying German and jurisprudence (16). He is as captivated as he is repelled by the "extreme modernness" of the view from Olive's window (15). It soon becomes evident that Basil's nostalgia supplies a convenient veil for a historical world inhospitable to his most concerted efforts. As the narrator observes at one point, Basil is literally at sea, "without means, without friends," and with little idea of how to make a place for himself (162). More than a world he wishes to revive, Basil's past affords an escape from a threatening present.[11]

Basil's sacred response is revealed in his visit to Memorial Hall, where he is in singular sympathy with his New England surroundings. So moved is Basil by the overall aura of "tradition" and "antiquity" (207) and the view of past foes and battles, that he returns "to read again the names of the various engagements, at several of which he had been present." His immediate repetition in the present reflects the welcome intensity of this recapture of the past. Yet Basil's view of the past does not yield any deep recognition of his own experience, nor does it effect his vision of history.

What is most pronounced about Basil's relation to the past is that it remains fixed throughout the novel. The most steadfast of the novel's central characters, his convictions remain unaltered by his experience. While Olive seems genuinely moved by a resuscitation of her past, Basil is consistently nostalgic. The novel's walk-

[11] Ransom represents the "antiquarian" perspective on history, as outlined above. Leo Marx offers an interesting view of idealized realms of pastoral space in *The Machine in the Garden* (New York: Oxford University Press, 1964); see also Henry Nash Smith, *Virgin Land* (Cambridge, Mass.: Harvard University Press, 1950), 145–54, on the myth of the southern garden as "inimical" to "change." Ann Douglas's analysis of the antiquarian "escape from history" in *The Feminization of American Culture* (New York: Knopf, 1978), 197–239, is also relevant here. But, curiously, while Douglas's view of the "static imagination" governing much nineteenth-century historical writing, which served to "absorb and mute . . . historical change," provides a critique of Basil's myth, her overall thesis concurs quite precisely with his own decrial of "a feminine . . . nervous, hysterical, chattering, canting age" (290).

ing caricature of a sense of the past, Basil represents a stereotyped South, immersed in volumes of Scott and images of medieval chivalry.

In the novel's final chapters, Basil's stratagems to capture Verena at Music Hall recall John Wilkes Booth's stalking of Lincoln. Basil explicitly likens himself to a young man "he could imagine . . . waiting in a public place, [having] made up his mind, for reasons of his own, to discharge a pistol at the king or the president." His fanatical ruminations emphasize difference: "He was apart, unique, and had come on a business altogether special" (371). As the moment of their climactic departure nears, the egoism of Basil's designs on Verena is increasingly evident. He views his "rescue" in chivalric terms, as a challenge to "all his manhood" (382).

Indeed, Basil is fixated with the idea of his own fixedness. Verena is "helpless" before his unchallengeable will. Imaging himself as a knight errant in an age grown weak and timorous, he notes the "tremendous entreaty" in the faces of Olive and Verena (382, 383). Before these weak women and the flimsy male front comprised of the two publicity mongers, Dr. Tarrant and Mr. Filer, Basil's sense of his own power grows. From his heroic height everything "looked small, surmountable, and of the moment only" (382). Verena herself is dwarfed and ineffectual: he "notice[d] her strange, touching tone, and her air of believing that she might really persuade him" (385). As in previous scenes where he watched her speak, enjoying the speech rhythms but disregarding the meaning, Basil easily dismisses her pleas before his own designs (53–55, 196–97, 230–32). Looking upon Verena, he sees only his own triumph, how she had "evidently given up everything now—every pretence of a different conviction and of loyalty to her cause" (385). Yet this sheds no light on the ominous disclosure of the novel's end: "though [Verena] was glad . . . beneath her hood, she was in tears" (390). Olive and Basil provide little insight into Verena's deeper nature, concerned as they are to simplify and still her existence, but Verena undergoes a significant transformation in the novel.

Because she is usually portrayed through the perspectives of other characters, the focus of the designs and desires of others, the remarkable change in Verena's own vision of history is often overlooked. Some critics simply dismiss her as a "nonentity," whose power of attraction for other characters is so improbable as to constitute one of the novel's major weaknesses.[12] But the hollowness often attributed to her character is more an outgrowth of others' intentions than a trait inherent in her personality. The question of her identity is a point of heightened speculation from her first appearance in the novel at Miss Birdseye's soiree. Miss Birdseye, through whose myopic focus we first lay eyes on Verena, seizes upon this "new" celebrity and pieces together a myth of her past that she links to a vision of her great reform destiny (29–30), just as all the party-goers reflect upon her identity and purpose (35, 39, 40).

Her personality dictated by publicity-conscious parents and acquaintances, Verena experiences a troubling discrepancy between her performing self and some vague inner being she barely perceives. Her repeated injunctions to her mother before the gathering audience, "It isn't *me*, mother" (48), rather than a sign of devotional humility, seems a haunting indication of the emptiness she feels beneath the "rehearsed" role she plays in public (46). It is telling that her dramatic red hair, a source of her celebrity, is described as looking as if her very "blood had gone into it" (51): it is yet another sacrifice to her profession. Yet the changing temper of Verena's speeches through the novel provides a key to the profound changes taking place in her character, and in her vision of history.

Verena's first speech consists largely of universal pleas against social injustice. "The great sisterhood of women," she proclaims,

---

[12] In his introduction to *The Bostonians*, Charles Anderson writes that Verena is "hollow and vulgar," a "nonentity" (27). Some recent attempts have been made to "fill out" Verena's characterization by exploring her possible connections to contemporary historical figures. See, for example, Sara Davis, "Feminist Sources in *The Bostonians*," *American Literature* 50 (December 1979): 570–603.

"should quench [suffering], we should make it still, and the sound of our lips would become the voice of universal peace" (55). A loose, ahistorical vision reflecting a desire to "still" time, this speech fails to challenge the actual social position of women. But a later speech, which bears traces of Olive's tutelage in its increased sophistication, significantly weds universal principles to specific historical applications. Calling for a return to "Eden," the speech also contains the striking image of woman's "convenient" conventional box "with nice glass sides." The box confines women to a "comfortable, cosy" domain while exposing an outer world they are prevented from entering. Verena's demand that the "lid . . . be taken off" confirms the suffocating nature of contemporary women's roles (232). So effective is the "simile" that Basil, though he quotes mockingly, is condemned to its repetition (276).

Another observation by Verena following this speech contains further "details" about the contemporary social system omitted from Basil's antiquarian perspective. His nostalgic reverence for traditional women is undercut by reference to the demographic realities of the women's movement. Reminding him of women without families, she demands, "What are you going to do with *them*? You must remember that women marry—are given in marriage—less and less; that isn't their career, as a matter of course, any more" (291). In light of Basil's own feminine home, comprised of a mother and unmarried sisters suffering the ravages of the Civil War, Verena's point seems especially penetrating. The women's movement, this view implies, accompanies deep alterations in society—changes in the marriageability of women, in their self-conceptions, and in their needs for new economic roles. Verena notes specific historical facts omitted from Basil's chivalric scheme, and manifests, of all the characters, the greatest capacity for an awareness of historical change.[13]

---

[13] The following works provide a starting point in describing the social setting for the rise of the women's movement in nineteenth-century America: Nancy Cott, ed., *Root of Bitterness*, (New York: Dutton, 1972), see esp. Carol Wright's "The Working Girls of Boston," 311–21; Aileen Kraditor, ed., *Up from the Pedestal* (Chi-

Verena's critical reputation as a character without ideas or preferences, which follows from the assessments of the other characters, clearly needs to be revised. Presumptions of her natural passivity, or in Olive's words, "unlimited generosity" (70), allow others to overlook her desires and invest her with their own. Olive's perception of Verena's inability to "account" for herself (74) facilitates the projection of her own self-image. Verena appears to possess "exactly the same tenderness . . . that [Olive] herself had" (75). And to Basil, who chooses to be "quiet" about his native land (44), Verena offers a "speechless smile" (77). In a similar projecting spirit, Basil denies that her speeches express any part of her true being. Enacting the objectification of women that her speeches expressly criticize, Basil locates the speeches' "effect . . . not in what she said . . . but in the picture and figure of the half-bedizened damsel" (53). Olive likewise fixes Verena in her mind as a "Joan of Arc" (74, 106, 126), and also seeks to establish her image in a natural setting, under a tree. This "oriental idea" (87) suspiciously recalls Basil's first perception of Verena as looking "like an Oriental" (52). Both seek to control Verena through such typecasting. But Basil's metaphors have another effect, that of exploding the image Verena has assumed through the agency of her parents and Olive.

What Basil allows Verena (that Olive cannot) is an opportunity to nurse the growth of something inside herself. Though his attempts to possess her are for his own idealized ends of private domesticity, he is able to do what her former lovers have not—kindle

cago: Quadrangle Books, 1968); Aileen Kraditor, *The Ideas of the Woman Suffrage Movement, 1890–1920* (New York: Columbia University Press, 1965); and Carroll Smith-Rosenberg, "Beauty, the Beast, and the Militant Women," *American Quarterly* 23 (1971): 562–84. Daniel T. Rodgers also has an interesting chapter on women's work in *The Work Ethic in Industrial America, 1850–1920* (Chicago: University of Chicago Press, 1978), 182–209. Verena's rhetoric of confinement is largely consistent with what Rodgers describes as a social group "who found their role as islands apart from the main channels of life stunting and acutely claustrophobic, it was natural to rise up against all the occupational taboos that so visibly hemmed [them] in" (208).

a deep response of desire in her. The alien quality of love to Verena appears in its first spontaneous assertion, so startling to her consciousness that, "like a person who had collected herself for a little jump . . . she seemed to herself strangely reckless" (202).

Verena's encounters with Basil manifest both the terror of her first deep feelings and the accompanying pleasure of the freedom they entail. Their outings remind her of the one time in her childhood that she felt free to "indulge all her curiosities." This exceptional instance of freedom, in which she and a companion ventured into the woods to play at being gypsies (282), suggests the games of deception and disguise that allow one to test various roles. Since she has been routinely deprived of such experimentation, it is fitting that Verena's experiencing of different desires with Basil is frightening. But her fearfulness also points to another possibility: that perhaps there is more of Olive in Verena than might be readily apparent.

Verena's comfort in the fixed role she has played for her parents and Olive is that it has allowed her the illusion of knowing who she is, freeing her from the pain of confusion and doubt. Her reaction to Basil's labeling of her as a "preposterous puppet" exposes the depth of her feeling, and her fear. "It isn't *you*, the least in the world, but an inflated little figure (very remarkable in its way too), whom you have invented and set on its feet, pulling strings, behind it, to make it move and speak, while you try to conceal and efface yourself there" (293). Basil displays a profound understanding of Verena's role with her parents and Olive. She has ever been a "figure" designed to please, "inflated" to fulfill the destinies mapped out by others. But this is perhaps obvious from the novel's opening. Basil's speech penetrates most perceptively in divining how Verena herself has actively conspired in the "invention" of a self designed for the purposes of others. She has not been a mere passive vessel; rather, she has participated in their "concealment and effacement" of her. And her reward for this complicity has been a relatively anesthetized existence.

Verena's response to Basil's speech confirms its truthfulness.

"That description of herself as something different from what she was trying to be, the charge of want of reality, made her heart beat with pain; she was sure, at any rate, it was her real self that was there with him now, where she oughtn't to be" (293). Her evasions unveiled by Basil, Verena reacts with a feeling of "pain," the first such pang she experiences in the novel. From this point on she comes to feel pain more and more, an exemplification of the sufferings incurred by being in time as opposed to living beyond experience at the height of a ropedancer.

It is revealing that Verena's first step in her growing fear of her feelings and of Basil is an attempt to repeat and delay, "to think and think again" (296). Most of her actions in the days preceding her decision about Basil take the form of compulsive repetitions. Her talk is "voluble, fluent, feverish"; she is "perpetually bringing up the subject" (328). The image of Verena courting Basil with "her watch in her hand" (331) symbolizes the hope that her previous image, the contained and invulnerable identity she holds for her parents and Olive, can remain intact—that somehow the clocks can be turned back and the uncertain state emerging from her love for Basil can be put away in favor of a condition of "permanent rest" (329).

The great burden of the days leading up to the scene at Music Hall is that, instead of experiencing the complex nature of her new feelings, Verena is compelled to face her predicament as a set of binomial oppositions. Like a passive subject miraculously converted by a wizard with a wand, Verena is considered by Basil and Olive to have experienced a transvaluation of principles at the hands of Basil. She is encouraged to believe that hers is simply the choice between two antithetical extremes: accept either Basil or Olive, give herself to a man or a movement. Yet warring beneath the necessity of choosing between irreconcilable opposites is the deeper purpose that she has discovered in herself: "the conclusion that she loved as deeply as a woman could love and that it didn't make any difference" (334). Verena's impulse is not to embrace either: caught between Basil's presumptions and Olive's speechless demands, she is paralyzed.

In the novel's final scene, Verena "temporize[s]" because of the "spell" of Basil's presence (382). Verena wishes to speak but cannot with Basil there—his being renders her mute. This dilemma encapsulates what has gone on throughout the novel. Basil, through whose point of view Verena's speeches are usually conveyed, effectively silences her by ruminating on everything during her speeches except their content. In this way, Verena is repeatedly silenced for the reader as well. Basil's final act of silencing Verena, as he is described as "indulg[ing] not in the smallest recognition of her request" (386), is thrown into an extremely questionable light. Given the narrator's enigmatic final remark, it is difficult to close the novel without misgivings about Verena's retreat. This brings us to the novel's narrator, a figure who plays a prominent role in the novel, manifesting, perhaps more surreptitiously than the characters, his own ambitious designs on time.

James's Democratic Narrator

Satirical and occasionally abusive in his treatment of the novel's characters, the narrator often turns his strenuous judgments of others upon himself. At times he is reminiscent of Northrop Frye's classic "eiron" figure, a Socratic self-doubter who undermines his own knowledge of and capacity to describe characters and events. The narrator's fluctuations between criticism of others and self-deprecation reflect an ambivalence toward power that is also evident in his assessments of his ability to control the pace of the narrative.

A notable feature of the narrative mind is the contiguity between his time consciousness and that of Olive Chancellor. Olive's habit of setting up the world, compulsively previewing and reviewing experience, is echoed on a grander scale by the narrator's efforts to manage his narrative. The similarity of their intentions can be understood in terms of a revealing remark the narrator makes about Olive: she "had a fear of everything, but her greatest fear was of being afraid" (14). For Olive, it is not the cause of fear that terrifies, but the condition of fearing. Being itself terrifies her: the circumstance of being fixed in an experience that cannot be avoided because it is future tense, or mastered because it is past, but must be simply endured.

Despite his insight into Olive, however, the narrator seems to share her fears, as evidenced by the parallel between her "greatest fear" and his own fondness for a construction that launches the novel's famously qualified conclusion. "It is to be feared that with the union so far from brilliant into which she was about to enter, these were not the last she was destined to shed" (390). This dramatic undermining of the union of Basil and Verena signifies the narrator's effort to qualify his impending loss of narrative authority by projecting beyond the novel's end, which signals a fear akin to Olive's peculiar fear of being afraid. Nor is this the only time in the narrative where this construction appears. In each of its uses it pertains significantly to Basil Ransom (38, 77, 243, 337) and betrays the narrator's fear and distrust of him. Basil seems to represent a force of reality to the narrator, and certainly to Olive, that cannot be underestimated or evaded. The introductory "it is to be feared" discloses the feeble effort to control by anticipation what the consciousness knows can never be contained.

A later description, though initially focused on Verena, illuminates further the fears held by Olive and the narrator. The narrator remarks that had Olive "been less afraid, she would have read things more clearly; she would have seen that we don't run away from people unless we fear them and that we don't fear them unless we know that we are unarmed" (323–24). Fearful circumstances, this passage suggests, can never be anticipated and evaded as Olive and Verena hope. We know to run only through experiencing our vulnerability; outside the fearful circumstances, we would not know a need to escape.[14] The narrator's profound un-

[14] This passage brings to mind the conclusion to T. S. Eliot's essay "Tradition

derstanding of Olive's predicament, which he replicates at times in his own discourse, clues us in to his own attitudes toward time.

Throughout the novel, the narrator complains that he is being rushed in his recounting of events, referring to details he might offer and suggestions that he might enlarge upon had he only more space and time. Assertions such as "I have not taken space to mention certain episodes of the more recent intercourse of these ladies, and must content myself with tracing them, lightly, in their consequences" (141) imply his subjection to a power other than his own artistic prerogative. In this example, the narrator significantly calls attention to his compulsion to forsake process (the intimate details of the lives of "these ladies") for results, the "consequences" of their developing relationship. Similar comments augment the portrait of a narrator at odds with some dictatorial force overseeing his project, and perhaps uncomfortable as well with his society's temporal perspective.

In the description of Basil's New York neighborhood, for example, the narrator anxiously excuses this apparent digression. The scene is rendered, he tells us, "for old acquaintance sake and that of local colour; besides which, a figure is nothing without a setting." While almost haughtily distinguishing his own artistic subtleties from the protagonist's "indifferent, unperceiving step" (not even "view" or "gaze"), the narrator still feels beholden to rationalize every detail. Not for memory's or art's sake alone can this brief sketch be justified. Instead, it must be explained as functional, a generic necessity. As he asserts, "a figure is nothing without a setting." "And after all," he concludes, "I have not taken so long as all that, having only 'briefly' indulged myself here" (160–61). In the next passage, the narrator pointedly denies himself a description of Basil's rooms, as if to reaffirm his obedience to his temporal censor. As the narrative proceeds, however, temporal re-

___

and the Individual Talent," where he asserts that "only those who know what emotion is would know to want to escape from it." An analysis could be made of the American form of this evasion of emotion. Such a study could consider, along with the concern for the exile of emotion, the issue of James's and Eliot's actual exiles.

strictions formerly perceived as external are increasingly internalized by the narrator (163, 164, 165, 325, 353). Thus he aligns himself with Basil's inattention to Verena's speech at the Burrages', announcing, "The historian who has gathered these documents together does not deem it necessary to give a larger specimen of Verena's eloquence" (232). But the narrator's various confessions of impotence are most significant in that they divert attention from his continual manipulations of the reader's perspective. The narrative is characterized by a curious and extensive series of anachronies: analeptic reversions to information and events already recounted, and proleptic anticipations of those upcoming.

Like Olive in her propensity "to forecast the consequences of things," the narrator consistently alerts the reader to the future significance of narrative happenings and personages.[15] During Basil's dinner at Olive's, for example, the narrator alludes to a future conversation between Basil and Mrs. Luna, whom, he also points out, Basil is "destined" to encounter often (17). Here, anticipating within an anticipation, the narrator forecasts both Basil's and Mrs. Luna's future assessments of Olive's dinner, as well as Basil's own predestined meetings with Mrs. Luna. He likewise frequently comments that a given event is occurring for the first time or that it will have profound future ramifications. Of the first intense exchange of looks between Olive and Verena, he says, "It was this glance that was the beginning" (69). While these prolepses might be expected to instill a sense of the future, they in fact function oppositely, to create a sense of the past, planting "insignificant seed[s]," whose importance may only be grasped "retrospec-

---

[15] The narrator jumps ahead to anticipate future events in his narrative, by my estimate, nearly twenty-five times in the novel. These jumps occur most commonly in the form of the following anticipation of the one time Basil hears Olive laugh: "Only once, in the course of his subsequent acquaintance with her, did [laughter] find a voice; and then the sound remained in Ransom's ear as one of the strangest he had heard" (18). The laugh itself is described on page 358. Other significant instances of anticipation include: 6, 10, 16, 17, 18, 20, 25, 27, 53, 68, 69, 72, 73, 74, 76, 79, 80, 95, 105, 202, 257, 270, 346–47.

tively."[16] The accumulative effect of the narrator's prolepses is to establish the process of narration as a backward glance for the narrator, placing him on a plane of knowing beyond the novel's reader.

By stipulating the reader's expectations, and elaborating his own sense of the past's significance, the narrator's prolepses also serve to evaporate a sense of the lived present, as indicated by a description of a dialogue between Verena and Olive. "It was one of those talks," the narrator says, "which people remember afterwards . . . in which they see signs of a beginning that was to be justified" (73). This obsessive reading of the "signs" of events, as well as the idea that experience needs to be "justified," implies that human experience has little pleasure or value except as a past validated by truths that it has served to anticipate.

More common than his habitual anticipations are the narrator's analepses. These remarks, which draw attention to what has been previously mentioned or described, often elicit a repetition of the past example in the reader's mind, or at least some fumbling effort at recollection.[17] These actual reversions to the past, unlike his prolepses, tend to establish a sense of complicity between narrator and reader by referring to knowledge they both share. Thus, in explaining the renewed energy of Basil's pursuit of Verena, the narrator remarks familiarly, "We know a little about his second thoughts, as much as is essential, and especially how the occasion of their springing up had been the windfall of an editor's encouragement" (338). The intimate "we," the assumption that "we" know what "is essential," seems designed to convince the reader that his view is merely the limit of common sense. Yet this mo-

[16] See Genette, *Narrative Discourse*, p. 76.

[17] The narrator refers to events already described, more often than he anticipates—about thirty-five times, by my count. These include: 11, 40, 61, 91, 93, 95, 96, 101, 117, 126, 134, 135, 136, 139, 141, 143, 157, 158, 164, 178, 192, 202, 216, 244, 247, 260, 262, 272, 310, 324, 329, 334, 338, 351, 355, 359. Finer distinctions among the various kinds of narrative prolepses and analepses can be made. This presents a subject for further research, beyond the scope of this chapter.

mentary "complicity" with *The Bostonians*' narrator typifies the subtlety of his coercion.

And there are more complicated forms of narrative recall, not confined to the narrator, that vividly further the connection between temporal perceptions and the will to power. The narrator's scrutiny of characters' processes of retrospective signification reveals a consciousness of the ways in which individuals still others in time as means of dominating them. In describing characters' willful imaginings of past experiences of themselves and others, the narrator betrays his awareness of one of the most common linguistic habits of characters in James's novels: the substitution of a figure or image for a particular historical experience.[18] Such an act of substitution is seen in Olive's imagining Verena as Joan of Arc. Though the figure is introduced by Verena herself, the narrator explains that "this analogy had lodged itself in Olive's imagination" (126). The figure becomes increasingly coercive through Olive's repeated allusions to it (74, 106, 126). Her desired mythic view of Verena as the "original" savior of women comes to replace the real person in her mind, as the metaphorical Verena becomes dangerously remote from the changeable woman in history. Yet Olive's desired image of Verena is eventually exposed as a delusion in her painful retrospection at Marmion, which brings Olive to see the reality of Verena's character. The scene suggests that only a retrospection leading to the recognition, however momentary, of

---

[18] Some fine studies have been done of conscious and unconscious acts of figuration by James's characters. In an essay on "The Jolly Corner," Deborah Esch argues that James's characters are actively engaged in "finding the 'terms' that will turn experience into a writable, readable, narrative . . . the crucial terms arrived at by the Jamesian consciousness (whether narrator or character) are invariably terms of comparison or metaphors." "A Jamesian About-Face: Notes on 'The Jolly Corner,' " *ELH* (Fall 1983): 587–605. Ruth Yeazell provides a discussion of the function of metaphorical thinking in James's late works. As she observes of John Marcher, the protagonist of "The Beast in the Jungle," the figure of the beast "allows [Marcher] to evade immediate reality and its demands, to avoid the risk of passionate confrontation." *Language and Knowledge in the Late Novels of Henry James* (Chicago: University of Chicago Press, 1976), 37.

the demands of a specific historical time and place constitutes genuine consciousness.

Another recurring figure (twice with Olive, and in the final scene with Basil) is the image of Verena concealed by a cloak or mantle. The first time, Olive flings her mantle over the "shivering" Verena, while demanding that she vow never to marry. The literal and figural acts of enfolding give rise to a seemingly infinite series of repetitions: Olive herself repeats the request three times; and the phrase also "echoes" in the "startled mind" of Verena—indeed, it is already a repetition the first time Verena hears it, for she has been expecting the request, "had already felt it in the air," prior to Olive's desperate voicing of it. The demand, imaged in Olive's mantle thrown over Verena, is recalled and nearly repeated in a later scene where Olive is described as "prepared to throw a fold of her mantle, as she had done before, over her young friend" (117, 134). She refrains, it seems, because she has learned from the pain of that previous entreaty not to subject herself and Verena to such a scene again. Because of Olive's restraint the second time, there is a troubling lack of hesitancy in the final example at the novel's end, where Basil "thrusts the hood of Verena's long cloak over her head, to conceal her face and her identity" (389).

This last effort to hide or erase Verena's identity carries forth the previous images with a greater force. What has been first an at least partial gesture of protection, and then, an impulse suppressed, is in this third instance an unambivalent act of "thrusting" and "concealing," which registers the replacement of her public role by a private domestic identity. The imperiousness of his action, and the tears beneath the hood, forecast a more troubled future than that afforded by conventional romance endings. Any closing promise of eternal domestic bliss is precluded by the gnawing echoes of this repetition with a difference. The only sense of resolution here may be the reader's conviction of Basil's permanent effacement of Verena.

Despite his rigorous self-scrutiny, and his surveillance of the characters' designs on time, there are instances (equivalent to Olive's moment of relaxation at the Burrages') when the narrator seems to relinquish his vigil, censoring neither the characters nor himself. In some examples, such as the visit by Basil and Verena to Memorial Hall, or their walk through Central Park, the description actually moves into present tense (210, 282), as the narrator seems to fully inhabit the imaginative act of describing his characters' world. The scenes read like still-life paintings set down amid his rushing satirical narrative, picturing a world removed from time. These descriptions usually begin in indirect discourse, and then distinguish themselves from the characters' point of view, adopting the sole perspective of the narrative consciousness.

One such passage is Verena's view of Boston from the western windows of Olive's house:

The western windows of Olive's drawing-room, looking over the water, took in the red sunsets of winter . . . the general hard, cold void of the prospect; the extrusion, at Charleston, at Cambridge, of a few chimneys and steeples, straight, sordid tubes of factories and engine-shops, or spare, heavenward, finger of the New England meeting-house. There was something inexorable in the poverty of the scene, shameful in the meanness of its details, which gave a collective impression of boards and tin and frozen earth, sheds and rotting piles. . . . Verena thought such a view lovely, and she was by no means without excuse when, as the afternoon closed, the ugly picture was tinted with clear, cold rosiness. The air, in its windless chill, seemed to tinkle like a crystal, the faintest gradations of tone were perceptible in the sky, the west became deep and delicate, everything grew doubly distinct before taking on the dimness of evening. There were pink flushes on snow, "tender" reflections in patches of stiffened marsh, sounds of car-bells, no longer vulgar, but almost silvery. (152–53)

The passage distinguishes sharply between Verena's view and the narrator's, as Verena's perceptions ("Verena thought . . .") and idiom ("tender") are specified precisely. What is most interesting about the two sets of perceptions is the alteration that takes place in the point of view of the narrator. The narrator seems to undergo a conversion over the course of his description, as if he steps into the single-spired New England church as he ambles through the scene, his attitude changing from critical judgment to a lyrical absorption with the landscape's details. The opening phrases, describing the "hard cold void of the prospect," with its "inexorable," "shameful . . . meanness" of detail, are evaluative assessments that betray a consciousness out of sorts with this American industrial scene. Indeed, the tone here is not unlike a particularly irritable passage from James's *Hawthorne*.

Verena provides another response: a difference not alone registered by the enchanting sundown that begins at the point where her consciousness enters. In an interval akin to the Emersonian moment where the mind infused with Reason harmonizes a disarray of farmhouses into a single image, Verena's sensibility provides a transforming "tint" that projects a "cold rosiness" on the scene. The narrator reminds us that this is seeming ("seemed to tinkle"), the *work* of perception ("perceptible"; the "tender reflections" of a mind), but he participates in the transformation of the scene. Through Verena's agency, he comes to accept the "sounds of car-bells" as "no longer vulgar, but almost silvery," a moment of elevated vision that occurs appropriately in a marginal realm, the transitional time of twilight.

The narrator's description of the decaying seaside world of Marmion represents an instance where he seizes such inspiration on his own.

The train from Marmion left Boston at four o'clock in the afternoon, and rambled fitfully toward the southern cape, while the shadows grew long in the stony pastures and the slanting light gilded the straggling, shabby woods, and painted ponds and marshes with yellow gleams. The ripeness of the summer lay upon the land, and yet there was nothing in the country Basil Ransom traversed that seemed susceptible of maturity; nothing but the apples in the little tough, dense orchards, which gave a suggestion of sour fruition here and there, and the tall, bright golden-rod at the bottom of the bare stone dykes. There were no fields of yellow grain; only here and there a crop of brown hay. But there was a kind of soft scrubbiness in the landscape, and a sweetness begotten of low horizons, of mild air, with a possibility of summer haze, of unregarded inlets where on August mornings the water must be brightly blue. (298)

The passage begins similarly on a note of criticalness, evidenced, for example, in the observation that "nothing" in the scene "seemed susceptible of maturity." The narrator is here concerned with maturation and process, with how to express the way this fairy-tale land at first resists, and then comes to incorporate, the processes of change, the inevitable encroachments of decay. This August landscape suggests an approaching autumn with its accompanying climate of death. Yet the narrator seems skeptical, perhaps asking, "How does this childish and immature land die?" "How does it broach the realities of time and change?" to which he responds, "Not easily." Finally, however, the narrator discovers in the apples the capacity for "sour fruition here and there," seemingly convinced that this world can, in its own "mild, vague" way, die.

Still, this portrait of natural conditions has certain limitations. It seems yet another evasion of the characters' specific historical circumstances. And it is appropriate that the narrator describes Olive and Verena's retreat as a pastoral romance. All of these restful descriptive scenes comprise efforts to naturalize the characters' world. Neither the "bravery" and "heroism" at Memorial Hall, nor the delicate pre-autumnal wasting away of the land at Marmion, can be considered the work of a historicizing consciousness. But there is a perspective in the novel that discloses an inescapable social history: I now turn to the marginalized historical details of contemporary politics which represent a will to domination as inherent in the acts of love and sexual desire.

The Politics of Sexuality

It has been argued that a central impulse of modernist literary texts is the management or repression of historical and political contradictions within the narrative form. The critical practice that emerges from this view treats the literary work as the rewriting or restructuring of a prior historical or ideological subtext. The text

169

serves as a reluctant midwife to the real, representing the very circumstances against which it also reacts.[19]

Such a view is especially pertinent to *The Bostonians*, which pictures its narrator and characters repeatedly and self-consciously retreating from their real historical experiences. Recurring allusions to an inability to face reality comprise a veritable chorus in the novel, suggesting the characters' consciousness of a specific set of social circumstances they are attempting to conceal. Yet critics have overlooked these patterned evasions, stressing instead the deficiencies of the American scene as the novel portrays it.[20] This critical emphasis on the disenchantment of the novel's American portrait has obscured the complexity of its critique of American society. A related tendency to view the novel as comic satire veils what is perhaps its most disturbing feature—the strain of paranoia and fear generated within its comic vision. What is needed is a reading that penetrates the novel's network of concealments and evasions to consider what such machinations reveal about American social and political arrangements. In Hawthornesque fashion, the novel questions the possibility of knowing another's inten-

[19] See Fredric Jameson, *The Political Unconscious* (Ithaca: Cornell University Press, 1981), especially 73–102. My view differs from Jameson's articulation of James's aesthetic as "a protest and a defense against reification [that] ends up furnishing a powerful ideological instrument in the perpetuation of an increasingly subjectivized and psychologized world . . ." (221). I argue that Jamesian point of view maintains a perspective on its own precariousness. James seems to me most perceptive and critical in his depictions of how the cultures of his novels foment the appetite for subjective voyeurism. James's works in general are more self-reflexive and ironic about the situatedness of subjectivity than Jameson allows. James in fact is closer to Conrad, who Jameson sees as not "unaware of the symbolic social value of his verbal practice . . . whatever the thoughts and awarenesses of the biographical Conrad—a reflexivity, a self-consciousness . . . is inscribed in the text itself" (237). I would argue that a similar awareness of the symbolic significance of verbal actions is present in James's narratives.

[20] It must be admitted that the novel invites critical propensities to stress the emptiness of the American social scene. Though I am not here concerned with psychobiography, I think an interesting study, if carefully done, could be made of James's curiously ambivalent American narrators (that is, narrators of works set in America, such as *The Europeans*, *Hawthorne*, and *The Bostonians*), in light of James's own tortured attitudes toward his native land.

tions, of perceiving what is concealed beneath the surface of what one sees. But in a way that is undeniably Jamesian, the novel represents these processes of coversion and subversion as inherent in dialogue—with narration and talk as the very vehicles of manipulation and coercion.

An obsession with lies and truth-telling prevails from the novel's beginning, where Mrs. Luna expresses disdain for the single-minded honesty of New Englanders. Basil's paradoxical retort, "I pretend not to prevaricate," affirms that the themes of truth's indirections and falsity's open claims will be hopelessly entangled throughout.[21] And the forms that concealment takes are particularly relevant to the novel's "salient and peculiar point": the situation of women and human sexuality.

At the first women's reform gathering, the guests can hardly contain the sexual excitement, precipitated by the delay of their leader, Mrs. Farrinder. Described as a continually "freshened" company of "pilgrims," this "anxious," "florid" crowd of limp curls and "dusky bonnets" is clearly awaiting release. And Verena's talk meets their expectations: her father's "stroking and soothing" to elicit the necessary inspiration brings spirit-tapping to the limits of decency. Basil's observation that "even a carpet-bagger [had] a right to do what he pleased with his daughter" (52–53) confirms the incestuous implications. The crowd itself is collectively overcome by Verena's speech: "powerfully" moved, the assembly "broke into exclamations and murmurs . . . a higher pitch of conversation . . . people circulated more freely" (56). And Matthias Pardon's exuberant cry, "There's money for some one in that girl," sounds more than a bit ironic, whether or not he is aware of it.

Most curious and telling is the narrator's apparent concern to mask any licentious overtones. The buildup and denouement of Verena's speech is portrayed in terms of negations, as what might

[21] For an illuminating discussion of heroic liars in James's early fiction, see Richard Poirier, *The Comic Sense of Henry James* (New York: Oxford University Press, 1967).

have been expected to occur but did not. The speech "was not followed by her sinking exhausted into her chair or by any of the traces of a laboured climax. She only turned away . . . smiling over her shoulder at the whole room, as if it had been a single person, without a flush in her whiteness, or the need of drawing a longer breath." As if attempting to avert a "flush" on the "whiteness" of his conscience, the narrator defuses the exploitative sexuality of the scene by emphasizing Verena's untainted innocence. This is no "labored climax," nor is there any trace of a "flush." Yet the image of the audience as a "single person" is explicit enough. And Selah Tarrant's repeated efforts to disembody his daughter, asserting the "impersonality" of her talent, may signify a last-ditch effort at discretion.

The scene captures one of the central ironies in the novel's movement for women's reform: it reproduces the coyness and domination that prevail in more traditional sexual relations. As Mrs. Farrinder's manipulative excitation of her audience makes clear, a commitment to gender equality in no way precludes the exploitative impulses that are built into the culture's model of human sexuality. One of the questions ultimately posed is whether in American culture desire can ever be dissociated from conflict and domination. Repeatedly, the novel exposes what the characters seek desperately to repress: the will to dominate that stands as the modus operandi of their love and sexual relations. Significantly, their concealment of the conflicts aroused by desire is portrayed as a reflex of democratic ideology: the ritualized denial of a will to power is an unspoken convention in the novel's culture.

This issue is elaborated through a recurring reference to one trait shared by all of the characters, their fear of "facing" things. Confronting reality is an action both rhetorically insisted upon and earnestly avoided. Although "reality" is differently defined by all as a phenomenon to be evaded its meaning remains relatively constant. In the novel's early chapters, the fear of facing things seems Olive's peculiar attribute, part of the tragic shyness noted by Basil Ransom in their first meeting. Olive cannot keep herself from averting her eyes, and the narrator adds that she is so evasive that at times, "she was unable to meet even her own eyes in the mirror" (10). Though the trait is exquisitely developed in Olive, however, it is hardly unique to her. And all of the characters betray contradictory tendencies toward openness and concealment. Basil may appear "friendly," but there is something "hard and discouraging" in his face. Mrs. Luna may seem "intolerably familiar," yet she fails to reveal "what body of doctrine *she* represented" a restraint reflected as well in her "tight bodice" and the "stiff plaits" of her petticoat (5–7). Indeed, the discrepancy between easy self-revelation and the withholding of a deeper self may be another key to the American social character. A later passage specifically suggests that such duplicities form the basis of a collective American psychology.

Olive's dismay over the arrival of Basil in her first interview with Verena gives rise to a mystifying breach of democratic decorum. The narrator observes, "For the first time in her life, Olive Chancellor chose not to introduce two persons who met under her roof. . . . Neither of her companions had an idea that in leaving them simply planted face to face (the terror of the American heart) she had so high a warrant" (77). In the novel's society, knowing someone's name is the essential term of social intercourse. This superficial formality ensures a surface intimacy that need never be penetrated. But the absence of this meagre but all-important convention, which seems to function as a stay against the characters' overpowering natures, signals social chaos. Deprived of the ritual of introduction, left "simply planted face to face," Basil and Verena are literally two raw outgrowths, experiencing "the terror of the American heart." There are enough allusions to Newton's laws, and to the characters' "natural" qualities, to support a reading of nature as the bottom-line threat of the novel. Nature is what can never be *re*formed as Olive dreams, or *re*written as Basil might wish. Yet a deeper level of inquiry exposes the graver dangers to be found in civilization itself.

Throughout the novel, characters' rhetorical insistences on the necessity of facing "realities" render doubtful the probability that they are in fact confronting their experience and one another. Thus in arguing for the sacred celibacy of their reform mission, Olive points Verena to a rarefied, self-serving reality. "Priests," she asserts, "when they were *real* priests—never married" (119, emphasis added). She takes similar license in labeling men who "pretend" to sympathize with their cause, "not really men." In both instances, Olive dismisses any challenge to her exclusive possession of Verena by undermining its reality. At the same time, however, Olive repeatedly insists that she and Verena "ought to face everything" (246, 249, 259, 260, 273).

Eventually, Verena comes to mock Olive's definitional freedoms. She reminds her at one point, "You know it's not our real life," to which Olive sadly replies, "Almost anything is better than the form reality *may* take with us" (260). The course of the novel for Olive may be seen as a growing awareness that terms alone, figures of speech, cannot contain experience. She comes to see retrospectively how her terms have falsified and evaded a reality very different from her desired conception of it. Later, when Verena adopts Olive's rhetoric, Olive detects Verena's evasiveness in its mirroring of her own. Their relationship becomes increasingly inverted, as Verena employs Olive's former terms of speech in her own effort to regulate their lives. The inversions reveal not only Olive's decreasing power over Verena, but also Verena's need to manage new, overpowering emotions.

Now it is Verena insisting that they must "work in the midst of the world, facing everything, keeping straight on, always taking hold" (261). Verena's rhetoric emphasizes worldly action, the "facing" of their secular mission. But as Olive is painfully aware, such moments of testimony are what most belie. The rhetoric of confrontation, redirected at Olive, exposes Verena's insincerity—that she is *working* to make Olive (and partly herself) believe, rather than operating from a true sense of conviction. The ominous closure to a particularly emotional exchange underlines the point. "[Olive] came to her slowly, took her in her arms and held her long—giving her a silent kiss. From which Verena knew that she believed her" (261). Olive, like her audiences, responds to Verena's eloquence, and Verena, as she has with her public, remains aloof. Yet the manipulative self-consciousness of Verena's closing knowledge adds a sinister register: what was perhaps self-protective about Verena's detachment from her public is here the subtle deception of one whose love the strategy depends on.

For Verena, growing up in the world, and learning what love is (through Olive's love of her) and to love (through the stirrings of her passion for Basil), means learning how to deceive and manipulate others. Verena does not change from a charming innocent to an evil demon. But, as is true for many Jamesian protagonists, acquiring a larger sense of experience involves the development of her powers of perception, with an accompanying knowledge of how to control and use others as means to her own ends. And Verena's growing aptitude for manipulation and evasion goes hand-in-hand with a mounting rhetoric of confrontation. Verena rationalizes one visit with Basil, for example, in claiming that to see him "is more dignified than dodging" him. This hallowing of directness actually masks Verena's true feelings—that she intensely desires to be with him—in part to herself. And the more Verena swerves from a sense of complicity with Olive, the more earnestly she attests to her loyalty (319). Olive is too much aware of the duplicities of her own rhetoric to miss the significance of Verena's. Thus, in recognizing "a tone in regard to their relationship that Verena has never used before," Olive knows that "Verena was not sincere" (325).

If Verena's maturation in the novel can be seen as the process of learning the manipulative strategies of loving and being loved, she has brilliant role models in Olive and Basil. Both simultaneously foment and evade the power struggle incited by their desire for Verena. For Olive and Basil, loving Verena means denying her historical being, and replacing it with a mythic image that accords with the fixed time scheme of their respective ruling visions.

Olive's developing love is punctuated by fearful assertions and retreats. The transformation of her interiors registers, metonymically, her aroused emotions. Where previously her house had merely been "passionately clean," now "daintiness" [was] "elevated" to a religion; her interior shone with superfluous friction" (151). Combining religious awe with the sensual note of "superfluous friction," the description reveals the double-edged nature of Olive's desire. Her aim to canonize their relationship merges uneasily with her physical passion. Olive's historical narrations to Verena, perceived as sacred and sexually thrilling, betray an equally ambivalent design. "Desir[ing] to keep her precious inmate to herself" (154), Olive spends hours alone with her in her "strenuous parlor" lecturing on the history of women. These narratives, which give Olive a feeling of power and "mastery," leave Verena feeling "immensely wrought upon; a subtle fire passed into her" (159).

Proving an even more irresistible force to Verena, Basil prides himself on possessing an absolute sense of reality. He proclaims a willingness to "face" truths most of his "womanized" generation evades, and defines confrontation itself as a masculine trait. "The masculine character," he tells Verena, is "the ability to dare and endure, to know and yet not fear reality, to look the world in the face and take it for what it is" (290). Despite his claims, however, Basil is no more willing to face "reality" than those he denounces. His desire to turn back the clock, in denying the advent of the "new old maid" and the social changes she portends, in favor of the "*old* old maid," attests to his inability to face his historical era, and to accept Verena's perceptions of it (292). Basil's idyllic vision of domestic bliss represents the dislocated urban man's pastoral longing. And his likening to the empyreal narrator of the preface to Hawthorne's *The House of the Seven Gables* is of central significance. Their respective efforts at "building castles in the air" are strategies for denying their relation to a world of historical change that they would prefer to imagine beneath them. It seems especially appropriate that Basil intends to "put [Verena] in the biggest and fairest of [the castles]" (318)—yet another attempt to delimit her in time.

Moving continually from an idealized image to actuality, Basil betrays a perspective twice removed. The highest compliment he can pay to an individual or scene is that it "please[s] him almost as much as if it had been a striking work of art" (310). Akin to yet another Hawthorne narrator, Miles Coverdale, Basil reads *into* his world as much as he reads *in* his world. Basil's coercive aestheticism suggests that he may be more resistant to reality than any other of the novel's characters. He denounces Verena's speaking career because it wars with his own antiquarian sense of time and history. Verena's profession is an insult to his manhood, a challenge to the aggressive passion she has stirred in him. Thus he sees her on the platform as "tremendously open to attack" (316). To "squelch" her engagement at Music Hall "would represent to him his own success, it would symbolize his victory. It became a fixed idea with him, and he warned her again and again" (339–40). The hint of obsession here presages the assassin-like air of Basil's "rescue" of Verena. And perhaps in foreclosing her speaking career he does kill a part of her that genuinely seeks expression. Verena's question to Basil, "What is to become of all that part of me?" trained for public life, is never answered (336). In striving to cut off this part of her life, Basil is committing "a violation" as great as Olive's effort to deny Verena men.

Verena's inability to choose between the stark oppositions presented by Basil and Olive suggests that there is something crucially lacking on both sides. And the novel's ending implies that Verena does want to talk, that she is struggling against Basil as she has struggled against Olive's repressions of the past. But his disposition precludes that he will see anything in her gestures and expressions but the reflection of his own triumph and desire. Basil assumes that Verena has given up "her cause . . . just as any plighted maiden might have asked any favour of her lover" (385). This image is clearly the product of Basil's own pastoral perspective. Yet it is curiously consistent with an earlier image, in which the narrator likens Basil and Verena's courtship to "Arcady" (331). This raises the question of to what extent the narrator can be seen to sympathize with Basil's Coverdaleian efforts to "turn the affair into a ballad." It is necessary to examine the narrator's game once more with an eye to its powerful effects, to ascertain what kinds of strategies he might be trying to conceal from the reader.

In the manner of the characters he describes, the narrator can be seen both to embrace and to evade his power over the perceptions and moral judgments of the reader. This tendency to disguise his engineering of the reader's responses may account for the often striking variations in narrative tone. In the early chapters the narrator openly mocks the characters in a biting comic-satire that prohibits the reader's sympathy toward them. Rather than fully dramatizing the characters, the narrator draws attention away from them to his own powers of humorous exaggeration.

One of the narrator's favorite methods of undercutting is to provide detail upon incriminating detail about the characters in the form of parenthetical asides. By offering the undermining information as interpolations conveyed in the characters' own idiom, the narrator implies that the best way to illustrate shortcomings is to let the figures speak for themselves. In one example, Mrs. Tarrant's self-serving interpretation of Olive's invitation to Verena is relayed parenthetically as her own, "one must know when to go forward gracefully" (67). In a later instance, Basil's treatment of Mrs. Luna, which he fears impolite, is excused in his own pompous terms, "still with all due ceremony" (227). Other parenthetical statements deflate the characters by exposing their self-deceptiveness or ignorance, while alluding to the narrator and reader's greater insight into their minds, or knowledge of their experience. Thus, Olive's narrative on the history of women's suffering asserts a conviction of "their softness," a condition "she knew (*or she thought she knew*)" (159, emphasis added). And Verena's talents are "superabundantly crude . . . happily for Olive, who promised herself, *as we know*, to train and polish them" (101, emphasis added).

But as dogmatic as he is at these moments, at other times the narrator seems to resist the authority of his narrative altogether. In his opening description of Basil, he timidly equivocates in asserting that "*apparently*" the character had "taken up" a book on entering Olive's parlor. A further attempt to evade an authoritative perspective is seen in his disclaimer, "It is not *in my power to reproduce* . . . [Basil's] charming dialect." And an admission following this one affirms the narrator's doubt: "He played a very active part in the events I have undertaken *in some degree* to set forth" (6, emphasis added). Repeated vows of impotence too numerous to examine in detail offer a portrait of a narrator incapable of accepting the authority of his perspective.[22]

The narrator's vacillations between satirical invective and doubts of his abilities to describe and judge reveal his equivocal will to power over the reader's perceptions and opinions. The narrator thus reproduces in his relationship to the reader the same dynamics that prevail in Basil and Olive's struggle for the possession of Verena. Like many of the democratic characters he describes, the narrator is decidedly ambivalent toward power. Some selected examples where the narrator denounces his authority of description or judgment, only to immediately assume it, will illustrate my point.[23]

[22] Chronic uncertainty is epidemic among James's narrators, who in Seymour Chatman's words, often "confess momentary ignorance" as a means of establishing the "necessarily approximative" nature of human perception. (*The Later Style of Henry James* [Oxford: Basil Blackwell, 1972], 41). Nevertheless, the narrator of *The Bostonians* takes what might be called a normal degree of Jamesian self-doubt to the level of obsession. Here again I offer an approximate catalog of examples where he confesses to an insufficient knowledge or capacity for judgment: 6, 31, 44, 54, 67, 70, 81–82, 90, 94, 125, 133, 141, 146, 148, 160, 164, 239, 244, 270, 287, 323, 328, 338, 354, 365.

[23] In this regard, the narrator is interestingly considered as a dim ancestor of democratic narrators in works by Timothy Dwight and Philip Freneau, who undermine the authority contained in their narrative roles. Emory Elliott provides an analysis of this tradition of narrative self-effacement as it relates to the quest for and fear of authority in American politics and culture; see *Revolutionary Writers* (New York: Oxford University Press, 1982).

In an early description of Olive Chancellor, the narrator point-edly resists judging her, commenting, "Whether, eventually, she was successful in what she attempted, the reader of her history will judge." Forthwith, however, he launches into what may be the most biting diatribe of the novel: "Such is the penalty of being of a fastidious, exclusive, uncompromising nature; of seeing things not simply and sharply, but in perverse relations, in intertwisted strands." The passage closes with the seemingly gratuitous aside, "I suppose it was because he was a man" (125). Beginning dispas-sionately, the narrator ends in a tone that appears to war with his original intent. Throughout the novel, the narrator voices such in-tentions of impartiality and then overturns them.

These ambivalent displays reveal the narrator's fear of another kind of reality—the reality of his personal perceptions and judg-ments, of his feelings for the novel's events and characters.

In a similar fashion, the narrator repeatedly embraces and relin-quishes his pursuit of the "real" point. Recounting Olive and Ve-rena's last days together, he professes to a "despair of presenting [the scene] to the reader with the air of reality." Further on he con-fesses, "It must be admitted that in reality [Verena] was very de-ficient in the desire to be consistent with herself." And finally he observes, "I scarcely venture to think now, what Verena may have said to herself" (328–29). Moving from denial of his ability to ren-der the scene, to an unequivocal criticism of his character's refusal to face reality, to more doubt about his descriptive capacities, the narrator seems to resist the judgment to which he "must admit."

Yet just as the scene at Marmion involves a pivotal recognition for Olive, so too can it be seen to evoke a realization for the narra-tive consciousness. The passage begins with the narrator's dis-claimer that Olive's painful retrospection represents "mysteries into which I shall not attempt to enter, speculations with which I have no concern." He then proceeds, however, to an extensive de-tailing of Olive's deepest confrontation with reality, even offering a final judgment of her "miserable musings," as he intones, "Posi-tive it is that she spared herself none of the inductions of a reverie that seemed to dry up the mists and ambiguities of life." This rather mocking outlook on the rigid clarity of Olive's backward glance is immediately softened by the admission that we all experience "these hours of backward clearness" (354–55). To engage occasionally in self-torment through contemplation of the past is understandable, the narrator seems to believe. He then continues on, openly censoring the excessiveness of Olive's review.

Moving from evasion through sympathy to criticism, this passage represents an important moment for the narrator as well as the character. Instead of disavowing the reflex to judge, the narrator appears finally to accept it. Analyzing human beings, describing them, like loving them, is here unavoidably linked to the act of judgment. Nor does the narrator refrain from criticism. Finally judging without apology, the narrator has become the critical historian who can look upon the past with a discerning eye and apply it to his present understanding. No longer denying the obligatory authority of his narrative role, he accepts the possibility that he knows more than his characters, whose rambles go "unnoticed" by them, and his readers, who may seek in him a way of understanding the world.

FIVE

American Innocence and English Perils: The Treachery of Tales in *The Wings of the Dove*

🦋

THE CONCLUSION to Henry James's *The Wings of the Dove* has been seen as typical of the renunciation that befalls the Jamesian protagonist. Kate Croy's "We shall never be again as we were!"[1] signals the end of her bond to Merton Densher, realizing the "temple without an avenue" (52) that has symbolized their relationship. Kate and Densher will go separate ways, their love destroyed by greed and guilt. Their union has been tainted from the start, such a reading supposes, and the ending merely confirms the air of deprivation and futility that has plagued them.

Yet the novel's close can be understood differently, and Kate's powerful declaration seen as other than an inevitable renunciation. Rather than a denial of Kate and Densher's love, the statement serves as a sobering recognition of history. More than formalizing an implicit strain in their relations, Kate is insisting that distinctions between past and present must be boldly confronted. This perspective contrasts with Densher's: he has fallen in love with Milly's memory, content to revere her image as he also reveres an image of his relation with Kate that is fixed in time. Densher clings to the past, attempting to ignore history's changes and thereby soften its blows, while Kate holds to its recognition.

The split between time as memorial and time as historical process in this final scene resonates with the novel's growing concern

[1] Henry James, *The Wings of the Dove* (New York: Norton, 1978), 403. All subsequent references to this edition will be included parenthetically in the text.

over gradations of historical consciousness as it nears its end. The novel throughout betrays an interest in the responsibilities incurred by characters' historical actions, and dramatizes their attempts to reshape history through the stories they tell about their past and present. Often it appears that a pact with reality has been achieved, and that the world has become a conspirator in the characters' efforts to supplant their historical experiences with aesthetic reconstructions of them. But these histories ultimately do more to reveal the characters' realities than any more obvious fictions they might have wished to create. And the fact that their narrative preoccupations return them to a confrontation with their social and historical circumstances illuminates an important aspect of history itself: that it may only be encountered through the act of narration, or the embracing of textuality.[2]

In *The Wings of the Dove*, the process of historical narration reveals the extent to which all are complicit in the actions of their contemporaries, and bound by the social and political demands of their world. This is the sense of Kate's insistence at the novel's end that Densher admit his love for Milly. Her challenge to Densher is self-implicating: "Don't speak of it as if you couldn't be. *I* could in your place" (403). Her willful substitution emphasizes that the historical participants in the novel's recounted events, including

---

[2] See Fredric Jameson, *The Political Unconscious* (Ithaca: Cornell University Press, 1981), esp. ch. 1, "On Interpretation." For Jameson, the "structuralist" or "textual revolution" is most significant in its potential effects upon individuals' experiences of social institutions. By allowing us to "extrapolat[e] . . . the notion of 'discourse' or 'writing' onto objects previously thought to be 'realities' or objects in the real world" (296), the concept of textuality alters our perceptions of our power to change them. He continues, "When properly used, the concept of the 'text' does not, as in garden variety semiotic practice today, 'reduce' these realities to small and manageable written documents . . . but rather liberates us from the empirical object—whether institution, event, or individual work—by displacing our attention to its *constitution* as an object and its relationship to other objects thus constituted" (297). By highlighting the fact that history is made, invariably by deeply interested interpreters, the view of history as text opens up the possibilities for critical thinking. Historians, as well as literary theorists, have become increasingly alert to the narrative dimensions of historiography. See, for example, Lawrence Stone, "The Revival of Narrative," *Past and Present* 85 (1979): 1–24.

characters, narrator, author, and readers, are accountable for its outcome. By participating in the imaginative reenactment of its scenes, we are accomplices: any of us could love in Densher's place, conspire in Kate's, and die in Milly's. Kate's claim for her ease of identification points to our own.

Moreover, the novel portrays the powers of narration as potentially destructive to suggest that telling is itself an incriminating act. In the most striking example, Lord Mark's disclosure to Milly supposedly leads straight on to her death. Though the novel features many different kinds of narrators, there seems to be a guilt inherent in this shared role.

In the following pages I examine the novel's treatment of storytelling as a means to self-realization and political power. I first study the various characters in their will to remake historical (and genealogical) circumstances, and to control others through linguistic manipulations. I focus on certain characters' attempts to deny their will to power by concealing their participation in narrative designs. I then examine the strategies of the novel's narrator, as well as the work's overall structure. The narrative's continual evasion of its ostensible story line parallels the characters' own desires for and fears of plotting. Finally, I explore the ways in which the novel implicates all in the social and political treacheries of its plot, thereby exposing the fallacy of viewing storytelling as a route to transcendence. Instead, the novel reveals the interconnectedness of everyone in society, and the fundamentally *social* texture of narrative. Any claim for an innocent American tale free of history is exposed as myth. I conclude with an examination of Milly's death in light of late nineteenth-century cultural stereotypes of women. Entering the debate among recent theorists about the potential avenues for women's power in this period, I consider Kate and Milly's different relationships to the problem of political action, showing how their varying degrees of social and political autonomy accord with their respective power over historical narration.

The Characters' Tales

The Wings of the Dove opens upon a different world from any encountered in this study so far. Unlike the gesture that severs the link between the work of art and the real world in the preface to *The House of the Seven Gables*, or the struggling evasions of "the real" by the characters of *The Bostonians*, *Wings* begins with a character who insists on confronting her familial connections and the circumstances of her origins. Though her consciousness of history and its conditioning in this scene is more easily avoided, Kate meets her own evasive impulses with renewed commitments to the necessity of awareness. Her instinct for flight, and consequent conviction of how deeply she is held by her father's world, is a warning to the reader that try as he might to discover transcendence in the novel's terms, he will be drawn back, as if in quicksand, to its most compromising implications.

> She waited, Kate Croy, for her father to come in, but he kept her unconscionably, and there were moments at which she showed herself, in the glass over the mantel, a face positively pale with the irritation that had brought her to the point of going away without sight of him. It was at this point, however, that she remained; changing her place, moving from the shabby sofa to the armchair upholstered in a glazed cloth that gave at once—she had tried it—the sense of the slippery and of the sticky. . . . Each time she turned in again, each time, in her impatience, she gave him up, it was to sound to a deeper depth, while she tasted the faint flat emanation of things, the failure of fortune and of honour. (21)

The word "unconscionably" suggests the insolence of the familial claim on Kate, the demands artfully cloaked or denied by a father too wretched in his own need to perceive hers. But each tormented recognition of her prison of "consanguinity" serves to preclude the possibility of flight; for Kate, confrontation itself offers the only means of escape. Just at "the point of going away without sight of him . . . she remain[s]." Each time she moves to give "him up, it was to sound to a deeper depth" his "failure of fortune and of honour."

Kate Croy's intimate relation to the energies of the novel's plot is borne out by the novel's opening with this visit to her father's rooms. It is also appropriate that our first view discloses her gazing into a mirror. As Otto Rank points out in his study *The Double*, the motif of a character confronting a mirror image affords "sociability with one's own self," allowing one simultaneously to be and see one's being.[3] We might consider Kate's gesture as exposing the duplicitous possibilities of her experience, allowing her to conceive of a duplicate or even contradictory self. The image plants the seeds of a character who throughout the novel will betray a facility for contradictory motives and aspirations. Though the critics most kindly disposed to her admire a consistency that they oppose to the hypocrisies of Merton Densher, these views overlook the great spring to Kate's consciousness: her "constant perception of the incongruity of things" (56).[4] Her genius lies precisely in her ability to accept the weight of past relations while putting that burden in trust toward her own freedom. This is the sense of the opening passage where her repeated conviction of her father's damning impossibility nevertheless compels her to remain, and even to renew her offer of closer involvement with him. Kate's character reveals the heroism of contradictory wagers, of being convinced of something and effecting its opposite.

Kate gains freedom by putting the past, as it were, in its place, which means textualizing it. In conceiving of her past as a debauched tale that has somehow gone awry, Kate establishes her

---

[3] Rank, *The Double* (New York: Meridian, 1971), 18–25. This image of Kate presages Milly Theale's confrontation of her own mortality in the Bronzino portrait, a recognition so powerful that it must be instantly denied. The Bronzino portrait allows Milly to see herself, and to escape from that vision, to witness her own death through a portrait frame. Milly's declaration, "I shall never be better than this" (137) is echoed by Kate's closing, "We shall never be again as we were." Both statements display a consciousness of time: but where Milly anticipates death, Kate gazes backward to distinguish past and present.

[4] For this view, see Dorothea Krook, *The Ordeal of Consciousness* (Cambridge: Cambridge University Press, 1962), 203–215, 221–29, and Sallie Sears, *The Negative Imagination* (Ithaca: Cornell University Press, 1968), 63–74, 90–98.

power to rewrite it. Her history, "dropped first into words and notes without sense," has been left "unfinished" by its author, in a gesture perhaps of impotence or disgust. It seems inexplicable why such "a set of people" should have been "put in motion" only to break down helplessly of their own accord, without even the aesthetic justification of an "accident." In Kate's characterization, the family chronicler is irresponsible in failing to give their story some artful closure. Yet his fallibility allows for her assumption of narrative power. Their history, in her hands, will not fail at a "sort of meaning" (21–22). Kate's action of "readjust[ing]" and "re-touch[ing]" her hat and hair seems a subtle testimony of her commitment to remaking the past. And quite apart from any conscious intent, Kate's aspect records her capacity to go beyond the givens of her experience. Possessing "stature without height, grace without motion, presence without mass," her body refuses genetic attributes as the limiting condition of self-presentation (22).

Yet the novel features as many tales as there are characters, and Kate encounters in Lionel Croy a challenge to her desired revision of the family script. Kate's respect for a certain aesthetic code is met by her father's refusal to abide by any common terms of artistry, his story lacking even "the moderate finish required for deception" (23). The epitome of narrative unreliability, Croy invalidates any rules of the fictional game, and thus, Kate's aspirations for a meaningful fiction. Mystification is the only apparent strategy in his fiction of misrule. His "indescribable arts" (24) prove immune to deconstruction, just as his appearance reveals nothing of his true circumstances. He relies on "plausibility" itself, and his banishment by Kate's mother, rather than an aspersion upon him, "reflect[s] . . . invidiously" on her (26).

Croy's unconcealed hypocrisies, his refusal even to try to make his claims consistent, exemplify the manipulative intent ever present in his dealings with Kate. What might be taken as clumsiness or buffoonery in another man is studied unscrupulousness in him. Like his previous refusal to lie adroitly (23), Croy doesn't respect others sufficiently to take the trouble of proper deception. With others, as we shall see, Kate's linguistic power proves formidable. At the very least she is always able to enter into dialogue on her own terms. But her father refuses even to engage her terms.

Though Aunt Maud is recognized as one who resists "easy analogies" (37), she is less elusive than Lionel. In contrast to him, she wears her manipulations on her sleeve, a method that is more adaptable to Kate's purposes. Kate's silent naming of Maud, "The Britannia of the Market Place," exemplifies her ability to compromise Maud's domination. Unbeknownst to Maud, Kate envisions her "with a pen on her ear," and perhaps, "a helmet, a shield, a trident, and a ledger" (37). The fact that Kate refrains from voicing the "Britannia" title indicates a fundamental principle in the novel's portrayal of naming. To confer a name is to enter into an agreement with its recipient. When the name is pronounced, it becomes the possession of its recipient, who may subvert it or otherwise shape it to his or her own uses. But where the name remains undisclosed, as in this instance, the namer retains exclusive power.[5] Kate thus invokes a secret sign system that Maud cannot challenge. Yet Kate is also aware of the limits to this power. As she

[5] The subject of naming has a long history among literary theorists. An early example, Plato's "Cratylus," features a dialogue between Hermogenes, the nominalist, who holds that all names represent arbitrary conventions, and Cratylus, the organicist, who argues that names convey essences. Socrates synthesizes these two positions: names are both conventional and natural, but above all, the work of "the chief artificer of language." Aligning the powers of the linguist and the legislator, Plato registers the political implications of naming. *The Dialogues of Plato*, trans. B. Jowett (Oxford: Oxford University Press, 1953), 1–106. More recent theorists have discussed the power of naming in Proust and others. Roland Barthes insists on the "Cratylean character of the name in Proust . . . no one is closer to the Cratylean legislator, founder of names, than the Proustian writer, not because he is free to invent the names he likes, but because he is obliged to invent them properly" (67). "A Cratylean consciousness of signs" examines language not as convention, but as "the writer constructs it." Barthes's view is consistent with Kate's reconstructing claims; for her, words forge a certain *relation* to the world, rather than simply reflecting it. "Proust and Names," in *New Critical Essays* (New York: Farrar, Straus and Giroux, 1980). Also pertinent here are Gerard Genette, *Figures of Literary Discourse*, trans. Alan Sheridan (New York: Columbia University Press, 1982); and J. L. Austin, *How To Do Things with Words* (New York: Oxford University Press, 1970).

observes, "There were some things, after all, of which Britannia was afraid; but Aunt Maud was afraid of nothing" (38).

Kate's recognition of family ties keeps her continually aware of compromising conditions. She is not above her sister Marian's experience, which leads her to doubt the viability of marriage—"if that was what marriage necessarily did to you" (41). Nor is she incapable of identifying with the despised Condrips, with whom she feels "something in common" (45). By refusing to see her own possibilities as beyond the circumstances of others, Kate derives a power to subsume their versions of experience in her own. She can enter into others' lives and perspectives, and use them as directives for her own constructions. Kate insists on working through the materials of the world, in order to get to her own more satisfying, but still applicable, fictions.

Merton Densher is the first to note the enormous fund of energies Kate devotes to the rewriting of her past. In one of their earliest meetings, he listens to her history, more alert to the form than the content of her narrative.

Kate confessedly described them with an excess of impatience; it was much of her charm for Densher that she gave in general that turn to her descriptions, partly as if to amuse him by free and humorous colour, partly—and that charm was the greatest—as if to work off, for her own relief, her constant perception of the incongruity of things. She had seen the general show too early and too sharply, and was so intelligent that she knew it and allowed for that misfortune. . . . It always struck him she had more life than he to react from, and when she recounted the dark disasters of her house and glanced at the hard odd offset of her present exaltation—since as exaltation it was apparently to be considered—he felt his own grey domestic annals make little show. It was naturally, in all such reference, the question of her father's character that engaged him most. . . . What was it, to speak plainly, that Mr. Croy had originally done? I don't know—and I don't want to . . . one cold black Sunday morning when, on account of an extraordinary fog, we hadn't gone to church, [Marian] broke it to me by the school-room fire. I was reading a history-book by the lamp—when we didn't go to church we had to read history-books—and I suddenly heard her say, out of the fog, which was in the room, and apropos of nothing: "Papa has done something wicked." (55–56)

CHAPTER FIVE

It is telling that Kate receives the original insight that motivates her "work[ing] off" of her past, in a fog over a history book. The circumstances of history, the scene suggests, are always a blur to present viewers, it is only by achieving some distance that details accrue into a pattern. Kate instinctively recognizes this principle of history making, and doesn't seek immediate edification. It is only slowly, later, through silent communications with her mother, that Kate comes to put some pieces in place (57), and here too she is cautious, attempting to suspend judgment.

The passage points to a significant upgrading of historical studies in the novel's contemporary world. History reading substitutes for church worship, the secular tale of human actions supplanting ritual homage to God's eternally unfolding plan. Though Kate connects the events of her family past with a still-mysterious and omnipotent "hand of fate," her "impatience" with that pattern reveals her conviction that it can be reworked by human hands. She decorates the past as she wills, adding "free and humorous colour," a cast that wars with the dismal tints supplied by fate. The "impatience," even "violen[ce]," that Densher detects in Kate's "talk" suggests the energy she directs toward the recasting of her experience. To see the past as she does, aspiring to give it new shape and sentiment, requires a power that can subsume the guilt incurred by its remaking. "The dark disasters," cast in "the hard odd offset of her present exaltation," reveal a past now made to serve its experiencer.

Milly shares Densher's admiration of the power and originality of Kate's past narratives. This becomes apparent to Milly early on in their relationship when they exchange "quantities of history" as a way of establishing their intimacy. Kate not only relates her own past, but provides Milly with so forceful a view of Milly's that she adopts it as her own. Thus, "Milly actually began to borrow from [Kate] a sort of view of her state; the handsome girl's impression of it was clearly so sincere" (113). The sincerity of Kate's "impressions," the element of *life* in her versions of experience, makes them stick. So energetic and full are her narratives that they overtake those of others. Kate's perceptions pass from one character to another, her images preparing the ground for the implantation of her larger design.

Kate's power lies in the cumulative impact of her impressions. It is significant that Jamesian metaphor has traditionally been seen to derive its power through precisely this process of accretion.[6] Milly is quick to recognize Kate's ability as "a tribute positively to power" (113), a perception that recurs. Kate's power is sometimes even fearsome; Milly likens her in one scene to the admittedly "violent image" of a "panther" (171). It would be imprecise, however, to conclude that Milly's relationship with Kate is based entirely on her own linguistic submission. One noteworthy instance reveals the equality that prevails between them: Kate's naming of Milly as "a dove."

As previously discussed, the act of publicly naming someone involves the complicity of namer and named, a process that also sheds light upon the relation of a narrator and a reader. In both cases, the supposedly passive member of the exchange—the named or the reader—actually assists in the final form of the design. The reader must comply with and help to create the narrative, just as the person named accepts his appellation, and in the process makes it his own.[7] When Kate names Milly, the term is accepted only as it suits Milly's own purposes. Though Kate's action accords with her genius as a labeler of the world, the real drama of the scene is found in Milly's reception of Kate's brand.

---

[6] On this point see Ruth Yeazell, *Language and Knowledge in the Late Works of Henry James* (Chicago: University of Chicago Press, 1976), and Deborah Esch, "A Jamesian About-Face: Notes on 'The Jolly Corner,' " *ELH* (Fall 1983): 587–605.

[7] Ross Chambers's study, *Story and Situation* (Minneapolis: University of Minnesota Press, 1984), redefines the function of narrative as distinct from the narratological tradition represented by Seymour Chatman's *Story and Discourse*. Chambers stresses the "textual indices of contractual and transactional understandings—that themselves realize the narratives as communicative acts" (10). He focuses specifically on the problem of "duplicity," understood as "the textual understanding of the necessarily *dual* input (of text and reader) into the communicative event and the consequent acknowledgment, in texts, of the irreducible *otherness* of the reader" (14).

Termed a dove, Milly "felt herself ever so delicately, so considerately, embraced; not with familiarity or as a liberty taken, but almost ceremonially and in the manner of an *accolade*, partly as if, though a dove who could perch on a finger, one were also a princess with whom forms were to be observed" (171).

The depth of Milly's awareness here is almost sinister. Milly's acceptance of "the name so given her," the way "she met it on the instant," yields the strongest impression of the exchange. Kate's action is preceded by Milly's enlarged sense "of how people . . . were often touched by her." Receiving Kate's name with a decorum that is hers alone, Milly is "embraced . . . ever so delicately, so considerately." Thus, Milly draws a circumference of her own imaginative light around Kate's deed. So fully do her own impressions introduce and receive Kate's name that it appears more the product of Milly's "inspiration" than Kate's. It is appropriate that Milly's first exercise of her powers as a dove involves her manipulation of a figure who has proved formidable even to Kate. Envisioning herself at her "most dovelike," with an expression "as earnest" as it is "candid," Milly lies to Aunt Maud about Merton Densher's return to London (172). Kate's name has conferred upon Milly the monolithic veil of innocence, a power she wields to the novel's end.

One further point about the power of private naming in this scene deserves mention. If a name is never pronounced, as we observed in the example of Kate's "quiet naming" of Aunt Maud, it remains the possession of the namer, a secret power held forever uncompromised by discourse. Thus, it is especially significant that Kate's naming of Milly is preceded by Milly *silently* designating Kate a "panther." When Milly actually does "find words," it is not to express this image, but to offer a remark that conceals her fear.

This is not to undermine Kate's linguistic powers, but to insist on a certain mutuality of exchange. In the worlds of James—and this is true of all the novels, early and late—characters are never passively exploited, but always mediate and compromise their uses by others. The subtleties of manipulation in these works reveal any act of domination to be partial and qualified.[8] Milly and Kate's encounter with the Bronzino portrait offers another instance of such a power exchange, though here Kate, not Milly, appears to win the upper hand.

Though Kate enters the scene after Milly's likeness has been established, her manipulation of a sentiment already set in motion is supreme. Kate's initial response to the realization that Lord Mark has anticipated her is the brave acknowledgment of his prior claim. "*You* had noticed too? . . . Then I'm not original—which one always hopes one has been" (138). Yet Kate's statement makes a mockery of priority. Suggesting the self-deceptiveness of any aspirations to originality, Kate next freely dispenses with Milly's. Acting as a "re-enforcement" to Lord Mark's sense of Milly's "great likeness," she overturns Milly's claims for self-origination. Surrounded by all these well-meaning guardians of her image, Milly is again struck by Kate's power, noticing through her fatigue that it is Kate who engineers everyone's departure (139).

Milly receives other strong impressions of Kate, though always, as in the example of the dove, it seems that Milly allows Kate her power, and even that she derives some personal benefit from emphasizing Kate's strength. Returning from her first visit to Sir Luke Strett's, for example, Milly considers Kate's relation to illness. "*She* would never in her life be ill; the greatest doctor would keep her, at the worst, the fewest minutes; and it was as if she had asked just *with* all this practical impeccability for all that was most mortal in her friend" (158). Kate's almost insolent vigor is seen to actively solicit Milly's debility. Personified as aggressive and demanding, Kate's health requires that Milly be "most mortal" so as to set itself in firmer relief. Kate's health is an imperial power, ex-

---

[8] James's insight into the mutuality of power relations approximates a recent discussion by Anthony Giddens. "All power relations," he writes, "manifest autonomy and dependence in both directions. . . . In all cases in which human agency is exercised within a relationship of any kind—power relations are two-way." *Central Problems in Social Theory*, 149 and passim.

ploiting Milly's illness by annexing her like a vulnerable pacific island. Yet these are Milly's perceptions, and they seem exaggerated for the sake of establishing the identity of her illness. In any event, she must protect herself from Kate, and responding to Kate's questioning with a one-word denial of her illness, she feels that she has "done something for her safety" (158).

Milly knows instinctively the perils of interacting with Kate. Consistently meeting Kate on her own terms, she nearly always separates from her with a sense of relief at how close she has come to danger. But Milly is also a challenge to Kate. Indeed, the fundamental sense of their relationship is that each respects the limits of knowing and controlling the other. Kate is the only figure in the novel, with the occasional exception of the narrator, apprised of the depth of Milly's awarenesses and self-consciousness. As she cautions during the dinner where the absent Milly is freely characterized by all, "One *sees* [Milly] with intensity—sees her more than one sees almost any one; but then one discovers that that isn't knowing her and that one may know better a person whom one doesn't 'see,' as I say, half so much" (208). Kate perceives that Milly's intensity is both intentional and cultivated. Like a star that blinds the viewer at precisely the moment where it most promises to expose, Milly's radiance is as masking as it is revealing. Her appearance of openness, her skill at convincing others that they are seeing fully, facilitate her secrecy. Kate recognizes that Milly's air of easy access is her means of keeping others out. Not suprisingly, Kate's observation is lost on the assembled guests, who call it "interesting" and then return to their easy classifications. But Kate and Milly do not miss one another's labyrinthine meanings.

Kate herself is sometimes subjected to others' terms. This is evident in her dealings with the sovereign claims of her Aunt Maud. Aunt Maud's strategy for undermining the love between Kate and Densher is to deny its existence. As Kate remarks, "Aunt Maud's line is to keep all reality out of our relation" (200), a silencing operation that like the manipulations of Lionel Croy seems indomitable. Maud's power is based in tyrannical displays of imagination that parade as natural or consensual actions. She "takes everything as of a natural . . . when she adopts a view she . . . fairly terrorises with her view any other . . . dares and defies her idea not to prove the right one" (287). Her authority is achieved through forcing the world into alignment with her desires by assuming that her reality is everyone's. Kate's subjection to Maud's will, for example, is presumed rather than negotiated.

In a scene witnessed by Densher, Maud scrutinizes Kate as she would a piece from her art collection. As Kate enters the room where Densher and Maud are already seated, he notes "the straight look" with which Maud acknowledges her claim. "The girl had to reckon with [it] as she advanced. It took her in from head to foot, and in doing so it told a story that made poor Densher again the least bit sick: it marked so something with which Kate habitually and consummately reckoned. . . . Densher saw himself for the moment as in his purchased stall at the play; the watchful manager was in the depths of a box and the poor actress in the glare of the footlights" (204). This is the most compromised view of Kate in the novel. Walking the gauntlet of Maud's gaze, a "poor actress" at the behest of manager and audience, Kate for once seems unequivocally vulnerable. Densher's disgust at Aunt Maud's appropriation is characteristic; throughout the novel he will denounce actions by others in which he explicitly (as here) or implicitly participates. As the purchaser of a box, Densher symbolizes the cash nexus in this scene, which hardly disqualifies him from participation. He struggles to dismiss his complicity, terming his role "*mere* spectatorship" (emphasis added), and insisting that "the drama . . . was between *them*." Yet he admits to "a paying place in front, and one of the most expensive," the hint of his own requisition by the drama in the sense of his great monetary sacrifice (205). Clearly, Densher has lost something here, and the suggestion is that it is his desired innocence.

Densher throughout holds to a view of aesthetic responsiveness as a form of immunity; art indicts its performer (narrator) and creator (author), but always stops short of implicating its audience (reader). Audiences approach art as acts of self-preservation, or self-cultivation: its role is to enlarge assumptions already held, not to alter or unhinge. As readers grow aware of the fallacy of these claims, in light of Densher's implication by his plot with Kate, they are led to the conclusion that art never acts passively upon its audience. Rather, the audience participates in and is responsible for the form of the artistic product in every stage of its production.

The central feature of Kate's character is her grasp of the complicity incurred through participation, either as narrator or reader, in the process of narration. This awareness is most clearly brought out in her series of dialogues with Densher. In one of their earliest discussions about Milly's health, Kate's illuminations contrast suspiciously with Densher's obfuscations. Her confrontation of her own experience and prejudices through Milly's opposes Densher's disengagement from Milly's circumstances. In the haunting manner of a mesmeric seer, Kate intones, "She doesn't see the future. It has opened out before her in these last weeks as a dark confused thing" (213). To which Densher responds dubiously, "After the tremendous time you've all been telling me she has had?"

Their conversation proceeds in this way, Kate offering insights and Densher doubts, until Kate "falter[s]": the precise facts of Milly's illness comprise details that Kate prefers to overlook. "I'm a brute about illness," she fairly hisses. "I hate it. . . . From illness I keep away" (215–16). Kate's sense of Milly's predicament yields a profound self-perception. We can imagine the physical suffering she has witnessed all too closely in her mother's "ache" (23, 56) and in the pathetic deaths of her "two lost brothers" (21). And Kate also thoroughly perceives Milly, anticipating that her illness will be her greatest performance. "She won't smell, as it were, of drugs," Kate tells Densher, "she won't taste, as it were, of medicine" (215).

Kate's fund of empathy, her ability to see herself in Milly's place, does not prevent her use of Milly—the step for which she is decried by Densher and by most of the novel's critics. Kate's actions, however, can be seen to follow from her double vision: her empathy, which allows her to see through Milly's eyes, and her objectivity, which provides a view of Milly in light of Kate's own needs. It is the latter possibility that precipitates Kate's use of Milly; but this view neither precludes nor diminishes the former one.[9] The key to Kate's character is that she is able to maintain both perspectives: the empathetic and the objective view. Her will "to make things pleasant for [Milly]" (214) is not incompatible with her desire for Milly's money. Kate's plan in fact goes awry not as a fulfillment of the notion that evil cannot triumph, but because others in her world hold her to impossible standards of consistency, which they themselves regularly betray.

The early sections of the novel picture the necessity of Kate's powers of invention. Her instinctive skill with language, her impatience with the tired forms of her past, and her disdain for conventionality as exemplified by the unimaginative authoritarianism of her aunt, all condition her regard for Densher's singular mind. The latter parts of the novel emphasize the call of convention upon her, raising to the fore her feelings of deprivation. The material world serves warrant upon her senses, appearing more and more to motivate her actions. This is perhaps in order that we may imagine Kate taking the money at the novel's end, and in turn inhabiting a grand home in pearls and splendid clothing, single like the Condrips, but still satisfied that she has in fact *done* something to redeem the family name. Kate, we can trust, will never again play the starving actress.

Thus, during the party at the Palazzo Leporelli, Kate regards Milly's pearls as the symbol of what she will never know as Densher's wife. Kate's bitter regret over her difference from Milly in this

---

9 The latter assumption is integral to the historical perspective, in Kant's view. "Human action as seen from the outside . . . is just as much nature as anything is." Hence, from any individual's perspective, others are merely objects in the world to be used like any other objects. See R. G. Collingwood's discussion of these ideas and their relation to the historian's task in *The Idea of History* (New York: Oxford University Press, 1946), 90–97.

pose strikes a note of extreme pathos. "There was nobody with whom [Milly] had less in common than a remarkably handsome girl married to a man unable to make her on any such lines as that the least little present" (304–305). Kate has here reached a point where the world resists her deepest desires. Her capacity for maintaining disparate truths, for feeling empathy while objectively envisioning another's usefulness, has reached its limit, refused by her world, or rather, her love. Densher will never lavish upon her gifts from another woman's money, and she is forced to choose between him and Milly's fortune.

The reality of Kate's diffused possibilities is contained in the image of what contrarieties have now become in her life with the Condrips. As Densher observes in his visit to Marian's home,

A part of the queerness . . . sprang from the air as of a general large misfit imposed on the narrow room by the scale and mass of its furniture. The objects, the ornaments were, for the sisters, clearly relics and survivals of what would, in the case of Mrs. Condrip at least, have been called better days. The curtains that overdraped the windows, the sofas and tables that stayed circulation, the chimney-ornaments that reached to the ceiling and the florid chandelier that almost dropped to the floor, were so many mementoes of earlier homes and so many links with their unhappy mother. (381)

Kate's deep sense of the incongruity of things, formerly her "greatest charm," here plagues her as incongruous pieces of furniture, relics from the past whose disproportionate mass seems to express disapproval at the family's fallen condition. Kate's fine feeling for contradictions is now materialized in the form of personal effects that suffocate the senses.

Kate Croy's power resides in her ability to rewrite circumstances, to confront and challenge, through naming and narration, the barriers to her aspirations and desires. Milly Theale, in contrast, is more receptive; given her terms by others, her power lies in transforming them. Though the pair has more in common than has usually been recognized, Kate's relation to forms is more original and active, her plots and appellations incite others to react, while Milly is a recipient of others' terms. Milly watches herself from the outside in, and through most of the novel her perceptions of others viewing her serve as her main source of motivation.

From her introduction, Milly lives in the spotlight, her personal history rendered in the tones of a press release or publicity campaign. In place of the partial indirect discourse that introduces Kate, Milly is seen exclusively through the adoring eyes of Susan Stringham, chief confidant, faithful servant, and, not incidentally, magazine journalist by profession. The sensational notes of Milly's opening history seem to indicate Susan's byline.

> "It was New York mourning, it was New York hair, it was a New York history, confused as yet, but multitudinous, of the loss of parents, brothers, sisters, almost every human appendage, all on a scale and with a sweep that had required the greater stage; it was a New York legend of affecting, of romantic isolation, and beyond everything, it was by most accounts, in respect to the mass of money so piled on the girl's back, a set of New York possibilities." (77)

There is something crude, even exploitative in this sensationalizing of Milly's grief. Moving from her lonely mourning to the excess money it has conferred, the transition suggests the extent to which Milly will be preyed upon in the novel. Susan regards Milly as an acquisition from the beginning, emphasizing the lure of Milly's personality, her quality of "strange[ness]." Throughout the novel she gains celebrity, and a parasitical glamour, as Milly's constant companion.

The key to Susan's view of Milly (and this holds true for all the characters with the exception of Kate) is that she sees her exclusively in objective terms, as a fixed and quantifiable entity. The image of Milly being caught in others' minds, catalogued and labeled like a rare species of bird, recurs. And this process is set in motion by Susan, to whom Milly is "the real thing, the romantic life itself" (78). Milly is everything this bookish Vermont widow with her literary aspirations and deprived New England sensibility has imagined as *different* from her life of "straightness and security" (78). Susan is perfectly disposed to feed from Milly's circumstances, to promote this "potential heiress of all the ages" (79).

In a novel that opens upon Kate's valuation by a profiteering father and sister, Susan's linguistic inflation of Milly appears yet another tactic for increasing the market value of one's chief possession. Susan's celebration follows from her sense of ownership. Indeed, her typecasting of Milly as princess has the force of a lock and key. "That a princess could only be a princess was a truth with which, essentially, a confidant, however responsive, had to live" (85). The irony of this observation is Susan's air of resigning herself to the inevitability of Milly's "nature," in light of her own fixture of the term. Susan attaches a conventional attribute, and like a fairy godmother, makes it nature. Her imaginary seizure of Milly is literalized in the scene where she follows Milly up the mountain, stalking her as if she were a beast of prey.

From the scene's beginning, Susan feels a certain guilt, proceeding "with a quietness that made her slightly 'underhand' " (86). The necessity of moving "softly," and the manner in which she deduces from markers along the way the exact route of her prey—questioning "a bewildered old woman" and noting the discarded "Tauchnitz volume"—seem the actions of a game hunter. Coming upon her kill, she carefully conceals "her own nearness." It matters little that this is a hunt of the imagination, Susan's only weapon perhaps the pen that may inscribe the daily habits of this captured princess. For the novel recognizes the power of language to aggrandize the self and to exploit others, to be as formidable as any more vulgar acts of betrayal or domination (86–87). That Susan's fear, as she holds her breath before Milly perched perilously on the mountain's edge, is the loss of a trophy she will accompany to concerts and dinners rather than hang on her wall, does not change the prevailing ethic of the hunt. Susan's weapon may appear far from violent, but it is she who at the novel's end aligns the powers of language with those of murder.

Susan's fear may also be compared to the civilized sentiments of a collector who sees a particularly fine item about to crash to the floor—which accords with later mention of Susan's "property in their young friend" (210). Susan's monopoly opens a world she could never have entered on her own, as noted insidiously by those bent on purchasing shares (99, 102, 117). To possess Milly is to type her, and Lord Mark so firmly "place[s Milly]" from an impression of her native land that Milly feels as if she has been "popped into the compartment in which she was to travel for him . . . with the door sharply slammed upon her" (104). This is Milly's fate before the Bronzino portrait as well, where the chorus of admirers, united in agreement over her likeness, seem almost to force her bodily into the picture frame (138).

Milly's similar perception at Luke Strett's is her own. She imagines herself captured in a photograph, "engraved, signatured, and in particular framed and glazed," set among the "circle of eminent contemporaries" decorating the walls of this renowned London surgeon (146). To be ill, and treated by Strett, is to be contained by "the listening stillness" of his inner sanctum. It is to be held in time, with the progress of disease, at least metaphorically, halted forever. But Milly is also aware that her own photograph is prematurely envisioned, and that Luke Strett recognizes her frantic necessity. "He knew . . . that she was secretly romancing at that rate, in the midst of so much else that was more urgent, all over the place" (146).

Milly's hunger for forms, her need to define a life that feels unjustified and undeserved, makes her especially vulnerable to others' images. Thus, she conceives of herself as a walking emblem of "the American mind," which must be tutored into the variety of ways for taking English society (168). This image of Milly's American innocence is repeatedly invoked by Densher (279, 302–303, 314, 316, etc.). Densher's adoption of Milly as a personal prize, like others' adoption of her, is confirmed through typecasting. To him she is "the American girl," which becomes a kind of "settled" agreement between them. Though she may at times "fall short of her prerogative of the great national," it is not due to Densher's want of "keeping her, with his idea" (322). Yet Milly is intricately involved with others' naming and typing of her, which is her means of power and participation in the novel's dramatic action.

Milly is also an active reader of her own and others' experiences, and as such, she accepts her active role in the novel's events. One of the targets of Milly's critical acumen is Kate. Milly is the first to note the hint of "brutal[ity]" that Kate converts into a kind of "strange grace." She also perceives the peril of Kate's quick ways, the flashing and fixed judgments signalling an impatience kept under reign, but still posing "danger[s]" for those around her (117). Most importantly, Milly sees that her understanding of Kate depends on her own intuitive powers, recognizing the "unnamed" passages in Kate's recounting of her past as the crucial ones (112). Resisting the inadvertent displays or slips that "convenien[tly]" disclose character (122), Kate's only revelations will be traps and contrivances. Even Milly's visit to the Condrips' seems to throw more light on the English social system in general than on Kate and her family. Kate would never allow Milly the compromising view of vulgar incongruity that she allows her lover at the novel's end.

For Milly, Kate's supremacy inheres in her periodic ability to sever all "connexions and lose her identity" (132). Like the romance as James describes it in the preface to *The American*, Kate can effect an illusion of freedom from all social ties, even while testifying to the impossibility of such transcendence. The paradox is contained in the description of Kate's facility for weightlessness, as an "attaching property." The greatest form of imaginative power is to acknowledge temporal and social constraints and defy them anyway. Her feat enlarges the possibilities of imagination itself, rendering the onlooker's mind more supple and aware of its own potential. Kate's illusion of disconnection also deprives the onlooker of firm ground, preventing her own precise situation in the narrative.

But Milly as reader still has ways of manipulating Kate, as evidenced by the recurring motif of Milly perceiving Kate through Densher's eyes. From the first, Milly's awareness of Kate and

Densher's connection yields a troubled sense of guilt and danger. Locating intuitively what will be the parameters of this triangular relationship, Milly seems proleptically apprised of some act of deception or treachery that will implicate them all. As if to insist from the outset on their shared incrimination, Milly denies Kate and Densher's role in the concealment, turning their manipulations into her own apology for suspicion. Attempting to "make it up to Kate" (140), she implicates herself with a gesture of self-immolation that characteristically follows Milly's keenest insights. Milly moves reflexively to convince herself that all is right during moments when she most deeply intuits otherwise, almost as if her fundamental guilt cultivates sorrow by allowing it to build knowingly. And though she forces herself to reject her knowledge as "pervers[e]," she thwarts Kate's plan to accompany her to Luke Strett's (144), and she denies her illness (156–57), thereby denoting her deeper suspicion.

Instead of being simply acted upon, Milly acts upon others as an interpreter and critic. She is, in short, a far better reader than the critics who read her as victim. If other characters seem empowered to interpret Milly in various ways, investing her with their own desires and plans, it is only because she wishes them to. This is clearly the case in the scene where Kate's naming of Milly is countermanded by Milly's interpretive terms.

Likewise, in Lord Mark's first visit to Venice, Milly repeatedly snatches his presumptions out from under him, through either willful enlargement or misunderstanding. Insisting on her own terms, she casts his overtures in a noble light that reflects favorably on both of them. "It didn't sit, the ugly motive, in Lord Mark's cool English eyes; the darker side of it at any rate showed, to her imagination, but briefly. Suspicion, moreover, with this, simplified itself: there was a beautiful reason—indeed there were two— why her companion's motive shouldn't matter" (268). Lord Mark's "ugly motive" is discarded because it wars with her preferred pattern. Though a "darker" possibility presents itself, Milly chooses to entertain it but "briefly." Milly's willful aestheticism insists on

203

her own more "beautiful reason," which disqualifies Lord Mark's version altogether. By privileging her own script, Milly evades a truth she has already intuited and fears.

This raises a crucial point: Milly has actually assisted in the construction of deceptions for which Kate and Densher are often exclusively held accountable. Those who, with Densher, believe Milly "successfully deceived" (224) ironically expose their own deception by Milly. At this point in the novel, Milly is already well aware of Kate and Densher's hazardous suppressions, a foreknowledge that makes her talk with Lord Mark an almost ludicrous dance of evasion. So forcefully does she struggle to keep him from coming out with what he supposes are revelations that she ends up appearing the aggressor. At one point in the dialogue the narrator steps back to observe, "They had a moment . . . during which neither pronounced a name, each apparently determined that the other should. It was Milly's fine coercion, in the event, that was the stronger" (274). Though Lord Mark's assertion of Kate's falsity is an unmistakable jolt to Milly's "presence of mind," Milly's resistance to his truth is consistent with her former evasions. At each point she steps in to defend Kate's actions to herself. "She could only be concerned to 'stand up' for [Kate's veracity]." And later, in lieu of the now "aspersed Kate," Milly feels that "she must claim her own part of the aspersion" (276–77). This is in part an attempt to establish sole control over the events. But also, as the image of her "caged freedom" suggests, Milly shares Kate's capacity to entertain incongruous thoughts and feelings. Lord Mark's view of Kate's betrayal, however real, does not preclude Kate and Milly from being "such tremendous friends."

This is because Milly, like Kate, sees experience with a great deal of moral complexity. Milly will come, as she notes, to confront Kate's actions in her own way. She will learn to "bear" what is in any terms a "loss." But Milly rejects Lord Mark's condescension toward Kate (276–77), as she would Densher's toward Lord Mark (343). While their terms of opprobrium allow Mark and Densher to evade implication in the evildoings they unveil, Kate and Milly know better. Aware of their own participation in the chain of events that effect them, Kate and Milly are prepared to embrace their roles in the histories they in part make. Milly recognizes her inevitable complicity in Kate's silences, acknowledging how she has watched Kate's suppressions take form with an almost scientific curiosity. She knows also that Kate and Densher's drama has served her, conferring a generous starring role.

Milly participates in the subtle establishment of terms that allow others to manipulate her, and through which she in turn controls or manipulates them. As we will see presently, the only process of self-imaging that Milly upholds unknowingly is her adoption of a cultural myth that designates death as her greatest possible act.

Merton Densher is marked from the outset by his detachment from social rituals. He is above the maneuverings for status and wealth that prevail in Maud Lowder's circle, and he also refuses the air of industry suitable to middle-class youths of his era. Despite the narrator's half-hearted disclaimer that Densher is not "unamenable, on certain sides, to classification," his distinctive trait seems to be an imperviousness to codes and categories. Professionally, he is "young for the House of Commons . . . loose for the Army . . . refined . . . for the City . . . and, quite apart from the cut of his cloth, sceptical . . . for the Church." Physically, he appears, "vague without looking weak—idle without looking empty" (46). His elusiveness is explained by his youth: like Holgrave in *The House of the Seven Gables*, Densher is too young to be captured by any fixed mold. He still inhabits "that wondrous state of youth in which the elements, the metals more or less precious, are so in fusion and fermentation that the question of the final stamp, the pressure that fixes the value, must wait for comparative coolness" (46).

One doubts youth to be the cause of Densher's vagueness. Densher's uncertainties insulate him from unwanted ties and involvements. Yet Densher is not altogether consistent in his resist-

205

ance to forms and expectations. He is in fact committed to an idea about his destiny that is only mentioned once in the novel and never told to anyone. Densher's great conviction, "the innermost fact . . . of his own consciousness," is "his private inability to believe he should ever be rich" (54). So inevitable is this idea that Densher never even tries to "understand it." A thing apart, beyond any of his experience, the feeling can never be tested or challenged.

The same note of predetermination characterizes Densher's career overall, as he envisions newspaper work as "part of his fate." Given Densher's self-limiting perceptions of fate, it is not surprising that he responds to Kate's refusal to be hemmed in by it. Her "impatience" before "the hand of fate" allows Densher vicarious confrontation with his own fate (56). Excusing his continual deference to her own narratives with the claim that "she had more life than he to react from" (56), he implies that it is Kate who most depends upon the method of their intimacy, their ritualized retellings of the past. By projecting all the discomfort and need upon Kate's engagement with her past, Densher evades working through his own. But his self-assured freedom wars with the weightiness of his deepest thoughts, which he need never acknowledge with Kate.

Densher uses the past in a way that is distinctly the opposite of Kate's. For him, the past is a static realm that provides a means of escape from his contemporary circumstances. He is not merely possessed of a *relation* to the past; rather, Densher drowns in it. A sacred place containing relics from his experiences, Densher's reified past rules his imaginative life. But his stilling of others in memory also allows him control over them. The intensity of his lovemaking with Kate, for example, is experienced in the aftermath, where he builds a retrospective effigy to their passion. "It was after they had gone that he truly felt the difference, which was most to be felt moreover in his faded old rooms. . . . What had come to pass within his walls lingered there as an obsession importunate to all his senses; it lived again, as a cluster of pleasant memories, at every hour and in every object; it made everything but itself irrelevant and tasteless" (312).

Drained of the subsuming, even threatening, aspects of Kate's presence, the encounter becomes, in memory, his acquisition. It is telling that the image is described as changing from a force with "an insistence of its own" to one so ruled by him that it seems a tamed animal kept under lock and key. "It played for him—certainly in this prime afterglow—the part of a treasure kept at home in safety and sanctity, something he was sure of finding in its place when, with each return, he worked his heavy old key in the lock" (313). "Night after night," Densher replays the performance in his private room—combination stage, orchestra pit, and auditorium. Employing one of his most preferred framing devices—the image of the spectator in the theatre—Densher becomes a voyeur to his own experience.

Kate is not the only figurehead in Densher's retrospective sanctuary. His encounters with Milly are similarly cast. His "still communion" with the spirit of Kate's surrender is replicated by "the charged stillness" that he experiences in remembering Milly (370). But Milly's memory is more accommodating to his imagination. There is no particular event, and little memory of any action, to limit his imagination. Recalling Milly's indeterminate "waves of sympathy" at her party in the Palazzo Leporelli, Densher feels that "something had happened to him too beautiful and too sacred to describe" (370). He "left it behind him . . . when he went out," but is assured of "finding it there" upon his return (398).

Yet more than a staged drama enacted again and again, Densher's new idol is a sense, a feeling for "the hunger of time." The dramatic loss of Milly's words, together with the loss of Kate, incites further need for his imaginative controls. Both incidents contribute to "the sacred hush" that rules Densher's days as the novel nears its close. It is consistent with Densher's particular uses of the past that he is not given the last word on time in the novel. His final hope is a resurrection of the past, a return into time that would render Kate and himself "as [they] were" (403). As one would expect, it is Kate who registers the truths of historical time. There is no going back, no escape from the knowledge conferred by one's own position in history. Human beings may be lost, but knowledge can not be. Densher, however, connects with the past alone. His escapes to the past epitomize an inability to confront his actions in history.[10]

The scene at Maud's dinner typifies Densher's evasions. Here, clinging to his role of detached spectator, he watches the beasts of prey circle restlessly around the image of the absent Milly. Significantly, this is preceded by the scene where Densher joins but denounces Maud's stalking of Kate. The terms of the hunt in the scene that follows are explicit: Densher is drawn in despite himself as the discoverer of "the wonderful creature . . . in her native jungle" (205). Unable to extricate himself completely—"He would have been amused . . . hadn't he been slightly displeased at all they seemed desirous to fasten on him"—Densher tries instead to downplay the violence of the hunt. Rather than a conquest by "lions and tigers," this is, after all, a mild display of "domestic animals let loose as for the joke" (208–209). But the overall tone leaves Susan "uneasy," and the concluding sense of their game is hardly "mild." The assembly is described as "the huddled herd [that] had drifted to [Milly] blindly—it might as blindly have drifted away. There had been of course a signal, but the great reason was probably the absence at the moment of a larger lion" (209). The "signal," referring either to Susan's letter or Densher's discovery, makes them instant participants. Densher is finally powerless to resist his complicity. And as we later learn, the admission "that he had been the first to know her" had "fairly become a habit" (286).

Densher's one concerted action in the novel is his confrontation of Lord Mark, where he attempts to piece together a historical explanation from the combined evidence of Milly's withdrawal,

[10] Examples of this include: 190, 279, 281–82, 287, 305, 312–13, 344, 348, 364–65, 369, 371, 378, 385–86, 399.

Lord Mark's presence, and his own sense of the past. Instead of evading the "shock" of his vision, Densher returns three times, until his "identity produced . . . all the effect of establishing connexions—connexions startling and direct." "Recognition" comes from deep and clear seeing, facilitated by his repeated encircling of the object of knowledge (327–28).

The scene serves as a metaphor for historical reconstruction. Densher's repeated revolutions around the figure of Lord Mark in the Venetian coffeehouse typify the historian's pursuit of his subject's tones and accents through repetition or reenactment.[11] For James, the historian's imaginative reclamation must include his experience of his own implication by past events. In this example, rather than provoking awareness of his role in the chain of events he reconstructs, Densher's explorations leave him feeling "remarkably blameless." Nor does his knowledge spur him to alleviate the effects of Lord Mark's visit. Densher looks upon his construction with "a sense of escape . . . an impunity . . . that was almost like purification" (329).

Densher's view of the past leads him to displace rather than to confront his own complicity. "Washed but the more clean" by his narrative, Densher refuses the identification with his subject's compromising actions that is essential to historical understanding. James's ideal historian is powerfully engaged with the past he frames: judging himself in judging it. Densher's glaring separation of his own past accountability from his recognition of Lord Mark's suggests a failure of historical imagination.

Yet however much he rationalizes, some part of Densher knows his complicity, which impels his obsessive conferences and correspondence with Susan (331–44) and with Kate (402–403). His discussions with Kate even incriminate him the more, by exposing

---

[11] I refer here to Collingwood's idea that the historian recovers the past through "reenactment." Collingwood's is a very Jamesian method: the historian must be one on whom nothing is lost. For Collingwood and James, historical reconstruction is an art, requiring both knowledge of one's subject and an indeterminate degree of sympathy. See *The Idea of History*, 205–282.

his failure to lie to save Milly. Densher's refusal to craft a salvational fiction may be his greatest evasion. He can only accept Maud's fictions for his own comfort following Milly's death (366). His final self-image is fearfully contained. He envisions himself "as from the page of a book . . . a young man . . . hushed, passive, staying his breath" (369). Given his preference for "passive" self-images in fiction, it seems inevitable that Densher resist the final act of the novel's script: opening Milly's letter.[12]

The closing image of Densher worshipping Milly reveals a "haunted," "harmless" man, in love with memory itself. The novel's characters exhibit various attitudes toward time and various apprehensions of their abilities to reshape their experiences. But the privileged characters seem implicitly aware of their complicity in the history set in motion by the plots they construct. This raises questions about the narrator's view of his complicity in the novel's larger plot, which is the subject of the next section.

The Narrative Evasions

In a letter to his brother on *The Wings of the Dove*, William James commented on the work's overturning of "every traditional canon of story-telling (especially the fundamental one of *telling* the story)."[13] The novel's striking tendency to diverge from the expected evolution of its plot bears further examination, as does its overall process of narration.[14] This section will consider the prominent features of the narrative: the varying treatments of charac-

---

[12] I view Densher's final refusal as an evasion, consistent with a history of suspended action, that is undermined by the novel's ethics of complicity. But see Allon White's interesting counter-analysis in *The Uses of Obscurity* (London: Routledge and Kegan Paul, 1981). White holds to the essential valor of Densher's renunciation. See 21–22 and passim.

[13] Quoted in F. O. Matthiessen, *The James Family* (New York: Vintage, 1980), 338.

[14] One of the few careful treatments of the narrative consciousness of *Wings* is Leo Bersani's "The Narrator as Center in *The Wings of the Dove*," *Modern Fiction*

ters, in particular the timid treatment of Kate, which contrasts
with an almost condescending familiarity toward Milly; and the
avoidance of the plot, which seems both to complement and to violate the evasions of the characters. The latter point will lead us to
speculate upon the complicities of reading, which are explored in
the next section.

The narrative reticence evident from the novel's beginning is
typical of James's late style.[15] If any ambition can be attributed to
the narrative consciousness, it is the achievement of clarity and
precision. Every vulgar particular in Lionel Croy's sitting room—
the "shabby sofa" with its "glazed cloth," the "sallow prints," the
"white centre-piece wanting in freshness" (21)—contributes to the
air of irritability that builds in the waiting Kate. The room itself
seems in attendance, its only "office" to hope for better days. The
narrator is meticulous in specifying the various perceptions. The
feel of the sofa—"slippery" and "sticky"—is Kate's, for "she had
tried it." Kate's sight of the street is placed precisely as "this view"
from the balcony (21). Almost afraid, it seems, of appearing intrusive, except to offer an essential detail here and there, the narrative
voice defers to Kate's consciousness.

Yet the narrator's apparent detachment does not lessen the fact

---

Studies 6 (Summer 1960): 131–44. Bersani's conclusions differ from mine. "The important point for James," he writes, "is that his characters' plasticity and passivity
make possible an extensive appreciation of Milly" (141). Yet the novel finally belies
the possibility of detached appreciation, and indicts an aestheticism that denies social entanglements. To remain detached is a failure of social responsibility. A parallel indictment of Densher's brand of aestheticism occurs in Bertolucci's film *1900*,
when the upper-class bride on the white horse cavorts with the lower-class laborer,
while the facists are bashing a boy's brains out. Their alluring romance of differences ignores the evil taking place below the romantic haze. Nor does the outraged
departure of the wealthy uncle at the scene's end offer a satisfactory response to the
atrocities.

[15] As Seymour Chatman observes of James's late manner, "There was a great
and increasing concern to insure that the descriptions of inner mental states were
by the character himself, as part of the illusion of central consciousness, rather than
by some intrusive narrator." *The Later Style of Henry James* (Oxford: Basil Blackwell,
1972), 41.

that Kate is as held by his terms as she is by her family. This is evident in the opening sentence, which typographically hems her in: "She waited, Kate Croy, for her father to come in. . . ." Bound by phrases on either side, Kate appears trapped in the sentence of which she is the subject. Seymour Chatman has suggested that such "grammatical submergences of character" tend to make them "recipients rather than actors" in the novel's events. Significantly, this is a rare moment for Kate, who more fully meets and constructs the events of her novel than many main characters in James's works.[16] Yet the novel's opening with Kate's grammatical submergence, a constraint that is consistent with her prison of consanguinity, confirms her need to gain control over her past and suggests that this control will involve a facility for narrative manipulations.

In establishing Kate's motivations, the narrative also reveals its own. There will be a concern for the embeddedness of human actors in familial and social affairs, and for the ways in which confronting or denying complicity effect the reconstruction of historical events. Just as the demands of Kate's relations are mirrored in her entrapment by the novel's language, so too are the characters' social complicities reflected in their embedment in one another's tales. And Kate's ambivalence toward her familial connections can be seen to parallel the narrator's ambivalence toward his tale. Representing the impulse to flee past entanglements while exposing the inextricability of those connections, the opening of the novel presages its foremost tension.

The narrator of *Wings* is far from the anxiety-ridden consciousness of *The Bostonians*, who seems more vividly at work orchestrating his novel's events; but there are notable similarities. For example, *Wings*'s often refers to a conspiracy of knowledge between

---

[16] Chatman, *Later Style*, 35–36. While a thorough examination of the issue is beyond the aims of this study, I would argue that where a character like Lambert Strether is linguistically "more domain than performer," Kate is much more actively rendered. An interesting study could be made of the varying degrees of "grammatical submergence" among the characters of *Wings*.

himself and the reader. More marked than the mere frequency of such allusions in *Wings* is the *pattern* of their frequency. Narrative intrusions, like "we have hinted, that our young lady . . ." (37), increase considerably in passages featuring Milly and Susan. Most often these self-reflexive observations function proleptically. The increase in such anticipations for Milly and Susan may be because this pair inhabits the territory of the self-conscious symbolic, a region of constantly anticipated and discovered meanings. Both are obsessed with destiny, acting in the name of some future design now only dimly perceived.

The proleptic note of their characterization is the designation of a given event as the "first" time, the initial instance of a continuing impression. Milly's sense of Lord Mark's intrusive prescience, for example, is "from this first of their meetings . . . what was most to abide" (103). Or, in another example, a "sense of quantities . . . was really, no doubt, what most prevailed at first for our slightly gasping American pair" (109). The overall effect of these references is to assert the primacy of the narrator's historical sense. What is an innocent beginning for the characters is a known past for the narrator. As was true of *The Bostonians*, such "insignificant seeds" distinguish the narrator's historical consciousness from characters and readers by pointing to what may only be "recognized . . . retrospectively," and also heighten the reader's sense of the past.[17]

Significantly, these observations usually accompany some gesture of appropriation. In their historical innocence, Milly and Susan become "our slightly gasping American pair." Or, "this proved sensibility of the lady of Lancaster Gate performed verily for both our friends during those first few days the office of a fine floating gold-dust" (110). Referring familiarly to "our young woman" while insinuating a future that he alone knows, the narrator seems condescending toward these characters. Susan, and

[17] See Gerard Genette, *Narrative Discourse*, trans. Jane E. Lewin (Ithaca: Cornell University Press, 1980), 76–77, especially chs. 1 and 2.

213

especially Milly, are the narrator and readers' trophies—"our young lady," "our friends," or "American friends" (122, 123, 132, 158, 168, 178, etc.). This approach would not seem significant were it not comparatively infrequent with Kate (37) and Densher (325, 352). It is as if Milly's symbolic resonance, seen in Susan's Madison Avenue style of introduction and in Milly's embracing of tags and characterizations, makes her more amenable to the narrator's objectification of her. The narrator, like all of the others, can type her as he wills. Her destiny fixed from the start, this ill-fated princess, "perched" on the edge of the Swiss mountains, is safe ground to the narrator and reader, who know that she will *never* have "all" the earth's kingdoms (87–88).

The narrator's cavalier treatment of Milly contrasts markedly with the deference paid Kate Croy, who seems to rival the narrator's authority. This distinction is exemplified by their portrayed relations to narrative. Milly is the simple American girl, who "in default of stouter stuff" must work her notion of England into a "light literary legend" (123). Entertaining "amusements of thought that were like the secrecies of a little girl playing with dolls when conventionally 'too big' " (132), Milly's aesthetic is innocent and undeveloped. In describing one of Milly's treacherous evenings with Kate, the narrator observes, "It might have been a lesson, for our young American . . . a lesson so various and so sustained that the pupil had, as we have shown, but receptively to gape" (168). If Milly is the star pupil, Kate is the classroom teacher, and the narrator's timidity toward Kate may be seen as fear of her authority. In contrast to the other characters, whose thoughts and motivations are frequently considered, Kate, with the exception of the opening sequence, is left to her own plottings.[18]

Like an earlier Jamesian figure, Madame Merle, to whom she is sometimes compared, Kate projects an air of privacy that prohibits

---

[18] Christof Wegelin's claim that "we never get inside Kate Croy" (521), though a striking oversight of the novel's opening, notes the narrator's marked *evasion* of Kate. *The Image of Europe in Henry James* (Dallas: Southern Methodist University Press, 1958), 106–109, 112–15, 117–21.

the narrator's familiarity. Neither Madame Merle nor Kate is presented to the reader with the assurance that informs portraits of Isabel Archer and Milly. Madame Merle first appears with her back turned, symbolizing her resistance to narrative revelations, in contrast with Isabel's innocent expressiveness.[19]

Though Milly is beyond Isabel's innocence, she is similarly appropriated by narrators and readers who presume to know her all too well. As Kate realizes, Milly is not so easily appraised and captured. Yet the narrator's perspective seems to deny her the respect of distance, and the power to mystify.

As the character who weaves plots, Kate exposes a truth that many would prefer to deny, that the word "plot" has connotations that are not altogether innocent.[20] The scenes that picture Kate and Densher guiltily stealing moments together are also, not coincidentally, their moments of plot construction. Two of these scenes particularly evoke the incriminating nature of narrative.

The first is at Aunt Maud's, following the dinner party Milly has missed. Seated together alone in the living room, Kate and Densher are for the moment secure that their openness actually "put[s] Aunt Maud off the scent" (211). Still, they know the "risks," and throughout their colloquy on Milly's past and future they "watch . . . the windows" (212), fearful that suspicions may be aroused. Twice they are interrupted, first by the arrival of Lord Mark, and last by Aunt Maud's emergence, which compels Densher to catch "his word as it drop[s] from him" (221).

A later instance of their guilty plotting is the scene at St. Mark's Square where Kate and Densher talk while Maud and Susan shop for lace. Here too, they watch like guilt-ridden conspirators to ensure that "their prospect was clear" (288). Yet now their fear has become internalized, just as their conversation itself focuses more

[19] James, *The Portrait of a Lady* (New York: Penguin, 1979), 171–72.
[20] The *OED* offers a definition of "plot" as "to plan, contrive or devise (something to be carried out or accomplished; to lay plans for. Now always in evil sense)" (2210, vol. 2). Peter Brooks includes the evil connotation in his array of definitions of the term; see *Reading for the Plot* (New York: Knopf, 1984), 11–12.

on their own past dissemblances than on Milly herself. Though these moments are singularly protected "with solitude and security" (290), their fear has become an entrapment over which they preside. Without a sign from the occupied pair in the lace shop, Kate suddenly asks the time, fearfully disrupting her inquiries into Densher's feelings for Milly. Though Densher points out that they've "taken but thirteen minutes," Kate insists on their return (288). Thus, the censorship they have all along externalized becomes the coda of their own intimacy. The novel's ending carries through this aura of mutual incrimination, as Kate and Densher supply their own trial and jury.

Densher and the narrator share an important similarity in their relations to guilty plots. Both are beneficiaries of Kate's plotting, which allows Densher access to Kate and to Milly's love, and the narrator to the novel's plot itself. And both seem to desire disengagement from Kate's narrative actions. This brings us to another major aspect of the novel's narrative: the question of how the story is, or in William James's view is not, told. The narrative at times appears to depart strikingly from the expected unfolding of its plot, a tendency that accords with the evasions and suppressions of the characters themselves. Kate, for example, has no desire to know the details of Lionel Croy's evil deed (56–57). And Milly's initiation into the novel's English society involves her growing sense of the need to conceal her own awarenesses and knowledge (142–51). Kate and Densher deceive Aunt Maud, only to find her a willing accomplice to their deceptions (200).

Given the characters' intentional mystifications, which are made possible by the consent of the mystified, a narrative structure that is itself replete with elisions and omissions becomes more suggestive.[21] The questions raised by the structural properties of a

---

[21] Sister Stephanie Vincec contends that James failed to re-read the entire novel before sending it off for final publication in *The New York Edition*, and terms the evasive plot structure of Volume 2 a compositional flaw. James's aim "to project a single, coherent picture," she argues, was disrupted by domestic complications, which distracted him from rigorously editing his novel. While James undoubtedly

work are usually more profitably conceived in terms of their relation to its achieved meanings than as tests of authorial competence. How do structural properties corroborate, disrupt, or even violate our understanding of a work's major concerns?

In the example of *Wings*, an evasive plot structure serves to elaborate issues central to the novel, including the obligations incurred by the act of narration, individuals' roles in historical events, and their inevitable complicities in the affairs of society. The method of narration can be seen as another link in the chain of concealments set in play by the characters. Thus, the relationship between the narrator and readers parallels that between various characters. I would suggest that the reader acts as an accomplice to the narrator's suppressions just as the characters aid one anothers' dissemblances. The narrative suppressions provide readers with what they desire: relief from the painful burden of knowledge. Yet readers also miss the omitted scenes, and may imagine them themselves. These omissions can therefore be seen to beckon readers into participation in the making of the novel's plot.

Volume I seems to develop as expected, introducing each of the main characters. Any evasions or omissions in the plot here appear as strategies of the characters themselves. It is only when we learn of details that Kate is withholding from Milly—the looming question of her relations with Densher—that the narrative itself begins to appear clipped and digressive. Book 4, for example, closes with Milly's mysterious reluctance to question Marian about Kate's relations with Densher. Her admission begs for illumination, but the narrative ends abruptly. Book 5 opens on Lord Mark's complaint that he has missed Milly and Susan far too many times in visits to their rooms (129), which is followed by Milly's conviction of the need for suppression, an observation itself deferred, not

---

held to some principle of organicism, it was far from "single coheren[ce]." Time and again, James's fictions challenge quests for monolithic truths. " 'Poor Flopping Wings': The Making of Henry James's *The Wings of the Dove*," *Harvard Library Bulletin* 24 (1976): 60–93.

"fully present . . . till later on," since she is distracted by Lord Mark (135). Next we see Milly before the elusive Sir Luke Strett, who has "but ten minutes to give" (142), followed by Milly's evasive prowl through the London parks. Embracing the whole of English life, Milly avoids the difficult confrontation with her intimates. The next section begins with Milly's evasion of Kate's questions about her illness. The last two books picture Milly's intuition of a relation Kate has suppressed (166), and Milly's trip to the National Gallery (177), which replaces one of the first scenes in the novel which the reader finds himself missing. The point of this brief catalog is to suggest the manner in which the narrative registers a central interest in and propensity for evasion prior to its major omissions in Volume 2.

Thus, the first time the narrative omits a dramatically significant scene is at the end of volume 1, where instead of rendering Luke Strett's meeting with Susan Stringham, it offers Milly's simultaneous visit to the National Gallery. Nor is the meeting portrayed in the chapter immediately following. Rather, it is withheld until the beginning of Book 7, sixty-six pages later, where Sir Luke's pronouncement is conveyed through the tactfully veiled discourse of Milly and Susan, but the precise details are never disclosed. Narrative omission and mystification are the keynotes of Milly's illness, underwriting her own desire for concealment. Thus, at the beginning of Book 6, where we might expect the scene, we have the history of Kate and Densher's reunion.

Indeed, Milly disappears until the beginning of Book 7. But her absence serves to heighten her dramatic role, as she dominates the common consciousness. Subtle changes in Kate and Densher's relationship record her effect. Densher notes that Kate has underplayed her intimacy with Milly, "hadn't wholly prepared him" for the situation he finds (191). And Densher is characterized as so consumed with the figure of Milly that one of his walks replicates Milly's "restless ramble" of the day before, to the detail of "troubled fancies" folding "their wings" dove-style around him (192).

218

Book 8 extends the evasiveness of Books 6 and 7 in retreating from Lord Mark's visit with Milly to an account of Densher's entrance upon the Venetian scene. We hear nothing about Lord Mark's call until Densher offhandedly questions his motivations in conversation with Kate one book later. Not until much later is Lord Mark's visit strongly, indeed alarmingly, recalled (327).

One of the most striking instances of plot disruptions in this book is when Kate and Densher's conversation in St. Mark's Square is interrupted midway by a history of "this colloquy" (288), which continues for two pages. The narrative steps backward in time to detail the affairs of Venice at this hour, and the chain of cause and effect that has led to Kate and Densher's free moments together. This backtracking midway through their heated dialogue, which concerns their refinement of their plot as well as setting of a trysting date, serves at once to defuse and to heighten the tension building between them. The disruption corroborates Kate's own censorship of their dialogue, her insistence that she and Densher "must go toward" Maud and Susan (288). Book 9 begins with the explicit omission of Kate and Densher's lovemaking scene. Instead, the reader is left with the reified language of Densher to fuel whatever imaginative vision he might conjure on his own. And Book 10 likewise disappoints, by omitting Densher's final meeting with Milly, who is banished entirely, though much discussed, through the remainder of the novel.

All of these evasions and wrenchings of sequence in the narrative of Volume 2, are more pronounced forms of features and concerns already in place in Volume 1. Like the characters he describes, the narrator pursues, then pulls away from the revelation of a plot that at times feels too treacherous to confront. These patterns suggest that the narrator does fear his plot, that he feels accountable for having in some sense helped to kill Milly. The issue of narrative guilt can also be framed in slightly different terms. Perhaps the narrator's resistance to his plot suggests a guilt over using Milly's life as grist for his fictional mill, "turning the affair into a ballad."[22] One might detect a Coverdalean strain in the narrative of *Wings*. Though this narrator is hardly so fully characterized, a set of narrative strategies can be identified that points to the process of narration as a guilt-ridden activity. Both narrators withhold details and scenes crucial to their characters' stories, in part to control the reader by quickening and lessening the dramatic action, but also from fear of the knowledge contained in their narratives.

The foiling of efforts to propel the narrative forward, which includes the omissions of key scenes, relates significantly to the novel's major subject—the passion and guilt generated by the making of plots. The narrator's refusal to confront Milly's illness directly is also a denial of his own incrimination. By never naming the details of Milly's circumstances, which retain their mystery to the end, the narrator remains detached from incriminating knowledge. The reader must gain knowledge through innuendo and imagination, and it is always possible that his interpretation is erroneous. Thus the narrative evasions force the reader to imagine key scenes, which makes the novel in part a reflection of the reader. Any reader's envisionment of the treacheries *apparently* taking place exposes his own capacity for evil.

This last point brings us to the subject of section three, the politics of storytelling. In *The Wings of the Dove*, plots represent quests for power, and whether tellers or readers, those who participate in their unfolding are implicated in the evil they effect. And the reality of ending, because it presages our own deaths, also implicates us all. The extent to which the novel becomes, as it nears ending, a lyrical meditation on the powers of time and death reveals a certain complicity between the narrator and these forces. But there is a more immediate and incriminating reality that the narrator does not appear willing to confront—treacheries of contemporary history and its reconstruction.

[22] This observation by Hawtorne's Zenobia of *The Blithedale Romance* (1852) refers to a habit of the novel's narrator, Miles Coverdale.

The Politics of Storytelling

As we have seen, the novel's narrator and characters, especially Densher, evade their complicity in the creation of plots that are seen to possess the power to kill. In revealing the details of Kate and Densher's designs, Lord Mark kills Milly. His "dreadful visit" is judged by Susan to have "done it," imparted the knowledge that results in Milly "turn[ing] her face to the wall" (339, 333). Consistently characters seek immunity from the construction of plots, a desire motivated by the common awareness of their injurious effects. But desires for "purity," typified by Densher's conviction that in passing the buck of disclosure to Lord Mark he is "washed . . . clean" (329), are repeatedly thwarted. One of the ways in which the novel exposes the interconnectedness of those who deal and die in its world is through its doublings and substitutions of characters. Often characters replicate one anothers' gestures or movements, or invert their actions. Such mirroring, which is sometimes apparent to the characters and narrator, but usually only to the discerning reader, demonstrates that no self is original or separate, and that the nefarious actions of one reflects the guilt of all.

The novel is built on a pattern of doublings and echoes. The earliest example of character doubling is the parallel between "Lionel" Croy and "the lioness," Aunt Maud—a pair of predatory beasts contesting for possession of Kate. Their wrangle ironically reveals their contiguity of interest: two lions, even when locked in head-to-head combat, have more to say to one another than to the kid (35). In a similarly reflective fashion, Densher recalls Kate's father seeming more "real" than his detractors (23–24), in making the mind "real" to her (47). And Kate associates the power of "make believe" with both (26, 56). By subverting common notions of reality, Lionel and Densher undermine the worth of being "believed." The fatalistic note of Lionel Croy's evil deed, with its air of "natural[ness]," resembles Kate and Densher's encounter on the Underground, just as Densher's view of Aunt Maud "build-

221

ing" on Kate recalls her father's terms (72, 32). Most strikingly, Densher's attendance on Aunt Maud during his first visit repeats Kate's irritable waiting in the opening scene (61–64). Like Kate, he moves restlessly through his resentment, scrutinizing ornaments and furnishings. But Maud's greater diplomacy results in the forging of an alliance between them, far from the rancor and misery between Kate and her father. Empowered to take others as she will, Maud can tell Densher that he is not for her niece, but can have him nevertheless in friendship. A visit that initially appears to Densher a valuable source for an article in fact yields "but a small amount of copy" (63). Hardly grist for anyone else's literary mill, Maud engulfs others in her own. Thus, this repetition with a difference also contrasts with Kate's visit to her father in that the earlier encounter serves to ignite all of her creative, plotting energies.

One of the most pervasive of the novel's doubling motifs is the paralleling of Kate and Milly's gestures and actions, a subtle but arresting set of images. Following their final dinner in the Swiss mountains, Susan sits while Milly revolves, her movements serving "as an inscrutable comment on *her* notion of freedom" (96). Three pages later, an identical fund of uncontrollable energy is associated with Kate, whose "incalculable movements" are viewed as "interfer[ing]" with attempts to see her (99). Though Milly and Kate's "differen[ce]" is stressed, the intensity of their relation itself incites the necessity of differentiation (101). And the idea of difference is itself a point of contiguity, since both define themselves as unique, and each is so regarded by the other. Their guardians corroborate this sense of their rarity (112), which accompanies the growing sense of complicity in their shared silences and suppressions. At Maud's dinner, Kate looks over at Milly in the company of Lord Mark, and "know[s]" his "effect on her." And Kate's knowledge is seen as "duplicating, as intensifying by a mutual intelligence" (105).

When consciously employed, doublings or substitutions serve as social weapons. Lionel Croy, for example, betrays a knack for inversion that makes his own sordid circumstances appear Kate's (24). And one of Milly's chief insights into this treacherous London world is the utility of such actions: the essential skill of having another "pick up the slack," or of "turning the tables on someone." Milly's view of the frantic banquet bustle where "plates were changed and dishes presented and periods in the banquet marked . . . while appearances insisted and phenomena multiplied and words reached her from here and there" (105), signifies her education in the surreptitious exchange of London social life. One must be quick to note altered alliances, alert to any compromise of one's position, adept at juggling and balancing others. Milly's sleight-of-hand substitution of Kate for herself as an object for Lord Mark's dissection demonstrates her developing awareness (107).

Milly also substitutes Densher for herself in the striking scene at the National Gallery, where she concludes for her own self-protection that the American women are exclaiming over him (176–77). Densher later notes Milly's powers of inversion, observing that "the case had turned round; he had made his visit to be sorry for her, but he would repeat it . . . in order that she might by sorry for him" (227). He takes her power to himself a moment later, "turn[ing] the tables" in their conversation (229), to establish an ease that is under his control.

Yet other moments of unconscious doubling reveal the characters' lack of control over these shifts and reversals. Lionel Croy's dishonor, the pain of an unsavory past that has to be for Kate "the great thing in one's life" (57), duplicates the idea of Milly's wealth, which "had to be *the* thing you were" (86). Both appear fixed in circumstances that would rule their lives had they less vision and energy. In the scene at Milly's rooms, where they spend the evening alone together, Kate plays the "restless and charming" Milly, "repeatedly quitting her place," moving "to and fro," to Milly's seated and admiring Susan (96, 167). Kate, held by Aunt Maud's proprietary glance, prepares for Milly's alternate possession by the various beasts of prey in the following scene (204–205). And though Kate feels herself immune to Milly's condition, convinced of her desire never "to change places" (114) with her, the desolate winter of Milly's death brings on the death of Kate's love.

Ultimately, only the unconscious doublings remain volatile, reminding readers of the interconnections and ensnarements that foretell their own complicity in the novel's events. The pattern of complicity that envelops the characters implicates the readers as well. Reading becomes an act of responsibility; to read involves a puzzling together that is close to the creative act of fiction making and also akin to the work of the historian. By bringing distinctive predispositions to their reading, readers alter texts in ways that are unique to them.

This is suggested in the novel's own featuring of different kinds of tellers and readers. Kate is the strong storyteller, offering designs so formidable that they threaten the narrator, who treats her more diffidently than any of the other characters. Lord Mark is a weak storyteller. The story he tells, though it is seen to eventuate in Milly's death, is derivative, a pale offshoot of Kate's design, whose sole motivating force seems vindictiveness. Milly represents the category of strong reader. Incapable of Kate's original storytelling energies, she nevertheless possesses the sensibility and perceptiveness to read deeply into the signs of her world. Reading for protection as well as for an expansion of consciousness, she derives greater self-knowledge. For Milly, reading is never a detached act, but implicates her whole being. Densher, in contrast, is a weak reader, who assumes that it is possible to be disengaged from one's experience of plots.

One of the most pronounced examples of the relationship of storyteller and reader in *Wings* is the series of dialogues between Densher and Kate. All the essential components of the relationship are present: one narrates, the other questions; one appears knowing, the other is repeatedly enlightened. Cast in a question-and-answer mode, with Densher asking and Kate supplying the details of the plan, their dialogues are in fact mutual constructions, scenes of linguistic exploration and discovery for both. The "game" they acknowledge playing with Aunt Maud (198) extends to their own conversations. Though it has usually been supposed that Kate leads Densher to a plan that is solely the product of her imperial imagination, close study of their dialogues suggests that they together define and refine a plan of action toward Milly. Densher's repeated requests that Kate spell things out for him lead her to solidify what has been vague in her own mind. Though he appears passive and yielding, his questions play an essential role in the act of design. In the first recounted dialogue following Densher's return to London, Kate lacks a clear idea or projected design, formulating a plan through give-and-take with Densher.

"[Densher] wondered. 'Prevent her loving us?' 'Prevent her helping you. She's *like* that,' Kate Croy explained. It took indeed some understanding. 'Making nothing of the fact that I love another?' 'Making everything' said Kate, 'To console you.' 'But for what?' 'For not getting your other' " (199). But a few minutes later Densher is still at sea. "Still," the narrator observes, "he didn't take it." And this leads to Kate's solidification of the point. "She threw out at last her own real light" (200). Densher's density forces Kate to articulate the details of their plan. But this refraining from pronouncements is a strategy for denying his complicity, which becomes evident at the dialogue's close. Marvelling at their excessive talk and Kate's increasing impatience, Densher muses, "It was he who was stupid—the proof of which was that he would do what she liked" (202). Densher's testimony of stupidity serves to absolve him of any intentional role in the scheme. Viewing his actions as mere acquiescence, he can deny complicity in their plan. But his consistent efforts to burden Kate with the act of assertion suggest, paradoxically, that Densher sees more than he would admit.

In a novel where narrating is a deed of the strongest kind, even aligned with the power to kill, Densher's repeated evasion of pronouncements is telling. His reluctance to testify or disclose seems almost a sinister kind of prescience. He struggles, "If our friend knows that all the while—?" a spasmodic halt that Kate must complete, coming "straight to his aid, formulating for him his anxiety"

(220). As the novel progresses, and Densher's lights into their design become more and more difficult to conceal, the tactical nature of his dimness becomes increasingly evident.

In the scene that follows, Densher's reluctance to take even the smallest step toward Milly indicates his fearful ensnarement. The choice of whether to accompany her on a drive is a moral dilemma. "He had been waiting for some moments, which probably seemed to him longer than they were; this was because he was anxiously watching himself wait. He couldn't keep that up forever; and since one thing or the other was what he must do, it was for the other that he presently became conscious of having decided" (234). Action has always been suspect to Densher, but his growing awareness of the impossibility of his detached perch makes him fear *any* action.

Brought to see his participation in the world of action and consequence, Densher responds fearfully, attempting to saddle Kate with responsibility for all action. "It was all doing what Kate had conceived for him; it wasn't in the least doing . . . anything he himself had conceived" (280). Over and over like a litany, Densher affirms his lack of will. "He hadn't really 'begun' anything," he contemplates at one point, "had only submitted, consented" (285). Even his effort to force Kate to his rooms seems a self-protective denial—contrived outrage at having exercised no will in their plan. His repeated allusions to her preeminent authority—"She was really fine" (201), or "he was to read into [Kate's] speech a kind of heroic ring" (309)—seem designed to support his own lack of volition. By inflating her strength and courage, and rendering her indomitable, Densher is able to invest Kate with sole responsibility for their plan.

But Densher's consciousness of his culpability is brought out in private ruminations, his gratitude, for instance, that "there was no male witness" to the chain of events (299). Though he admits merely to a desire not to have appeared "asinine" before this imaginary male figure, the term "witness" implies that he has in fact *done* something he would prefer to conceal. Densher is well aware of his conspiracy of ignorance. As he concedes at one point while meditating on his "sacrifice to knowledge" and the "truth he hadn't been ready to receive," "[Kate] had mystified him enough, heaven knew, but that was *rather by his own generosity than by hers*" (309, emphasis added).

The major contrast between Kate and Densher is that the process of narration brings her to sympathy for others, and confrontation with herself, while he avoids both. And Kate comes to see the insidiousness of Densher's passivity. Her growing awareness of Densher's conspiracy impels her insistence that he admit responsibility for his insights. When she discovers him at Milly's, his response is protective: he is there "at [her] so lively instigation." Yet this time Kate challenges him, first in refusing to restate their plan as she says, "Oh you know!" or "I've told you that!" Later she asserts, "You're free . . . act as you think best," departing with, "Say that, you know, from yourself" (236–38).

Still, Densher pursues the "transcendent motions" that make "the pressure lighten" (316), a desire consistent with the novel's end, where he declares his freedom from history. Densher's renunciation of historical constraints, like his willed detachment from narrative, is an effort to disavow the complicity of all the novel's characters. For Lord Mark's "gouged out" tale is a collective burden, a vessel of duplicities and deceptions filled by everyone.

The most far-reaching implication of Densher's characterization as reader is its parallel to a type of reader external to the text, who remains unchallenged and unchanged by its most perilous messages. The apparent tale of "American innocence," a monolithic history of the death of a beautiful woman, with a cathartic moral on the eternal powers of nature, is in fact a story of "English perils," a convoluted, guilt-invoking narrative of treachery. Ultimately, everyone—characters, narrator, author, and readers—shares the guilt over what happens to Milly.[23]

[23] Densher, with his "transcendent motions," can be seen as Georges Poulet's

CHAPTER FIVE

Yet this raises another crucial aspect of the novel's portrayal of storytelling: Milly's death is not the inevitable and natural event it is consistently perceived to be. Rather than a condition fixed from the novel's beginning like Hester Prynne's adultery, Milly's death can be seen as brought about through the treacherous dealings of the novel's many plotters. Milly's is a death by language, effected through the unfolding of story, indeed, by the very *need* for story. Milly's death seems to result from two circumstances: her personal guilt over a veiled past that precludes her right to live is exploited by her society's need for a victim to appease the communal appetite for meaningful stories.

Thus, the novel opens out into an examination of the storytelling process: what impulses account for its necessity, and what sacrifices are required by the demand for experience's illumination or heightening that appear its *raison d'être*. Repeated references to the characters as readers and texts (55, 191, 211, 220, 306, 366–67, 369) exemplify the novel's attention to its own task of fiction making. "[Susan] would like—Milly had had it from her—to put Kate Croy in a book and see what she could so do with her. 'Chop me up fine or serve me whole'—it was a way of being got at that Kate professed she dreaded" (211). Susan's perspective on Kate is consistent with the novel's overall view of her plotting capacities. Kate is a mine for the storyteller, a character with the dramatic force to activate many books. Kate's sense of her violation by Susan's literary scheme serves ironic commentary on Kate's role as the instigator of plots and Kate's use of Milly for her imaginative plan.

The novel features layers of plots, and various uses of human subjects for fictional designs. Other characters also exhibit some consciousness of the trap of being situated in someone else's plot. They betray, as Kate does here, an awareness of the dangerous

---

ideal reader, for whom reading provides a "transcendence of mind," revealing the subject "to itself . . . in its transcendence over all which is reflected in it." A "pure" activity, reading involves a movement of consciousness, a moment of sheer "being." See *The Metamorphoses of the Circle*, trans. Carley Dawson and Elliott Coleman (Baltimore: Johns Hopkins University Press, 1966), 311.

power of narrative schemes. Milly accepts the dove label because she can make it serve her own ends. Likewise, in Lord Mark's first visit to the Palazzo Leporelli, Milly struggles against his version of their shared history. Milly must subvert or refuse others' terms in order to survive. The characters' heightened awareness of the power of narrative helps to dissolve the barriers between the novel and its reading audience, inciting readers to recognize the ways in which they too are empowered or compromised by narrative processes.

As previously discussed, the reader is beckoned into creative engagement with the novel through its omission of key scenes. Kate's comment to Densher, "If you want things named you must name them," can be taken as a warning to readers (308). This novel will not deliver up its dramas on silver trays, nor tie them into discrete bundles of truth. Any reader desiring a well-paved plot with a readily accessible meaning had better look elsewhere. In *Wings of the Dove*, every reader must imaginatively access the drama and meaning for himself: its only truth is the relativity of meaning in all meaningful tales. Placing great technical demands upon readers, the novel's evasive style ultimately insists upon their political responsibilities as well.[24]

Most interpretations that discover come monolithic moral place Milly Theale at the novel's center as the reservoir of innocence and eternal truth, her figurative death "wash[es] clean" all who have participated in the entangling and muddled drama, which overall

[24] One of the first to discuss the effects of Jamesian obscurity was Vernon Lee. Observing that James's works possess their own screening process, she argued that their difficulty demanded subtle and attentive readers, capable of benefiting from an accumulative process of illumination, and of piecing things together on their own. *The Handling of Words* (London: John Lane, 1923), 241–51. The issue is also taken up by Seymour Chatman, *The Later Style*, and Allon White, *Uses of Obscurity*. White observes that James "associates . . . the idea of obscurity of information with purity . . . ; overt representation becomes a source of moral danger, and it is only by staying as far outside communication as possible, by remaining outside the letter, that one might get off" (21–22). Yet it is precisely the point of *Wings* that no one "get[s] off." If Milly teaches us anything, it is that no one remains unimplicated by society's treacheries.

belies the idea of singular meaning.[25] The hope of innocent storytelling originates in the preface, where James expresses his reluctance to embrace the treacherous demands of his impending
task. There is a similarity between James's drama here and Kate
Croy's vacillations in the novel's opening scene.

James begins with the difficulty of his prospective task: "Long
had I turned it over, standing off from it, yet coming back to it;
convinced of what might be done with it, yet seeing the theme as
formidable" (3). Every retreat confirms his conviction of the need
to confront his subject; each desire to defer or flee establishes further the necessity of taking his task in hand. A similar dynamic
prevails for novelist and character: action is essential but subtlety
is key, and one must have a constant sense of "the attaching wonderments" (3). Both face the demands of design and interpretation,
and both hope to fashion the truest possible script from the available materials. Yet they are reluctant: James perches on the periphery of his *donnée*, just as Kate perches on the margins of her
father's life demanding to be let in, while wondering at her own
demand.

The most revealing metaphor for James's ambivalence toward
his novel involves the "parent" watching "the child perched for its
first riding lesson in the saddle." This mixture of anxiety and detachment persists in the historical record that follows, where
James remembers his experience of writing in terms of a passenger
on a train (7). In a similar vein, James celebrates the lack of "conditions" upon his novel, declaring the good fortune of its rejection
for serial publication (8). The author's happy disengagement from
his work is repeated in its freedom from compromising monetary
constraints.

Yet material concerns reemerge with a vengeance in the language of the preface's final paragraph. A certain direct appeal contains a special "value," incurring a decided "expense," which must

[25] For a reading of Milly as the symbol of the arbitrary signifier, see John Carlos
Rowe, *Henry Adams and Henry James* (Ithaca: Cornell University Press, 1976), 191–
92, 196.

be held to "account" and "re-economised" at some later point (15). Apparently, James's work cannot escape the economic terms that pervade any artistic production. Before we conclude, however, that we have caught "the master" in the act of denying his vulnerability to social and economic pressures, we should remind ourselves that the novel is about the cash requirements of English life. The inescapability of financial arrangements is hardly an unacknowledged register for James the novelist.

The preface in fact discloses the novelist's conviction of the limiting exigencies of his craft. The business of novel production demands attention to "momentary" as well as "permanent" conditions (8). James in part laments such necessities: the writer needs space to expand his work's imaginative possibilities, he must be free of arbitrary monthly prescriptions. This plea is interestingly related to James's justification for his work's "merciful indirection[s]" (16). The distinction between the "permanent" and the "momentary" in novel writing parallels the distinction between narrative deviation and confrontation. The hope that the novel can exist in a timeless realm, disassociated from any historical constraints (like earning a living), is like the freedom to unfold one's plot by "a merciful indirection," unobligated to spell things out for any purpose, commercial or otherwise.

Significantly, such a privilege is associated with the figure of Milly Theale, the "unspotted princess." Inhabiting a world in which treacheries abound, "the pressure all around" can nevertheless be "kept easy for her" (16). To the novelist, for whom making a living is neither a small nor a dismissible pursuit, the only alternative is declarative—to assert his work's freedom from compromising conditions. These assertions made, the author still knows their essential fabrication, a knowledge that exposes. And just as James knows, so does Milly. Though seen as one whose path is set by the eternal workings of destiny, a character fundamentally disengaged from the demands of "momentary" historical conditions, Milly herself knows the cost of that symbolization. This may illuminate the preface's cryptic closure: the "painter's" confession

231

that he has failed to bring his subject fully to light. What remains veiled is the self-conscious measure Milly takes of her own tragic destiny. For those who, for the sake of a better story, wish to retain James's ostensible directives, the veil may be preferable. And most critics have held to James's impossible ideal of a character immune to the direct implications of the novel's plot.

A look at some exemplary views of the novel reveal the extent to which Milly has served as the critics' savior, absolving all of the plot's most costly social and political implications. For F. O. Matthiessen, Milly's circumstance provides "the greatest possible subject for poetry, the death of a beautiful woman . . . representative of a phase in our history when . . . the heiress of all the ages, was the sign by which cultivated Europe knew us."[26] As a statuesque symbol of America and an eternal inspiration for great poetry, Milly is seen as suitable to any literary enterprise: a "find," readily extracted from the novel's context. She can exemplify either the quintessential subject or the representative image of America, through a wresting operation not unlike the manipulation of her image by many of the novel's characters. The crucial difference, however, is that within the novel's confines Milly can qualify her appropriation. Ironically, what is done to her outside of the novel is more limiting, since she cannot directly challenge it.

Ernest Sandeen's view of Milly accords with Matthiessen's. Milly, in his words, "has proved her superiority but she has also had her revenge: without intending it she has heaped coals of fire upon the heads of those who tried to wrong her" (520). Thus, Milly can maintain her essential innocence, as well as obtain revenge. Her act of generosity has miraculously and justly metamorphosed into a plague. For Christof Wegelin, Milly remains "innocent" but "ravish[ed] . . . by a worldliness so knowing that it has forgotten the knowledge of innocence" (523). The novel, in this view, is founded on binomial oppositions, a conspiracy of

[26] See F. O. Matthiessen, *Henry James: The Major Phase* (New York: Oxford University Press, 1944), 42–43, 50–52, 55–60, 62–80.

blindness between a good character unable to recognize evil, and evil characters incapable of recognizing good. J. A. Ward argues that Milly's final act, by utilizing the novel's primary "destructive force"—money—is "tainted," through the "motive is not." Milly's "possession" of money causes her destruction, though she herself "is not corrupted by [it]" (532). And Laurence Holland concurs that the novel's end reveals Milly as "sacrament, the sacred thing . . . the treasure, dove, and muse of James's imagination" (573). All of these critical views provide a picture of Milly complementary to the preface's claims. Existing in a world of hypocrisy and guile, she remains innocent.

Given the movement of the novel's preface, and the tendency for critics to carry out James's less-than-clear directives for reading, it is not surprising that Milly has emerged in critical scholarship as the novel's still center, the abyss of innocence and eternality that swallows up most critics. I think it important to recognize the consequences of reading her in this way: what such views of Milly provide for and preclude. Claims for Milly's unalloyed purity, it seems to me, provide a path of escape from the most treacherous implications of the novel's plot. The belief in Milly's freedom from the entanglements of her society allows the reader a vicarious outlet for his own implication by the circumstances he has helped to reenact. By holding to Milly's innocence, it is possible to avoid one's implication by the novel's designs. But the novel insists that no one can stand by and watch another "perched" to his peril without somehow participating in that imperiling. The belief that reading can be liberating—that it can alleviate our anxieties, political, intellectual, emotional, or other—wars with James's deepest aesthetic.

Most importantly, such views obscure a whole side of Milly's characterization. One-sided visions of her betrayal overlook how she herself conspires in the designs of Kate and Densher. Milly's characterization raises a more complicated set of concerns than those suggested by readings of her blind innocence. The insistence on Milly's innocence, both within the text and without, reveals her exploitation by a set of cultural assumptions that she herself shares: assumptions that prize death over life as the greatest source of feminine power.

As the critical opinions above confirm, Milly's tragic death becomes the novel's still center, absolving the guilt of characters and critics. Densher's feeling at the novel's close, that he can live in Milly's memory, cherishing a guiltless love, parallels critics who retreat to Milly's death as the novel's center of meaning. The monolithic truth contained in Milly's demise is summarized by one view that Milly's "values, in short, her exemplary qualities of heart and mind, provide the moral standard in relation to which Densher and Kate must come to see themselves."[27] Milly's death is thus seen to provide a sacrificial meaning both within the novel's society and among the work's critics.

Whether or not her illness is perceived as a tragic necessity, it is undeniably a condition that she cultivates. Milly's association of her illness with power is evident in her first meeting with Luke Strett, where he appears to her "half like a general and half like a bishop" (143). These images together of martial and religious authority suggest Milly's subjection to the arbiter of her illness. Yet it is far from complete domination; their association, like any power relation, gives her power as well. Milly views their acquaintanceship as her "absolute possession" (143), just as she will become his possession, as a photographed image on his wall (146). Her illness is a "weapon" with which she moves in "the fashion of a soldier on a march" (152–53). Milly's enlarged view of Strett's medical knowledge fuels her own self-empowerment. Her "being found out about" by him, rather than something she evades, "was truly what she had come for . . . something firm to stand on" (146).

Milly derives a sense of identity from her condition. The firm ground it provides "prove[d] how little she had hitherto had to

[27] Stephen Donadio, *Nietzsche, Henry James, and the Artistic Will* (New York: Oxford University Press, 1978), 131.

hold her up," and releases her from her "queer little history" (146). This link between Milly's illness and her sense of the past helps to illuminate her vulnerability to the societal cult of suffering that she eventually fulfills. Conceived here innocuously as a means of "order[ing]" her "loosely rattling" life, Milly's illness is also a repayment for her past. Milly accepts the burden of illness because it feels right to her psychologically. Her deceased family produces for Milly the guilt of the "survivor" (149). In a sense, their deaths preclude her life. Thus when she learns of her condition, it seems a realization of something.

Even prior to this, Milly has cultivated an odd and sickly appearance. And later, looking for herself "in people's eyes," Milly pursues the feeling of distinctness that comes from roaming streets "not haunted by odd-looking girls from New York" (153). She feeds on "the curiosity she clearly excited in by-ways," envisioning herself as a dramatic "character." Though Milly's walk among the "grimy children" and "smutty sheep" is an attempt to feel herself into life again following her tragic knowledge, it rather enforces her sense of singularity and high drama. She ruminates, "It was perhaps superficially more striking that one could live if one would, but it was more appealing, insinuating, irresistible in short, that one would live if one could" (156). Milly stages a drama of her ensnarement by death in which she serves as director, manager, and star. With its "appealing" pull of inevitability, her death becomes the greatest possibility of her life.

Milly's first staging of the dramatic action is her arrangement of Luke Strett's visit with Susan Stringham. Instinctively aware that setting in motion alone is insufficient, that the success of "her plan" depends on retrospective management, Milly reviews the scene carefully with Susan. Highlighting the romantic interest, Milly demands, "Didn't you hit it off tremendously together and in fact fall quite in love?" (240). Her sequestration at the Palazzo Leporelli provides the height of her drama. She and Eugenio are a pair of veteran actors, rehearsing a scene so well known that no script is necessary. Her illness is "a conceit" with a "beauty and intensity" that allows her to "float on and on" (264). Her romance is so captivating that she draws Lord Mark in simply by noting "something poignant in which her visitor also participated" (266). Projecting upon Lord Mark a compassion he cannot feel, Milly incorporates him into her drama.

Here it is essential to clarify my point. Rather than her way of garnering power over her inevitable doom, apart from any sense of a tragic destiny, Milly's imagination of her illness is her means of establishing control over her present and accommodating her past. I am therefore questioning the assumption that Milly's death is fixed from the novel's beginning. Instead, Milly herself dramatically manages a death that is necessitated more by the demands of the collective plot than by the workings of some universal fate. Milly's romancing of "intensity," of a spiritual suffering predicating death, culminates at the party she gives in Luke Strett's honor. Likened to "wide warm waves . . . of a general, a beatific mildness" (301), her wealth and spirituality rule the scene.

Milly's compositional feat here, the arrangement of her guests as an Italian still-life, seems a repayment for her own previous "re-enforcement" into the Bronzino frame. In the manner of Henry Burrage, another powerful Jamesian aesthete, Milly arrays her guests to throw her own virulent energies into relief. "Let loose among them in a wonderful white dress . . . circulating with a clearness intensified . . . happily pervasive," Milly realizes the power of her dove image. The composition of the "Veronese picture" may "not quite [be] constituted" by the present assembly, but the resistant contours are "qualified by beating down" with her wings. This image of the splendid dove using her wings to smother those elements jarring to her image indicates the powerful thrust of Milly's artful aspirations. Her arrangement suggests a will to dominate that is hardly innocent. Indeed, Kate is "efface[d]," even "damage[d]," and all are compelled to recognize that "doves have wings and wondrous flights, have them as well as tender tints and soft sounds" (303–304). On this night a single glance from Milly composes Kate and Densher; as they stand to the side conspiring, her one look "brought them together" (310). But Milly's power depends on her evasion of any direct confrontation. As with her twisting of the dove image, and her conversation with Lord Mark, Milly rests quietly in her solitude, secure in the knowledge of what they don't know she knows.

Yet significantly, it is Kate and Densher's conversation that is highlighted, and spiritual knowledge of Kate, not Milly, focuses Densher's attention. The scene can be read as a paradigm of the type of power Milly wields in her illness. For it is Kate who really works on Densher here, as it is Kate who has the power to choose at the novel's end, despite the appeal of Milly's memory. Milly's great "intensity" (318) is vaporous, derived, she seems to know, from a self-deceptive view of its potential power. And Milly conveys this recognition to Densher that her illness is cultivated, and she can choose to live if she wills (318). Milly's real tragedy is that death comes to seem to her more "magnificent."

Indeed, by fully embracing death, Milly loses whatever dramatic control she has formerly exercised. The star of scenes she no longer directs, entirely controlled by others' imaginations, her final months are relayed through the voyeuristic dialogues of Kate and Densher. Milly gives up on life because death has always seemed a more powerful part. Yet, paradoxically, her yielding to that role is the final surrender of any power she might hold. The psychological factor in Milly's romance of death has already been suggested. As a self-proclaimed "survivor" of a "wreckage," Milly looks upon death as inevitable, even comforting. The cultural aspect of Milly's impulse raises more controversial questions.

Milly's cultivation of suffering exemplifies a phenomenon prevalent among upper-class women in the late nineteenth century. Susan Sontag recognizes this worship of physical delicacy and illness as a feminist issue. "The tubercular look," she writes, "which symbolized an appealing vulnerability, a superior sensitivity, became more and more the ideal look for women—while great men

CHAPTER FIVE

of the mid and late nineteenth century grew fat, founded industrial empires, wrote hundreds of novels, made wars, and plundered continents."[28] Though Sontag allows for a possibly "subversive" edge to the romance of tuberculosis, she concludes that it more often provided "a way of retiring from the world without having to take responsibility for it."[29]

[28] Sontag's analysis is useful in its cross-cultural emphasis. See *Illness as Metaphor* (New York: Farrar, Straus and Giroux, 1977), 31. Jackson Lears provides a complementary picture of the self-congratulatory girths sported by American male leaders of the era, with a look at the neurasthenic underside to this ideal solidity. According to Lears, neurasthenic symptoms, which he unites with a number of conditions under the category of "a paralysis of the will," took on "historical importance . . . not because nervous ailments had actually increased—that point is impossible to substantiate—but because observers *believed* nervousness was on the rise, and treated its spread as a cultural problem." *No Place of Grace* (New York: Pantheon, 1981), 50–51, and especially ch. 1. The problem was considered to be particularly acute among women. Charlotte Perkins Gilman's "The Yellow Wallpaper" portrays the escalation of a woman's nervous illness by her physician husband. Significantly, the woman's anxiety is heightened by being deprived of a writing instrument. See Gail Parker, ed., *The Oven Birds* (Garden City, N.Y.: Doubleday, 1972). Also relevant to this discussion is the family connection—the issue of Alice James's neurasthenia. A history of her case is found in *The Death and Letters of Alice James*, ed. Ruth Yeazell (Berkeley: University of California Press, 1981).

[29] Sontag, *Illness*, 34. It is important to recognize that the issue of feminine frailty in the late nineteenth century was divided along class lines. Middle-class women of the period were propounding a stronger image of "the new woman" that directly challenged stereotypes and helped to promote social changes such as Margaret Sanger's opening of the first birth control clinic in New York City in 1910. Though "the new woman" was often the target of satire, satire served to affirm her by drawing attention to alterations in women's roles. For a view of "the new woman," see Peter Finlay Dunne's "Mr. Dooley" series, "On the New Woman," 1898. On the changing roles of middle-class women, see David Kennedy, *Birth Control in America: The Career of Margaret Sanger* (New Haven: Yale University Press, 1970); Sarah Stage, "Out of the Attic: Studies in Victorian Sexuality," *The American Quarterly* 27 (October 1975): 460–85; Aileen S. Kraditor, *Ideas of the Woman Suffrage Movement, 1890–1920* (New York: Columbia University Press, 1965); June Sochen, ed., *The New Feminism in Twentieth-Century America* (Lexington, Mass.: D. C. Heath, 1971); and Lois Banner and Mary Hartman, eds., *Clio's Consciousness Raised* (New York: Harper and Row, 1974), especially essays by Ann Douglas and Carroll Smith-Rosenberg. For the depiction of these issues in other literature of the period, see novels such as Kate Chopin's *The Awakening* (1899), Edith Wharton's *The House of Mirth* (1905) and *Summer* (1913), Ellen Glasgow's *Virginia* (1913), Sarah Orne

The question of the power contained in the prolonged illnesses and deaths of American heroines of the late nineteenth century has been hotly contested by cultural historians. Some scholars have censored the cultural stereotypes that prized death over life for the era's women. For Ann Douglas, such tendencies were the pathetic strategy of an economically displaced ministerial and feminine class, which she sees as the nineteenth-century precursor to the modern American consumer.[30] Douglas's analysis, like Sontag's, has a certain air of blaming the victim, which is revealing in itself. Yet this does not weaken the validity of her observations, which convey a deep concern for the ways in which women in particular have been manipulated by stereotypes that circumvent and assuage, rather than engage and alter, the cultural limitations on their self-expression and political power.

Douglas's arguments are significantly qualified by the work of Jane Tompkins. In an essay on Harriet Beecher Stowe's *Uncle Tom's Cabin*, Tompkins views Little Eva's death as a source of salvation that is neither "naive" nor "unrealistic."[31] Modern readers,

---

Jewett's *The Country of the Pointed Firs* (1899), and stories by Mary Wilkins Freeman, including "The Revolt of Mother," which pictures the lives of quiet women harboring "the elements of revolution."

[30] "Women and ministers," Douglas writes, "in an effort to rationalize and glamorize their position, were engaged in subordinating historical progress to biological process. . . . The tombstone is the sacred emblem in the cult of the overlooked. It is hardly accidental that the ornate statuary which increasingly decorated Victorian graves has some resemblance to enlarged victory trophies. . . . If the insignificant could be proved significant, if the dead could live, ministers and women could establish a new balance of power in the free-for-all, intensely competitive democracy of American culture." *The Feminization of American Culture* (New York: Knopf, 1978), 243. Of particular interest in Douglas's book is her brief discussion of ideology, adapted from the ideas of Karl Mannheim and Georg Lukács; see 197–201, 448.

[31] As Tompkins argues, "The political and economic measures that constitute effective action for us, [Stowe] regards as superficial, mere extensions of the worldly policies that produced the slave system in the first place. . . . She recommends not specific alterations in the current political and economic arrangements, but rather a change of heart." "Sentimental Power: *Uncle Tom's Cabin* and the Politics of Literary History," in Elaine Showalter, ed., *The New Feminist Criticism*, (New York:

she argues, misread "sentimental," "popular" works by imposing modernist categories on historically precise subjects that demand historically appropriate terms of analysis. But this still leaves open the issue of power. As the portrayal of Milly's party at the Palazzo Leporelli suggests, the question of what *types* of power the larger society privileges remains difficult. We still must ask how effectively certain forms of resistance engaged America's prevailing systems of authority. Little Eva's and Uncle Tom's deaths are placations rather than challenges. They seem not to threaten the powers that be. Even to emphasize their effects outside the novel is to avoid the question of why "minority" power is so represented within its bounds. And whether spiritual transcendence is the greatest form of protest available is another moot issue. In James's novel, Milly's death appears to represent a complicated evasion of the world, which substitutes for an active confrontation with its terms. Caught equally by an oppressive psychological inheritance and by exploitative cultural categories particular to her social position, Milly is disposed to idealize death. Though, in comparison, Kate also suffers from limiting social conventions, she seems in the end less compromised by them.

There is little point in privileging one character's response over another's, but it is important to recognize their political as well as narrative implications. Just as Kate and Milly exemplify different nineteenth-century notions of women's health and political power, they also represent different models of women's writing. The two women's contrasting senses of their personal strengths and weaknesses are linked to their potential for reworking and rewriting their life scripts. Milly, who is too guilty to live, dramatizes suffering and death as her sole means for power in the world. Rather than embracing a transcendent destiny, Kate rebels against a meaningless family script by vowing to invest it in *life* "with a sort of meaning" (22).

Pantheon, 1985), 89–90; and *Sensational Designs* (New York: Oxford University Press, 1985), 132.

A comparison of Milly's imaginative creation, her romance of
death, with Kate's plotting, which directly confronts her contemporary experience, suggests two poles of women's authorship.
While Milly can be seen as the author of myth who images herself
in eternal categories of spirit and nature, Kate's designs function
in the society of the novel, in the name of changing its conditional
patternings. The different strategies and consequences of the two
women's narratives point to a central debate among theorists concerning the relative political impact of a biological view of wom-
en's authorship, and a view focused on the social institutions and
roles that are seen to define the possibilities for women writers.

As Ann Rosalind Jones argues, any evocation of man's or woman's "nature" obscures the fact that gender labels refer to socially
contracted roles, products of highly stratified political and economic categories. Men and women are confined by their particular
gender, Jones suggests, only to the extent that society so defines
them. The terms "masculine" and "feminine," are never "natural,"
but register a range of social and political prejudices and necessities.[32]

The point is that women must work through the terms presented by their societies, and strive to change those terms, if they
are ever to secure social roles that allow for greater self-expression.
We are never free of the worlds that have created us, nor is there a
primitive or original state to which we can return as a way of transcending undesirable social categories and relations. This is a vision with which Kate Croy would be in agreement. A character
committed to the necessity of working through her social circumstances, Kate represents an earlier moment of a radically social
consciousness of feminine political change. For Kate, such change
can never come about through Milly's vision of transcendence, nor
through Densher's nostalgia, but only through confrontation with
her society's essential terms.

[32] In Showalter, *New Feminist Criticism*, 373.

SIX

The Power of Mere Fable:
Reconstructing the Past in
An American Tragedy

CRITICS OF *An American Tragedy* have puzzled over the title and its generic implications. "Can a tragic vision," some have asked, "govern a Deterministic universe?" The question of the novel's title is often attributed to carelessness—yet another example of the author's (or the army of editors') ineptitude.[1] It is more revealing, however, to take this inconsistency on its own terms, to consider how the tension between a tragic and a deterministic philosophy might pervade the novel.

Most definitions of "tragedy" assert some degree of free will—that the protagonist's actions are "neither wholly predetermined nor wholly free."[2] The genre depends upon a world where human choices have discernible consequences, and where the potential for human initiative is present. The predetermined world of Dreiser's novel seems to lack the expected components of a tragic universe. Its characters "all act out the drama of determinism," in a "God-abandoned and sanction-stripped world of natural process."[3] Yet

[1] On the editing of *An American Tragedy*, see Donald Pizer, *The Novels of Theodore Dreiser* (Minneapolis: University of Minnesota Press, 1976), 227–32. Among those who discuss the concept of tragedy in the novel are Irving Babbit, "The Critic of American Life," *Forum* 89 (February 1928): 168; F. O. Matthiessen, *Theodore Dreiser* (New York: William Sloane, 1951), 207; Ellen Moers, *Two Dreisers* (New York: Viking, 1969), 286–90; and Pizer, *Novels*, 280–81.

[2] For a discussion of "tragedy" and "tragic flaw," see *The Princeton Encyclopedia of Poetry and Poetics* (Princeton: Princeton University Press, 1974), 860–65.

[3] Irving Howe, "Afterword," in Dreiser, *An American Tragedy* (New York: Signet, 1964), 817; Robert Penn Warren, "An American Tragedy," *Yale Review* 52

the ambiguities and contradictions of the novel, which build as it progresses—the problem of the protagonist's "character," the strain of sardonic echoes in the narrative voice, the inconsistent ideology of the American work ethic—all suggest that the determinism of *An American Tragedy* is not as self-evident as most critics have assumed. Indeed, so complex is the novel's portrayal of its deterministic vision that it can be seen in part as a meditation on that vision. Rather than simply a confused blend of deterministic philosophy and tragic pathos, the novel rises to the level of probing the social-psychological and political implications of these ideas. And the introduction of tragic concerns into a deterministic world might lead us to scrutinize the power of generic terms themselves, which serve as often to foreclose as to facilitate our access to textual meanings.[4]

In the following pages, I show how *An American Tragedy* is involved in exploring the social-psychological and political effects of its deterministic vision. All of the significant features of the novel's society—the rags-to-riches aspirations of Clyde Griffiths, the social stratification of Lycurgus, the increasingly rationalized world of Clyde's American odyssey—are disclosed to be within the range of human agency. The novel exposes a tension between an eternal rhetoric that portrays social organization as unalterable, and more localized details that reveal the controls over social processes, and individuals' perceptions of them, to be variously accessible to society's members. This concern for the links between temporal consciousness and political power is extended to a con-

---

(October 1962): 3. All subsequent references to *An American Tragedy* in the text are to this edition.

[4] One of the novel's chief questions involves the protagonist's viability as a tragic hero. Just as Joyce's *Ulysses* redefines the possibilities for heroism in the modern age, Dreiser's novel ponders the appropriateness of tragic terms in the twentieth century. Clyde's character seems a blend of naturalist and tragic categories. Neither completely passive nor completely fixed, he is likewise alternately insensible and self-aware. And he does achieve some perspective on himself by the novel's end. Most important, the point where naturalist and tragic categories clash reveals the pervading political contradictions of the novel's society.

sideration of the manipulative potential of historical narration it-self.

The novel's final book depicts Clyde as caught between the par-tisan political squabbles of an approaching election and the moral outrage of Bridgeburg County's rural inhabitants. Compelled to narrate a version of his past that his lawyers hope will satisfy a lo-cal jury, he is dumbfounded and, as the book progresses, increas-ingly obsessed with his inability to achieve an articulate narration of his personal history. Clyde's public execution is a silent agony, "his eyes fixed nervously," his final look, perhaps an "appeal," per-haps a "daze," left to the bystander's interpretation (811). Clyde's "tragedy" is inseparable from his incapacity to achieve a clear view of his experience, his failure as a storyteller or historian of self. He is a pawn of social authorities, a test case for the intricate legalities of those more knowledgeable and powerful than he. And Clyde's speechlessness testifies to the extent to which American authors have always aligned political power with the powers of historical narration.[5]

These links are established from the novel's beginning, where narrative authority seems to reside in the capacity to obscure his-torical consciousness. "Dusk—of a summer night. And the tall walls of the commercial heart of an American city of perhaps 400,000 inhabitants—such walls as in time may linger as a mere fable." We have entered upon the nervous interim between day

[5] It is interesting to compare Dreiser's novel to Norman Mailer's recent crime novel, *The Executioner's Song* (Boston: Little, Brown, 1979), which seems remarka-bly close to Dreiser's structurally. Each offers a brief history of its protaganist's life preceding his "crime," and devotes the remainder of the novel to society's "use and abuse" of a celebrated murder case. Mailer's novel may suggest what has changed in eighty years. The expansion of hype goes hand in hand with society's chaotic inability to take responsibility for judging the criminal. Gary Gilmore's manipu-lative management of his personal history contrasts strikingly with Clyde's befud-dlement. But this contrast raises the question of who is exploited more: Clyde, who is incapable of controlling the remaking of his past, or Gary Gilmore, who is the ringleader of his history's representation, rubbing shoulders with the media giants of modern America.

244

and night—with the world in transition, marginality reigns, and crime perhaps flourishes. Despite their air of immediacy, however, these clipped sentences offer few precise historical details. The opening emphasizes the subject of time without grounding us in a specific moment of history; the setting is the amorphous "heart" of a large American city around the turn of the century. But the tacked-on final phrase, "such walls as in time may linger as a mere fable," reveals the hidden claim of this vagueness—the designation of narrative as an eternal power. Juxtaposing the substance of the city, the aggressive facade of this business landscape, and the delicate image of a "linger[ing] . . . fable," the phrase points to a time when the reliable bluntness of America's urban world will be found in ("mere") fictions alone. Aligning narrative artistry with the power of permanence, the novel implies that the only accessible past is that which someone has chosen to transform into story.

This brief opening prepares us for a novelistic world in which anything that anyone possesses is already faded, already not sweet, because to its possessor it is so short-lived. The narrator's sense of time here presages Clyde's remark to Roberta at their love's inception: "We have so little time" (274). Yet the novel portrays striking differences among its characters' perceptions of time—differences that reveal control over temporal perceptions to be a distinctly political power. Throughout the novel, we see characters engaging in the kinds of manipulations the narrator attempts here. Specific historical moments are cast in terms of an obscure and remote temporality as a means of rendering unchallengeable a preferred point of view. The blurring of the reader's time sense here facilitates the narrator's powerful claim that fiction may be the sole adjudicator of reality.

In this chapter, I shall first explore the respective relationships to history of Samuel Griffiths, Clyde Griffiths, and Roberta Alden. I then analyze the novel's narrator, whose own relationship to time is revealed in the ironic repetitions that pervade his narrative. Finally, I turn to the novel's implicit political vision. Focusing on the clash between the rhetoric of determinism and the rhetoric of free will, I explain how the philosophy of determinism functions as a "containment strategy," employed by the powerless to assuage their despair, and by social elites to maintain the status quo.[6] By depicting characters' *differential* abilities to manipulate the temporal perceptions of themselves and others and to rewrite their pasts, the novel points to the political nature of time-telling and historical narration. Characters' capacities to define their experience beyond the demands of historical circumstances parallel their respective positions in the novel's social hierarchy. This is particularly relevant to the issue of Clyde's "inevitable" downfall, which is usually seen to result from some predetermined combination of inherent weakness and destiny. My reading suggests otherwise: that Clyde's experiences must be considered to follow from social-psychological and political factors in his historical present.

As I conclude, repeated allusions to Clyde's lack of education or training as explanations of his failure contradict implications that Clyde has learned his society's stories all too well. Clyde's tendency toward passivity and drift reflects the myths of a power elite whose tales of the way to wealth stress divine election over initiative. Thus, Clyde's experience fulfills his relationship to American ideology: within the terms of the novel's critique, his is the logical end for an ambitious young man dedicated to following his society's codes of behavior.

[6] For Fredric Jameson the notion of a "containment strategy," as distinct from ideological blindness, is "one of structural limitation and ideological closure. . . . From this perspective, Hegel's notion of Absolute Spirit is seen as just such a strategy of containment, which allows what can be thought to seem internally coherent in its own terms, while repressing the unthinkable (in this case, the very possibility of collective praxis) which lies beyond its boundaries." A containment strategy thus functions to prematurely foreclose the possibilities afforded by a dynamic view of the totality. *The Political Unconscious* (Ithaca: Cornell University Press, 1981), 52–53.

Narrating the Road to Wealth

Samuel Griffiths is the novel's exemplar of power and success, as well as its prime temporal manager. The details of his successful rise, recounted from his point of view, are the material of legend. Son of a moderately wealthy farmer, Samuel has managed to exploit his share of the paternal estate, and he views his success as primarily resulting from personal qualities of "determination" and "acumen." True to the paradigmatic Horatio Alger tale, luck is held to be a strategic factor in his social advancement, but it is luck rationalized in terms of Samuel's inherent virtues.[7] As the narrator comments, Samuel's "new collar enterprise which had been proposed to him" had "succeeded . . . beyond his wildest expectations" (153), yet the very next sentence reveals how Samuel, now "naturally . . . vain" about his success, has incorporated the strenuous and coincidental details of his rise into a mythic estimation of his life's course. Redefined as the pattern of predestined success, the role of effort and chance in Samuel's rise has been retrospectively subsumed. Similarly, his "calm and judicial air," though described as a cultivated aspect he is "always striving" for, becomes his "mere" acceptance of "the value that others placed upon him" (153).

[7] As John Cawelti writes of the Horatio Alger stories, "Alger is obsessed with luck. The chapter which contains the crucial turning point of the book is invariably entitled, ——'s Luck, and every accession to the hero's fortunes stems from a coincidence." *Apostles of the Self-Made Man* (Chicago: University of Chicago Press, 1976), 115; see esp. 101–123. On this theme of the American success ethic as portrayed in late-nineteenth and early-twentieth-century factual and fictional works, see Irvin G. Wyllie, *The Self-Made Man in America* (New Brunswick, N.J.: Rutgers University Press, 1954), and Herbert G. Gutman, *Work, Culture, and Society* (New York: Vintage, 1977), ch. 4, "The Reality of the Rags-to-Riches Myth." And for a sample of contemporary journalistic views on the role of luck in the rise to success, see "Their Strength Was to Sit Still," *American Magazine* 108 (October 1929). Also relevant to this discussion are two recent studies of Social Darwinism in turn-of-the-century America: Richard Hofstader, *Social Darwinism in American Thought* (Boston: Beacon, 1955), and Robert C. Bannister, *Social Darwinism* (Philadelphia: Temple University Press, 1979).

Throughout the novel, Samuel can be seen at work reshaping the cause-and-effect rhythms of his life into a narrative of the inevitable. Thus, the manufacture of cloth collars transcends the aim of monetary accumulation, and becomes a benevolent, virtuous activity. As Clyde is told at a party, "There was some social importance to making and distributing collars, giving polish and manner to people who wouldn't otherwise have them, if it weren't for cheap collars" (321). The idea of providing a social service allows Samuel to rationalize his factory empire's ruthless absorption of human energies. For everything is conceived in terms of the profit and utility motives that govern his factory. Clyde demonstrates his worth by instinctively mouthing the Griffiths ideology (175), and is thereby seen as "very adaptable" (174). Samuel's wife is noted for her efficient operation of the domestic front, commendable for letting "no disharmony" (155) inhibit its smooth functioning. Even his beloved youngest daughter Bella is "the most pleasing and different *thing*" (154, emphasis added).

Samuel's assuagement of his utilitarian objectives through invoking moral and spiritual ideals is most obvious in his view of his employees' lives. Like monastic monks, his workers are to be impressed with the transcendent nature of their factory calling, "the only really important constructive work of the world" (176). Reified as a labor process requiring religious devotion, the production of cloth collars is a rite not to be profaned by the glitter of extravagant salaries. The godhead of his factory world, Samuel expects his employees' personal habits to reflect his own self-restraint. His "intolerance" for those lacking "acumen and commercial ability," his immediate attraction to Clyde's "efficient and unobtrusive manners" (173), his regular refusal of dessert in favor of reviewing his stock and banking interests, all suggest a monastic dedication to his work. Yet Samuel's vision overlooks the fact that it is his own choice to lead such a life: were he to desire dessert one evening, it would be there. His workers' poverty-level wages predetermine the regular absence of dessert at their boards.

The lone threat to Samuel's collar empire arises in the form of a loose thread from the past. Habitually "cautious" and controlled, Samuel experiences a slackening grip on his judgment from his earliest dealings with Clyde. Following their first meeting, he is overtaken by tenuous ruminations. He "had always *felt* that *perhaps* an injustice had been done Asa. . . . [Clyde] *seemed* bright and ambitious—so much like his own son, and he *might* readily fit into *some* department. . . . *At any rate* he *might* let him try it. There could be no *real harm* in that. Besides, there was his younger brother, to whom *perhaps*, both he and his older brother Allen owed *some form* of obligation, if *not exactly* restitution" (173–74, emphasis added). Clyde's entrance as the "return of the repressed" into Samuel's carefully wrought world puts Samuel off balance. Even his announcement of Clyde's move to Lycurgus is impetuous. He blurts the news "suddenly" (156), though "he had not intended to set forth at once . . . but rather—to wait" (157). Significantly, the scene announcing Clyde's move *precedes* that which portrays Samuel's deliberation over whether or not to invite him. Often the characters' lack of free will is built into the novel's very structure, which indicates the uselessness of characters' choices by picturing their deliberations as aftereffects. In confirmation of the great power accorded him within the novel's deterministic vision, this is the only time that one of Samuel's deliberations is portrayed after the fact.

Samuel's experience of his past might appear to affirm the novel's essential determinism: even for one so powerful as he, the weight of the past may be his undoing. Following Clyde's conviction, he must endure a disgrace that necessitates the removal of his family to begin "life all over again" (745). Yet it is precisely because Samuel can emerge as unscathed as he does that the novel's determinism is undermined. For Samuel is able to dismiss unequivocally his one indulgence of memory. His decision to bring Clyde on has been a misreading of his past, based on "a mistaken notion" of what was denied his brother Asa. Despite the hints of compulsion in his encounters with Clyde, Samuel notes retrospectively how things might have been otherwise had the human agents involved acted differently, and in the process betrays a rather muddled conception of free will. Deploring Clyde's "ungoverned . . . carnal desires" and "uncontrollable brutality," he nevertheless insists on his responsibility for them (586).

Samuel himself "naturally" transcends even the most "deadly crisis." And his son's and his lawyer's perceptions of him in his handling of Clyde's downfall reaffirm his mythology of self. "The power of him! The decision of him!" (587). As he contemplates where "a main plant might be erected," a renewed but essentially unaltered self seems to emerge from the bricks of his projected factory (745). His immediate steps to begin again suggest that the past can be overcome and human selves remade, as if process and aging were beyond the range of possibility. In Samuel Griffiths's world of masonic self-mastery, historical conditions need not be limiting.

In contrast to Samuel Griffiths's capacities to withstand the vicissitudes of historical events, the novel's two main characters, Clyde Griffiths and Roberta Alden, are repeatedly overcome by the pressing historical circumstances of past and present. It is no accident that they are often pictured either on water or in terms of water imagery. Their internal worlds are characterized by fluid desires and dreams, and by the troubling waves of their past history.

From the novel's opening, Clyde is an alienated figure, caught between his aspirations and his family's circumstances. Participating in the street-corner performance of his evangelist parents, he is tormented by the "shabby thing that [their calling] appeared to be in the eyes of others" (14). The narrator dwells on the remarks of a drifter who sees what is obvious to everyone but Clyde's own family: "That oldest boy don't wanta be here. He feels outa place, I can see that." The aimless public prattle of one anonymous "idler and loafer" to another "seemingly amiable stranger" penetrates Clyde's feelings more deeply than his parents' conversations ever do (11). So perversely drawn are the lines of sympathy in society that there is an inverse relation between the closeness of two human beings and the degree of understanding and sympathy they can extend to one another.

Throughout the novel, it is the sympathy of strangers that is often most acute. Those who by their position might be expected to understand repeatedly fail this expectation, as evident in the cloudy mutterings of Clyde's father following his conviction. "He had never understood Clyde or his lacks or his feverish imaginings, so he said, and preferred not to discuss him" (743). The curious "so he said" implies that Clyde's "feverish imaginings" may be too painfully close to Asa's own quixotic dreams to bear careful scrutiny. Likewise, despite, or perhaps because of, their dispositional kinship, Clyde and Roberta are incapable of extending sympathy to one another. They are failed by each other and their respective families, but both receive much abortive sympathy from anonymous strangers, Roberta after death, and Clyde en route to the death house.

In considering Clyde's portrayal it is crucial to understand how he changes over the course of the novel, due less to the narrator's treatment of him than to actual alterations in his personality.[8]

---

[8] The question of Clyde's character has received less extensive analysis than one might expect. Whether dismissing Clyde as an empty-headed naturalist puppet (for this argument, see Moers, *Two Dreisers*, 228–34) or offering a new, "environmental" category of selfhood for naturalist works (as Philip Fisher has brilliantly done in "Looking Around to See Who I Am: Dreiser's Territory of the Self," *ELH* 44 [1977]: 728–48), most critics have tended to dismiss prematurely the issue of Clyde's character. Robert Penn Warren departs from this to some extent, observing, "Dreiser's method of presenting [Clyde] is far deeper and more subtle than that of mere accretion. The method is an enlargement and a clarifying, slow and merciless, of a dimly envisaged possibility" ("*An American Tragedy*," 6). But Warren's essay is for the most part impressionistic. Donald Pizer argues that the narrator's treatment of Clyde undergoes a change from ridicule to sympathy (*The Novels of Dreiser*, 259, 284). But I find the narrative attitude toward Clyde largely consistent. The following descriptions occur near the end of Book 3, before Clyde's execution, and convey as much irony at Clyde's expense as early narrative commentary. Clyde now felt "a desire to present himself honestly to his Creator, if at all (he did not then explain that as yet he had scarcely attempted to so present himself)" (792). "McMillan talked on about faith and the refuge which the mercy and wisdom of God provided—Clyde, standing before him with more courage and character

Clyde becomes more and more detached from his own feelings and needs, in response to his captivation by the American ideology of success. His increasing inability to weld desire to action seems to arise from his identification with an alienating elite ethic vividly described in the beginning of Book 2.[9]

In the novel's first book, Clyde appears relatively capable of executing his will, even demonstrating at points a decided acumen for moving up a modest ladder of success. He secures a job at the soda fountain because the manager is moved by his "innocent tribute to the superiority of his store" (32). The manager of the Green-Davidson is similarly impressed by Clyde's "skill and . . . will to be diplomatic" (35), and so offers him an opportunity. In both cases, Clyde wins favor through the small displays of deference so important in any hierarchy. He rises through his all-but-sudden awareness that "if he wanted to get on he ought to insinuate himself into the good graces of people" (34). Yet such eager displays seem alien to the Clyde of Book 2. Rebounding from the Kansas City accident that closes Book 1, he now manifests "much more of an air of caution and reserve" (160). Partly in terror of discovery by the police, and partly from guilty self-effacement, he skulks through the underworlds of various cities, "St. Louis, Peoria, Chicago, Milwaukee—dishwashing . . . sodaclerking" (161). On meeting Ratterer again, Clyde's tenuous narrative of his wanderings presages his predicament in the novel's last book, where he is entirely unable to narrate his past.

Though at this point Clyde is sufficiently self-possessed to at-

---

showing in his face and eyes than at any time previously in his brief and eager career" (800).

[9] Clyde can be seen in terms of false consciousness as analyzed by Louis Althusser in "Piccolo de Teatro," *For Marx*, trans. Ben Brewster (New York: Vintage, 1970), 131–51. Also see Althusser's discussion of the link between significant actions and significant beliefs in the essay entitled "Ideology and Ideological State Apparatuses," in *Lenin and Philosophy*, trans. Ben Brewster (London: New Left Books, 1971), 123–73. For an application of Althusser's theories to another novel by Dreiser, see Sandy Petrey's "The Language of Realism, the Language of False Consciousness: A Reading of *Sister Carrie*," *Novel* (Winter 1977): 101–113.

tempt a narration, the novel focuses increasingly on his failure as a historian of self, a lack of narrative authority that derives from his lack of insight into a contradictory American creed of success. Clyde's unconscious ambivalence is revealed in his somber contemplation of those who frequent Chicago's Union League.

To this club from day to day came or went such a company of seemingly mentally and socially worldly elect as he had never seen anywhere before, the self-integrated and self-centered from not only all of the states of his native land but from all countries and continents. . . . Here also, a fact which impressed and even startled his sense of curiosity and awe, even— there was no faintest trace of that sex element which had characterized most of the phases of life to be seen in the Green-Davidson. . . . Here was no sex—no trace of it. No women were admitted to this club. These various distinguished individuals came and went, singly as a rule, and with the noiseless vigor and reserve that characterizes the ultra successful. They often ate alone, conferred in pairs and groups, noiselessly . . . but for the most part seemed to be unaware of, or at least unaffected by, that element of passion, which . . . had seemed to propel and disarrange so many things in those lesser worlds with which up to now he had been identified. Probably one could not attain to or retain one's place in so remarkable a world as this unless one were indifferent to sex, a disgraceful passion, of course. . . . After he had worked here a little while . . . he had taken on a most gentlemanly and reserved air. When he was within the precincts of the club itself, he felt himself different from what he really was—more subdued, less romantic, more practical, certain that if he tried now, imitated the soberer people of the world, and those only, that some day he might succeed. (169)

Clyde's view of America's bloodless elite, the lean exemplars of the Dream, may be the single most important passage in the novel. The key to his downfall lies in the painful admission that here in the Union League, he "felt himself different from what he really was." This sense of difference from what he feels himself to be, the intense alienation fostered by his new creed, sets him on a course that leads directly to his "tragedy." Yet Clyde's tragedy is a paradoxical one; it is not based in tragedy's usual terms—the hero's recognition of his flaw—but rather lies on a "metatragic" level. His tragic flaw is precisely his inability to assimilate or fashion any sense of a self. His dream of "difference" exemplifies the thwarted vision of his entire life.

As the novel reveals, American ideology offers both an escape from ideology and an escape from the self. Critics have analyzed the underlying assumptions and political effects of American liberal ideology. America, from this ideological perspective, is pluralistic, a society of free and open debate where built-in inhibitors to specialized interests and factions ensure that no one group ever achieves political dominance. Yet the conviction that elite rule is impossible, the ideology of ideological immunity itself, serves, paradoxically, as a perpetual cloak to the prevailing power of select groups in America.[10] And this veil in turn functions to co-opt action for social change.

American ideology also inhibits action by undermining the idea of method and process. Betraying a contradictory blend of self-effacement and self-aggrandizement, the American success myth minimizes the claims of present existence. The successful individual conceives of himself and is seen by others as both a vehicle of divine intention and an enlarged image of human power. In either case, the links between actions and consequences are blurred by the miraculous details of the road to wealth.

Clyde's perception of the purified monastic life of America's elite locates success in terms completely alien to his formerly sensual and romantic aspirations. The elegant efficiency of the men he views, gliding "noiseless[ly]" in pairs, or most often alone, is reminiscent of the "yachts" described in William Carlos Williams's poem of that name. These effortless hulls, like Clyde's elite, are "unaware of the cost," Williams says, as they move always beyond the uncontrolled and "disgraceful" passions of the rabble. The

---

[10] See Theodore J. Lowi, *The End of Liberalism*, 2nd ed. (New York: Norton, 1979); G. William Domhoff, *Who Rules America?* (Englewood Cliffs: Prentice-Hall, 1967); Albert O. Hirschman, *The Passions and the Interests* (Princeton: Princeton University Press, 1977); and Morton Horwitz, *The Transformation of American Law, 1780–1860* (Cambridge, Mass.: Harvard University Press, 1977).

elite's famed impassivity in relation to their own "chemisms" signifies the extent to which they remain aloof from the lower classes.
Passion is expurgated from their circles, redefined as a lower-class
trait known only in "those lesser worlds with which up to now
[Clyde] had been identified." In adopting these upper-class role
models, Clyde turns their monkish leanings into a devotional
rite.[11]

At the close of Chapter 3 in Book 2, Clyde virtually takes an
oath in the new order of American business saints, vowing to "conduct . . . himself with the greatest care" (169). The remainder of
the novel pictures his continual falls from and rededications to his
faith. Examples of Clyde's devotional swings can be seen in his
early weeks at the collar factory. In his meeting with Gilbert
where the latter details what is expected of their managers, Clyde
envisions the "very distant and cold attitude" he will maintain toward the factory women working under him (233). Struggling
against his first attractions to Roberta, Clyde obediently recalls his
vows (243, 265).

Ultimately, Clyde's inability to fully embrace this creed makes
him vulnerable to exploitation by others. And as the novel progresses, his habitual form of alienated self-identification becomes
an increasingly formalized and imprisoning feature of the worlds
he enters. No longer merely a temperamental weakness or a means
of self-differentiation, his alienation becomes an externalized fact
over which he has no control. Now politically as well as psychologically marginal, Clyde is alienated from all the worlds he inhabits or aspires to. In Lycurgus, Clyde finds himself caught between
a lower-class community that eyes him suspiciously and an upper-
class community that denies him access. Alienated from the only

[11] Though critics, in particular Donald Pizer (*The Novels of Dreiser*, 252–53), have
noted Clyde's creation of a religion around Sondra, citing his repeated references
to her as a "goddess in her shrine" (314), or the picture of Clyde "dreaming into her
eyes as a devotee might into those of a saint" (366), they have overlooked the extent
to which Clyde's behavior following his "vision" at the Union League reverberates
generally with apocalyptic overtones.

available societies in Lycurgus, Clyde pursues his own society with another socially marginal character, Roberta.

Significantly, Clyde is described as perpetually at sea in the novel, spending much of his time either literally or figuratively afloat (73, 256, 309, 423, etc.). He appears most desperate during moments when he is forced to a standstill, "arrested" by circumstances. At his first elite affair, for example, Clyde's discomfort amid the luxurious "college chatter" is expressed in a feeling of being "beached" (318). But his drifting is hardly a comfort. Clyde's position in the novel's closing chapters, where he is viewed as a callous member of the elite by the humble inhabitants of Bridgeburg and as a bungling outsider by his wealthy relatives (who deny him funds for an appeal), provides the most destructive example of his crippling marginality.[12]

Clyde's self-perceptions can be seen as the inverse of Samuel Griffiths's. Where Samuel erects a monument to himself in the bricks of his factory, Clyde's self-image is one he is eternally incapable of substantiating. Clyde's fragile sense of self is the psychological corollary to his political manipulation. Both Clyde and Roberta are test cases for the American Dream of social mobility, their experience suggesting the deceptiveness of the rags-to-riches myth. Yet Dreiser's critique of the American Dream seems to take us one step beyond this. For in the novel's terms, any conclusion as to the inflexibility of the American class structure might be the logical outcome of elite rhetoric.[13] The effect of social tales that ob-

[12] The Griffithses' prohibition of Clyde's insanity plea stands as the apotheosis of his marginality—too close of kin to be termed insane, he is not dear enough to be saved.

[13] Among social theorists and historians contemporary to Dreiser who treat this complex issue of the myth versus the reality of social mobility in early-twentieth-century America are Pitirim Sorokin, *Social and Cultural Mobility* (New York: Harper, 1927), 164–83, and "American Millionaires and Multi-Millionaires," *Journal of Social Forces* 3 (1925): 627–40; and Helen and Robert Lynd, *Middletown* (New York: Harcourt Brace and Co., 1929). For useful surveys that range from the turn of the century to beyond the period of Dreiser's novel, see C. Wright Mills, "The American Business Elite: A Collective Portrait," *The Tasks of Economic History*, Supplement 5 (1945): 20–44; William Miller, "American Historians and the Business

scure the method of achieving success and attribute it to the work of unknowable forces is to inhibit any impulses toward change. The major irony in Clyde and Roberta's circumstances may be that neither is marginal enough in spirit—that they have over-internalized ultimately paralyzing social mores. Clyde is closest to self-determination in the moments of happiness he experiences with Roberta. The scenes of their developing love are the most poignant and beautiful of this bleak novel. So deprived and bitter are they that neither can quite believe the other's reality, a dilemma that plagues their relationship.[14] From the beginning, each views the other as an "apparition" (258). Clyde's first impression of Roberta is of "wistfulness and wonder," her face "haloed by bright, light brown hair," her gray-blue eyes "translucent" (241). Their first encounter has that quality of accident found in dreams. Clyde, afloat, pictures Roberta in his mind's eye, only to round the bend and see her standing there. Clyde's face, the narrator remarks, is "lit by the radiance of one who had suddenly, and beyond his belief, realized a dream." And Roberta reacts similarly to Clyde. It is "as though he were a pleasant apparition suddenly evoked out of nothing and nowhere, a poetic effort taking form out of smoke or vibrant energy" (258). Each is for the other too much the realization of desire to be true. And prior to their encounter they see one another in elevated terms: Clyde wonders if Roberta is "not really above" factory labor (241), and Roberta fears that Clyde is "too good or too remote" (250).

Elite," *Journal of Economic History* 9 (1949): 184–208. Among recent analyses see Stephan Thernstrom, "Urbanization, Migration, and Social Mobility in Late Nineteenth Century America," in Barton J. Bernstein, ed., *Towards a New Past: Dissenting Essays in American History* (New York: 1968); Reinhard Bendix and Frank Houton, "Social Mobility and the American Business Elite," in Bendix and Seymour M. Lipset, eds., *Social Mobility in Industrial Society* (Berkeley: University of California Press, 1959), 114–43; and Herbert Gutman, *Work, Culture, and Society*, esp. chs. 1, 5, and postscript.

[14] Donald Pizer offers an illuminating discussion of their tendency to view each other in the mythical framework of conventional romances. *The Novels of Dreiser*, 249–50.

As Clyde awaits Roberta on their first date, he is unusually calm and content, described as "dreaming and watching, the rustling corn behind him stirring an old recollection." Clyde seems exceptionally at home in his soul, so much so that he even looks expansively backward, viewing himself in terms of his past, taking pleasure in the difference between his new love and the more manipulative or crude women he has pursued formerly (272–75). Exceptionally warm and enthusiastic, Clyde laughs "ecstatically," feeling that "life had presented him a delicious sweet at last."

The scene provides the novel's most (arguably, only) attractive view of Clyde. "Too overcome to speak vigorously," his emotions are strong, and there seems no discrepancy between his desires and actions. But Clyde makes an assertion here that throws a veil of sadness over their encounter, a temporal articulation of social pressures that will punctuate their courtship. Clyde "felt a wonder of something—he could not tell what." "It seemed at that moment as though life had given him all—all—that he could possibly ask of it." But he tells Roberta, "We have so little time" (272–75). This remark contradicts the expression of plenitude and envelops the scene. The phrase may simply refer to their abbreviated meeting, yet it captures Clyde's sense of life as a discontented rush forward—a hurling beyond himself and what is to prevent present fulfillment.

This overriding self-denial, which seems connected to the suicidal impulse some have ascribed to Clyde's role in Roberta's death, precludes contentment in time. Tied to a boundless image of self and world, Clyde's time sense here parallels the narrator's own in the novel's opening, where he pictures vaguely a world of "such walls as in time may linger as a mere fable." Despite different ends, both convey a conviction of experience as ephemeral and irretrievable. But where the narrator turns his fear of a fleeting world into an assertion of narrative power, Clyde cannot superintend his fear of time.

Like her lover, Roberta is caught equally between grand desires and doubts over the possibility of their realization. Her sister

Agnes's marriage to Fred Gabel exemplifies, in Roberta's view, a capacity to live within a moderate range of expectations. As Roberta wonders, "Was it not better . . . to be married to a man even as inefficient and unattractive but steadfast as Fred Gabel, than to occupy the anomalous position . . . with Clyde?" (347). Roberta's position seems always to have been "anomalous." Sensitive and observant, like Clyde she feels alienated from a home environment that is "reduced," "melancholy," and "nondescript" (244), and from parents sunk in "depriving and toilsome poverty" (245). Displaced even in terms of physique, Roberta is described as "too delicate for [her] region" (245). And her marginal consciousness leads her to distrust and thwart the advances of most men. Perceiving herself as too intelligent for men of her own class, and too poor for better educated ones, she is "well satisfied that no one . . . in whom she was interested would be interested in her" (246).

Although Clyde and Roberta share psychological traits, there are also significant differences between them. Though Roberta is plagued with fears over her unorthodox love affair, she is in many ways stronger than her lover—less self-destructive and more capable of wedding desire and action. The two are from similarly impoverished backgrounds, but Roberta's view of her parents and their world lacks the resentment that characterizes Clyde's. Perhaps because she has no point of comparison between her family and any other, in contrast to Clyde's heightened view of the Lycurgus Griffithses, Roberta is more bonded to her own. Unlike Clyde, who denies his mother money in her need, Roberta contributes most of her earnings to her parents. And where Clyde responds angrily to his father's weakness, Roberta notes feelingly how her father's "gaunt face and angular elbows" contrasts with the "hopefulness of the younger generation" (346).

Roberta's capacity for sympathy arises from her greater insight into her own desires. In contrast to Clyde's rather vague and fumbling desire to get ahead, her goal of self-improvement is articulate from the start: Roberta must break the oppressive pattern of the family history. Her burden is perhaps greater than Clyde's, for she is driven by a success dream expressly nurtured by her family; her parents' special child, she is the one in whom their "hopes rested most" (346). Contemplating marriage to Clyde, Roberta's thoughts are twofold: it would raise her from her own degraded circumstances, as well as alter the repetitive bleakness of her family's rural life. Were Clyde to refuse marriage, "then all the results of her yearning, but possibly mistaken, dreams would be not only upon her own head, but upon those of these others, her mother's first" (346). While her family role as "emissary of a slowly and modestly improving social condition for all" (342) is demanding, it serves as an important source of strength. Unlike Samuel Griffiths, who denies the limitations of the historical past and present, and Clyde, who cannot accommodate his past through either denial or incorporation, Roberta is conscious of the fearsome pull of her past and the demands it places upon her present.

Their respective attitudes toward their origins accounts for the distinction between Clyde's outer-directed diffuseness and Roberta's inner-directed determination. From the beginning, while the urban Clyde gazes resentfully outward, coveting others' possessions, dreaming of "a better collar, a nicer shirt, finer shoes, a good suit" (19), all trappings of a self, Roberta nurtures an internal life, corroborated by the joy she feels in the world of nature. "In the orchard of a spring day later . . . when the early May sun was making pink lamps of every aged tree and the ground was pinkly carpeted . . . she would stand and breathe and sometimes laugh, or even sigh, her arms upreached or thrown wide to life" (245). Her exuberant and self-expressive dreams contrast with the bitterness and frustration of his. Their different outlooks are perhaps attributable to their contrasting artificial-urban and natural-rural environments. But Roberta's farm life is as dismal as Clyde's urban one, and her parents as repressive and hopeless as Clyde's.

Their crucial difference is reflected in their historical consciousnesses: Roberta's regard for a personal and a collective mission yields a deep sense of history. Her sense of the past informs her present, and fuels the greater initiative and purpose that is repeatedly set against Clyde's dependence and passivity. On her first day at the factory Roberta is remarkably adept. "A quick and intelligent worker, [she is] soon mastering without much advice of any kind all the tricks of the work, and thereafter earning about as much as any of the others" (251). While Roberta's "speed and accuracy" leads to her self-impelled rise (242), Clyde's "speed[y]" rise and "sudden jump in salary" results from his uncle's "choos[ing] to do all this for him" (234). His progress in the factory is, from the first, entirely dependent on the good will of Samuel Griffiths.

Yet Roberta's greater activeness and resolve seem to benefit her little, either in the kind of social rise she envisions or in her life generally. This is especially evident in the cruel irony of her drowning. For it is her action of rising in the boat that precipitates a death the would-be murderer Clyde is incapable of effecting. Finally a betrayed folk heroine to the trial audience, she is also a valiant victim to novel readers. In the last book, where the powers of historical narration are most vividly evident, her dramatic letters force all of her auditors, including Clyde, the public, and readers, to confront the past as inescapable. Less alienated from her origins and hence from herself than Clyde, Roberta possesses the crucial capacity to tell her own story. The simple expressiveness of her letters, the antithesis of Clyde's forced recitation of a past he is unable to simply or movingly retell, exemplifies the ambiguous wealth of Roberta's historical consciousness. Roberta's confrontational stance makes her a genuinely powerful figure only in death; it is only a deceased Roberta who can serve as an agent of the past. Roberta's experiences may suggest that despite her life, justice will be done in the afterlife. But they may more importantly imply that human initiative and historical consciousness are empty categories to the novel's lower classes, for the potential for realizing these terms resides in the novel's elite alone.

None of the characters seem to penetrate the rhetoric of eternal time to recognize their responsibilities as actors in history. It is crucial, however, that the veil of eternal time allows the wealthy characters power and contentment *in* the world. The novel's poor characters exercise power, if at all, only from the grave. It remains to be seen whether the narrator offers the potential for viewing society historically, as a plane of human responsibility and action.

The Narrator as Ironic Historian

The narrator of *An American Tragedy* is an exceptionally subtle voice in the Dreiser canon, less prominent and judgmental than is typical, and less given to sentimental rhetoric. The kinds of florid decrees found elsewhere in Dreiser are largely alien to this persona, who seems convinced of life's "ragged edges." In part, the narrator's greater reticence arises from the fact that this novel, more than any other by Dreiser, is recounted through indirect discourse from its protagonist's point of view. Still, the question remains as to why this technique would prevail, why the novel would tend more toward descriptive detail than philosophical judgment. Allusions to the novel's incorporation of the detached techniques of journalism as *explanations* for the deflation of its narrative voice merely beg the question. Given a novel in which the judgment of guilt or innocence is central to the plot, the significance of the narrator's judgments, whether absent or marked, cannot be overestimated.

The most obvious feature of the narrative voice is its excessive irony. What has not been noticed is how often this irony is directed at the novel's own repetitive patterns, serving as underhanded commentary on its deterministic philosophy. In addition to the larger repetitions of scenes and doublings of characters, there are smaller repetitions that reflect ironically upon such scenes or upon the characters themselves. These anachronies, which point either forward or backward in time, serve to heighten the novel's overall sense of time.[15] But they are so subtle (and so

---

[15] Gerard Genette uses the term "anachrony" to "designate all forms of discordance between two temporal orders of story and narrative." This includes prolepsis

uniformly missed by critics) that they appear as the narrator's private jokes.

In the novel's first book, for example, one of Clyde's fellow bellboys, Hegglund from New Jersey, an "over-sized youth" habitually attired in a "tight" uniform (37), is described reclining expansively in the chop-house, looking "not unlike a large and overzealous rooster" (59). Some three hundred pages later, in Book 2, at an elite ball in Lycurgus, the self-possessed escort of Sondra Finchley is portrayed in what seems a clear echo of the previous description. Freddie Sells in his "closely-fitting dress coat look[s] down on Clyde about as a spring rooster might look down on a sparrow" (321). Thus, the sophisticated Princeton man appears a repetition of the ignorant bellhop Hegglund, just another product of New Jersey, though less polished. This echoing metaphor functions to reduce the upper-class youth contemplating Clyde from his great height. But it is an ironic parallel unavailable to Clyde, enjoyed by the narrator and perhaps the reader as well. Other instances of such repetitions create an impression of the narrator as a bitter, mocking figure, standing to the side of his suspenseful plot of doom, jeering subtly at the rushing pursuits of the characters and at the static complacency of the conservative caste system he describes.

Most consistently the narrator's scornful repetitions are directed at religious faith. The Griffithses' evangelism, for example, is undermined by narrative juxtaposition as well as by more overt commentary. Their "collapsible" missionary religion, it is suggested, is not only a passive creed, but may be downright dangerous. An early description of the urban marginals who find their way to the Griffithses' mission ironically, even sinisterly, foreshadows Clyde's spiritual fervor at the moment of Roberta's death. These "botched and helpless who seemed to drift" into the mission are heard continually "testifying as to how God or Christ or Divine

---

and analepsis. *Narrative Discourse* (Ithaca: Cornell University Press, 1980), 40, and esp. ch. 1 on "Order."

Grace had rescued them . . . never how they had rescued anyone else" (17). Given the dramatic emphasis on Clyde's inaction in the climactic drowning scene, this detail seems more than coincidental. Though he rejects his parents' creed, Clyde, like the derelicts at their mission, summons its self-immolating message to absolve himself of responsibility for acting in his own behalf or, as the drowning scene will bear out, in another's. Yet Clyde will find rationalization for temporizing in more powerful creeds as well.

The entire drowning scene is cast in the repetitive rhythms of biblical verse. From the first mention of Clyde's "climacteric errand" (484) to the closing moments picturing "the peace and solemnity of this wondrous scene" (493), the portrait of Roberta's death exudes a sacramental aura. Recalling the derelicts at the mission, Clyde's unconscious during Roberta's drowning offers a retreat from the real world of action and consequence. Though Clyde's evasion cannot be said to cause her death, it does prevent his acting to save her, an eerie echo of the mission visitors who have never saved but only been saved.

Sitting in the boat with Roberta, Clyde dissolves into a realm of "endless space where was no end of anything—no plots—no plans—no practical problems to be solved—nothing." So gripped is he by this "sacred" revery that Roberta appears no more than a "shadow or thought, really, a form of illusion more vaporous than real." Caught between his desire for Roberta's death and his abhorrence of murder, Clyde enters a different temporal domain—a static order where no action or consequence exist. Akin to the lap of religion symbolized by his parents' mission, this "still" realm signals a "quiet, unprotesting type of death" (489). Inhabiting this mythical time, Clyde, like those at the mission, can deny responsibility for action. And his spiritual retreat from a deed that he has desperately pursued until the decisive moment absolves him, in his own mind at least, of a sense of responsibility for Roberta's death. Of interest here is the notion of religion as a kind of social welfare system whereby the lower classes may escape responsibility for past action or inaction. The way in which the charity mission allows the lower classes to evade their historical responsibilities parallels the method by which upper-class characters (such as Sondra and Belknap) *purchase* their evasions.

Another example of the narrator's ironic repetitions involves the portrayal of Roberta's all-night vigil following Clyde's sexual demands. She spends the night roaming about her room, gazing into the mirror, alternately sitting and standing. The most pronounced echo in the scene is Roberta's restaging of Clyde's anxious departure from the corn fields of Kansas City. Like Clyde, Roberta moves blindly in the dark of the dimly lit room; her physical gropings convey her mental anguish as she weighs the abandonment of her beliefs. Both characters' vigils end in resolutions to defy the self: Clyde concludes fearfully that he must "lose himself and so escape" (145), Roberta that "she must arrange not to have Clyde leave her" (295). Clyde's adoption of a self-effacing plan of sobriety and efficiency in the following chapter fulfills his aim, just as Roberta's forsaking of her deeply felt principles in yielding to Clyde leads to her end. The portrayal of Roberta's vigil is followed by a reading of her present in light of Clyde's past. The description of Clyde—"although the present conditions and situation are different," he is "in danger of repeating . . . what had befallen him" in his previous relationships—is in fact a description of Roberta, for it is she who is now in Clyde's former position.

The outcome of Roberta's night might appear fundamentally predetermined. She will not do other than what might be expected of a naturalist character—yield to physical impulse. Yet the fact that the scene is cast in terms of deliberation and choice is itself important. Though in her case movement is emphasized over thought, to reflect the predominant physicality of her concerns, Roberta's watch compares interestingly to Isabel Archer's motionless night before her fire in *The Portrait of a Lady*. Of course, the portrayal of that exemplary realist character pondering the weight of Gilbert Osmond's involvement with Madame Merle seems devoid of Roberta's physical struggles. Isabel's deliberation is primarily intellectual, whereas Roberta's is impelled by physical passion, however real her effort at conscious judgment. Where Isabel's vigil ends in the reaffirmation of a responsible self, Roberta's concludes with the embracing of an action she will later define as self-destructive. Still, this scene of intense deliberation, unusual for a naturalist work, serves as another indicator of the novel's wavering determinism.

The portrayal of Clyde and Roberta's first encounter on water exemplifies further the elaborate irony of the narrator's repetitions. A number of critics have noted how this scene anticipates the death scene of a year later, a perverse prolepsis recognized even by the historically insensible Clyde (475). Yet the extent of the scene's foreshadowings has not been fully analyzed, nor has it been noticed how the characters themselves set the predetermined course of their affair. In depicting Clyde and Roberta stifling their love before its inception, the scene ultimately reveals how deterministic assumptions are invoked in order to offset fears of the new and uncontrollable. The couple's thoughts just prior to their meeting delimit and distort their responses to one another in the actual encounter.

Roberta appears in Clyde's mind's eye in two forms before he recognizes her standing on the dock, giving his perception of her the appearance of an infinite regression. First, he sees her in memory, "shapely" and "smooth," as "she worked with her swift, graceful movements at her machine." Next, she is an anonymous, "very pretty" figure, standing on the dock, alive to his immediate perception. Finally recognized, she is a "realiz[ation]" of a "dream," her lips a "wavy line of beauty." And Roberta's developing view of Clyde is similar. She is "just the least bit abashed by the reality of him," for "she had been," the narrator informs us, "thinking of him so much and wishing for him in some happy, secure, commendable way. And now here he was" (257–59). Roberta's first view, like Clyde's, is a "commendable," secure vision. So pleasurable are their permissible images of one another that the actual encounter seems unwelcome.

The scene pinpoints a discrepancy between the imagination and the world it encounters, ascribing a perpetual gap between expectations and actual experience. By this logic, a fear of possessing a desired object arises from doubts that it can satisfy expectation. Yet more is at issue here. There is a fear of attaining the object of desire, precisely because it might meet and even unimaginably supersede expectations. The fear of what is not preconceived and thereby not bounded by imagination strikes most terror in this novel. Clyde and Roberta's fear of a pleasure uncircumscribed by convention inhibit and eventually destroy their bond. Each is too much the realization of a dream to the other to be deserved and fully encountered. Thus, the narrative appears to suggest that the "drama of determinism" has more to do with self-inflicted limitations than with impersonal forces. The imagination of fixity itself delimits human possibility. The idea of determinism is a construct, a socially functional and politically fused projection fantasy that incites guilt over human capacities for freedom or fulfillment. Yet some of the characters are more disposed to accept these social provisions than others.

In some instances, the narrator alludes directly, either playfully or sinisterly, to his anachronies. Most notable among these is Clyde's "accidental" view of the Alden farm at Biltz. What is striking about this second of three descriptions of Roberta's birthplace (the first is from Roberta's point of view, the last from the district attorney Mason's) is the narrator's dramatic distancing of himself from the responsibility for its "com[ing] to pass." As he intones, "Some might think, only an ironic and even malicious fate could have intended or permitted [Clyde's glimpse of the farm] to come to pass" (426). Merely a humble recorder of predetermined events, the narrator can hardly be held responsible for an incident that might be considered pivotal in bringing about Roberta's drowning. The narrator's disavowal of responsibility here carries forth and anticipates similar evasions, which include those of the derelicts in the Kansas City mission, Clyde before the sinking Roberta, Samuel Griffiths as he contemplates the prospects for Clyde's appeal, and the authorities of the inhumane modern death house.

The narrator's disavowal seems to confirm and parody this trail of denials, but there are other wry parallels here as well.

Clyde is "called to witness" a scene that is as much a depiction of his past as Roberta's, presaging ironically his forced recapitulation of his past at his trial. At this later point, however, where the memories of other witnesses prove far superior to his, he will be an impotent observer of others' versions of his experience. Here, Clyde recognizes his own past in Roberta's. "This lorn, dilapidated realm," by being connected with Roberta, is identified with "himself. . . . It even occurred to him, in a vague way for the first time, how strange it was that this girl and he, whose origin had been strikingly similar, should have been so drawn to each other in the beginning." And to further the parallel, Clyde's irresponsible dismay—"What was it about his life that made things like this happen to him! Was this what his life was to be like?" (427–29)— echoes Roberta's recent hopelessness incited by the same dismal rural scene: "Life was always doing things like this to her" (335).

For both, the oppressive scene signifies the past come back to life, a testimony to the inescapability of origins. By not living up to her expectations, Clyde becomes Roberta's past. As symbols of "inefficiency and lack," the farm and its surroundings are the "antithesis of all to which her imagination aspired . . . [which] was identified with Clyde." Yet if Clyde did not really love her and would not take her away from all this, then "the bleakness of it all" would come upon her with additional force (345–46). Likewise, Roberta's home in all of its decline signifies Clyde's past. Clyde's view of his origins in this glimpse of the Alden farm foreshadows his imaging of Roberta while she is drowning. Unless he "disengag[ed] himself," Clyde reflects desperately, gazing upon the farm, "this other world from which he sprang might extend its gloomy, poverty-stricken arms to him and envelop him once more, just as the poverty of his family had enveloped him and almost strangled him from the first" (428). And from the boat, looking upon Roberta drowning, Clyde sees her as "a form! It came nearer—clearer—and as it did so, he recognized Roberta struggling and waving her thin white arms out of the water and reaching toward him" (490).

The force of the camera blow can be seen to express Clyde's anger toward his past, revealing his inarticulate rage about his lower-class origins. Yet it may be equally the case that his inability to unite desire to action in his mute confusion prior to Roberta's rising in the boat also arises from his inability to accommodate his past. The scene contains an extraordinary paradox. Clyde's past projected onto his alter ego Roberta symbolizes the barriers to his present aspirations. But his repressed past—the uneasy fusion of a commercialized romanticism and the American success ethic— thwarts his enactment of his will in critical situations like this.

The narrator's repetitive ironies often hinge on questions of human responsibility for past actions. By hinting at the social and political effects of perceiving events as predetermined, and human beings as unaccountable for their actions, the narrator seems to prod the assumptions of the novel's deterministic vision. But though this scene at Biltz reveals the narrator's partial awareness of his own and others' willed detachment from their most compromising historical entanglements, his ironic sensibility never becomes a tool of critical insight. In order to clarify what appears from the perspectives of the characters and the narrator to be a hopelessly confused vision of individual responsibility, we must examine some of the novel's deeper political implications.

The Lycurgus Class Structure

An American Tragedy offers a critique of its determinist vision through the links it establishes between characters' social class positions and their abilities to manipulate temporal perceptions and historical narratives. In considering how the novel might be challenging its dominant philosophy, we can examine where individual responsibility for the past is borne and where it breaks down. Although most critics concur that rich and poor, powerful and powerless alike are at the mercy of time—pawns in the hands of predetermined circumstances—a deeper view implies otherwise, that crucial variations exist in the characters' subjections to time. Moreover, the novel suggests that the semblance of fixity functions to inhibit social change, and portrays determinism itself as a rhetorical instrument.

A recurring motif in Clyde's experiences is his incompatibility with the temporal frames of the worlds he enters into. This is not as true of the novel's early scenes, but from the moment of his arrival in Lycurgus his striving aspirations seem to jar with the town's apparently static social caste system. Walking through the streets of the town, Clyde is alarmed by the stark oppositions of its poor and wealthy sections. The slum is comparable to the worst of Chicago or Kansas City, while the palatial splendor of his relatives' neighborhood across the river is "arresting" (187–88). During his first days in Lycurgus, the modest circles in which Clyde circulates convey an air of relentless immobility. The placid aspect of Walter Dillard's aunt, who turns upon Clyde at a church social to "beam . . . a fatty beam," typifies the complacency of her world (201).

The air of fixity is further suggested by the repetitive lives of the Griffiths factory workers. Their daily march toward their workplace, joining the "general inpour" for other factories, and nightly return, "the same throng re-forming . . . and returning as it had come" (248), replicates the oppressive procedures of shirt collar production. The factory's workers seem hardly distinguishable from its products, which flow in "a constant stream . . . through several chutes from the floor above" (230). The production line absorbs all human beings and objects into its utilitarian processes.

Clyde himself inadvertently exposes one of the linchpins of the Griffiths factory rule. The "hundreds" of women workers, like the collars they produce, are indistinguishable sensual baubles to Clyde, each one a mild replication of the other (231). Thus Ruza Nikoforitch, with her "swimming brown eyes" and "snub fat nose," seems another version of Flora Brandt with her own "swimming . . . eyes" and "snub nose" (238). These "piece workers,"

Clyde's superior Ligget informs him, might be "freely take[en] on
. . . and then, once the rush was over, as freely dropp[ed]" (240).
Though Ligget's terms are strictly business, his allusion to the factory's constant need for "new blood and new energy" suggests a
different meaning of "rush," and facilitates Clyde's translation of
his words into sensual terms. The linguistic ambiguity conveys
the point: a factory ethic that dictates the exploitation of human
labor underwrites sexual exploitation as well. The repetitive
rounds of factory labor prove a dehumanizing temporality to its
workers.[16]

The objectifying routine of their workers' lives spurs much phi-
losophizing by the Griffithses. As Gilbert tells Clyde, "The men
and women who work for us have got to feel that they are employees first, last and all the time—and they have to carry that attitude
out into the street with them" (232). The adoption of circumspect
lives, in accordance with their routinized daily labor, ensures the
workers docility, which in turn guarantees the steady production
of shirt collars. The Griffithses' theory of factory management
"miraculously" discovers that what is "good" for human beings—
the commitment of their entire lives to their factory labor—is consonant with the interests of the factory. As the Griffithses "saw it,
there had to be higher and higher social orders to which the lower
classes could aspire. One had to have castes. . . . [There were]
those who were destined to rise. And those who were not should
be kept right where they were" (176).

The Griffithses' inclination to be "practical rather than . . .
charitable," to inveigh their workers with a feeling of "necessity
and compulsion" toward their work, and to inculcate "these lower
individuals to a clear realization of how difficult it was to come by

---

[16] Georg Lukács describes the temporal frames of capitalist society in his discussion of "reification": "Neither objectively nor in his relation to his work does man
appear as the authentic master of the process; on the contrary, he is a mechanical
part incorporated into a mechanical system." *History and Class Consciousness*, trans.
Rodney Livingstone (Cambridge, Mass.: MIT Press, 1971), 89–90. The ideology
of determinism can be seen, in Lukács's terms, to divorce human beings from the
sense of "authentic master[y]" over their existences.

money," represents their profiteering wages as morally and educationally beneficial. Serving to justify an exploitative labor system, the Griffithses' rhetoric on the nature of society transforms what is humanly interested and contrived into an image of inevitability. Their methods of labor management, the Griffithses maintain, fulfill their workers' social and spiritual destinies (176). But the novel's narrative undermines this rhetoric to suggest that far from the effortless outcome of a world whose social facts are as constant as nature, these forms of life and labor serve the special interests of an identifiable elite in a particular historical time and place.

As Georg Lukács writes, "When the ideal of scientific knowledge is applied to nature it simply furthers the progress of science. But when it is applied to society it turns out to be an ideological weapon of the bourgeoisie. For the latter it is a matter of life and death to understand its own system of production in terms of eternally valid categories: it must think of capitalism as being predestined to eternal survival by the eternal laws of nature and reason." What this vision omits is history itself: "the knowledge of the real, objective nature of a phenomenon, the knowledge of its historical character and the knowledge of its actual function in the totality of society . . .".[17]

The novel reveals the class structure of Lycurgus to be less natural or fixed than many of its inhabitants wish to believe. Repeatedly, the narrator records the discrepancy between the rhetoric of the town aristocracy and the specific historical details of their circumstances. This is evident in the contrast drawn between the Griffithses' established airs and the actual length of their lineage. Though their twenty-five-year residency establishes them as "if not the oldest, at least among the most conservative, respectable and successful in Lycurgus" (153), Samuel himself appears a bit

---

[17] The alternative to this capitalist perspective for Lukács is dialectical method. By dialectical, Lukács means that the members of a relation should be seen as fundamentally interactive, continually changing in response to one another. *History and Class Consciousness*, 10–11, 13, 14.

provincial as he gazes in awe at the bigger elite pond of the Union League in Chicago. He works hard for his relatively small stature, and is sufficiently aware of the effort of image-making to feel dismay over the Finchleys' "sudden and rather heavy expenditure for social reasons only" (155). Samuel carefully hides the signs of deliberate struggle. But his wife is less circumspect, and takes limitless "satisfaction in the grace and rank of her own home . . . she and her husband had been so long climbing up to it" (215).

Clyde may appear a picaresque hero in a world whose natural social hierarchy thwarts his ambition, but Lycurgus's class structure is more expedient than immutable. Indeed, the middle and elite classes of Lycurgus seem determined to mask the social and political maneuverings of their world, and with it the relationship between actions and consequences. Clyde and Roberta are the only characters who experience time as necessity, who are made to bear responsibility for their actions in history. Throughout their courtship, Clyde and Roberta are besieged by the public's censoring eyes, a projected vision of a community surveillance that is figured as a kind of temporal coercion.

The fugitive quality of their love is captured in the scene at Starlight Park:

Outside of Fonda a few miles they came to a pleasure park called Starlight where, in addition to a few clap-trap pleasure concessions such as a ring of captive aeroplanes, a Ferris wheel, a merry-go-round, an old mill and a dance floor, was a small lake with boats. It was after its fashion an idyllic spot with a little band-stand out on an island near the center of the lake and on the shore a grave and captive bear in a cage. . . . And as commonplace and noisy and gaudy as it all was, the fact that at last he had her all to himself, unseen, and she him, was sufficient to evoke in both a kind of ecstasy which was all out of proportion to the fragile, gimcrack scene. (278–79).

What resonates most in this description is the sense of captivity, which pervades their boundless joy. The "ecstasy" they feel is disproportionate to the meagre scene. Images of confinement, the "bear captive in a cage" who in his "grave[ness]" appears wisely conscious of his predicament, and amusements that purport to liberate, repeat rather than relieve the routinized constraints of their daily lives. The aeroplanes are "a ring of captives," the merry-go-round "a grinding machine" that carries its riders "round and round" in monotonous repetition. And the Ferris wheel, the source of freedom through height, is a set of "suspended cages." Each of these rides suggests a world of stasis, where human impulses are unleashed and immediately recontained. The sad park with its delicate "gimcrack" aura signals this world's continual manipulation of hope, as it kindles the dream, then demands its revocation.

It is significant that the designation of perspective here ("unseen") is grammatically ambiguous: it could be that Clyde and Roberta are unobserved, or that Clyde cannot see Roberta, so fully governed by his own needs is his image of her. In both cases, there is an emphasis on the limits to perception either directly imposed by society or internalized by the individual. The passage implies that dreaming itself is a public and commercialized affair, that hopes in this world may only be realized in a certain way, through carefully controlled public rituals that ensure that no dreamer gets too far away with himself. The solemn bear in the cage seems to know the reality of life in the novel's society as the ultimate in captivity—significantly, an exposed imprisonment, where an integral part of the punishment is its sufferance under the community's watchful eyes. The motif of Clyde and Roberta's relationship is their fear of obtrusive public eyes, standing perpetual guard on their moments of ecstasy. In pursuing, apprehensively and then exultantly, their sexual affair, moving beyond the static sources of release available to them, Clyde and Roberta's guilt is projected in the image of their vividly exposed deviance.

But the union of Clyde and Roberta is designated as deviant only because of their ignorance of the available conventions for circumventing their predicament. The couple's foiled attempts to abort Roberta's pregnancy indicate the existence of a social underground where undesired products of illicit affairs are easily disposed of. The narrator cryptically discloses that there were at least three "midwives . . . here in Lycurgus at this time" (384) who might have been called upon to perform an abortion. Roberta's habitual detachment from the other factory girls (412), Clyde's own isolation (373), and their lack of money handicaps them. The Lycurgus barber explains concisely, "In the first place it's agin' the law. And next it takes a lotta money" (409). As the order of summary suggests, the law can be elided if one has the essential connections and funds.

Most important, however, is the extent to which Clyde and Roberta's own self-incriminations inhibit their pursuit of likely alternatives. In a circular way, their guilt furthers their entrapment as both masochistically doubt the potential to rid themselves of their unwanted child. Though they are socially marginal, they are also deeply conventional, their sense of morality blocking the way out of their dilemma. Both feel unalterably defined by their past action, just as they feel irreversibly held by their lower class backgrounds. In fact, as Dr. Glenn's hypocritical stance in refusing them his services suggests, their act is labeled and dealt with according to their class position. Dr. Glenn's price for the suspension of morality in his mystifying blend of provincial piety, self-aggrandizement, and opportunism is beyond them for both financial and social reasons.

On first appearance Dr. Glenn epitomizes small-town reliable conservatism: all "grayness, solidity and stolidity." Informed of the true facts of Roberta's case, he refuses the request outright, declaring the immorality of abortion. But though his refusal to "rescue" Roberta gives him a feeling of superiority, his resistance is explained otherwise. He is "opposed to aiding, either by his own countenance or skill, any lapses or tangles *not heavily sponsored by others*" (emphasis added). In other words, Dr. Glenn will break the law to protect the reputations of wealthy girls, but stands his moral ground in the cases of poor ones. By his logic, it is moral to erase the "folly" of girls of "good family," but impoverished girls must endure the consequences of actions that their poverty explains (398–400). Their deeds divorced from the world of action and consequence and regarded as play, wealthy girls are aided in rewriting their pasts. Poor girls, on the contrary, reveal their low origins in every action they take, and must accept responsibility for what they are. Glenn's moral circumlocutions force Clyde and Roberta to bear the burden of their pasts, making them responsible for past actions in a way that contrasts strikingly with the novel's other main characters.

In the chapters leading up to Roberta's death, Clyde's dilemma of historical doom with her is played off against the static contentment of his trysts with Sondra. She and her friends revel in an irresponsible youth of sports and car trips that opposes Clyde and Roberta's subjection to the cause-and-effect processes of historical time. While Roberta exemplifies Clyde's "necessity," compelled to "speak out definitely and forcefully," Sondra is calm and still, "the panorama of the bright world of which [she] was the center" (414). Sondra is once again associated with stillness at the novel's close, where Clyde holds her unsigned letter "quite still" as he contemplates her freedom. "She was free. She had beauty—wealth" (790). Like Dr. Glenn's "girls of good family" and Clyde's lawyer Belknap (592–93), Sondra has the money and connections to erase the consequences of her actions. Her father's wealth and position ensure that her name will remain disentangled from Clyde's sordid experiences (580–81). And this is precisely how the novel defines power—as the ability to buy time and rewrite circumstance, to transcend the fixed conditions of its deterministic logic.

In the third book, others' abilities to manipulate and rearrange the facts of Clyde's past for their own uses are played off against his inability to gain any perspective on it. Book 3 opens upon a world obsessed with history's linear progress in the face of a hotly contested November election. No longer able to dream and delay with the wealthy set, Clyde must confront the localized concerns of a provincial town in early-twentieth-century America. The introductory emphasis on the immediate historical context of

Clyde's indictment and trial implies that he has fallen headlong into history. Given the importance of Clyde's sense of the past in Book 3, it is worthwhile to review his relation to the past in Books 1 and 2. Clyde's historical insensibility is established early on.[18] One rare recollection, stirred by his sister Esta's unhappy pregnancy, evokes a memory of Esta, "sitting at his father's little street organ . . . looking so innocent and good" (99). This momentary review arouses uncharacteristic sympathy in Clyde, an almost tearful conviction of how "strange" and "rough" life is. There are other examples of Clyde recalling the past (195, 278, 359–60, 425, 429). But it seldom brings him to an understanding or articulation of a sense of self, or place in the world.

A noteworthy exception is his first stroll through the streets of Lycurgus. Following an unhappy interview with Gilbert, Clyde's misery is mirrored in his view of a depressing slum. So struck is he by its "angularity and crudeness" that he "at once retraced his steps and recrossing the Mohawk by a bridge farther west soon found himself in a area which was very different indeed . . . very broad and well-paved and lined by such an arresting company of houses" (187–88). Clyde's retracing here takes him eventually from the dismal slum neighborhood to the wealthy environs of his relatives' home. And his initially impulsive retracing and recrossing gives way to a deeper process of self-review. Coming upon the Griffithses' mansion, Clyde is struck full force by the reality of "who the Griffiths were here," as opposed to "who the Griffiths were in Kansas City." As he becomes aware of his great "difference" from the Lycurgus Griffithses and his own identity as a "nobody" (189), Clyde's repetitive action brings him to a profound

[18] It is interesting to note that in revising the novel, Dreiser deleted numerous passages devoted to the various pasts of his characters, in particular the past of Clyde's parents. The deletion of their history, as well as the rather pointed dismissal of history that replaces it (14), supports the novel's overall suggestion that the key is not how one is created by one's past but instead how one may reshape those materials. For details about Dreiser's excisions, see Pizer, *Novels*, 210–14, 227–32.

CHAPTER SIX

recognition of how he has been made by his past. The volitional nature of this retracing, as distinguished from later ones, provides for a moment of self-awareness.

Clyde's only retracings and returns in Book 3 are forced upon him by his lawyers, the prosecuting attorney, and the parade of court witnesses who render him powerless by unfolding a past panorama in which he is the subject, but completely under their direction. All these recounters of Clyde's past give the impression of telling it more accurately than he, and most of them exploit it for their own uses. Clyde's past becomes a saleable commodity, a "hot" item serving others' interests. Thus, Clyde's inability to frame a believable version of his past makes him a victim of those who can. The defense lawyer Jephson's rhetorical question to Clyde under cross-examination, "After all, you didn't make yourself, did you?" (674), seems more than a little ironic given the emphasis placed on his inability to narrate his own history.

In fact, Jephson exemplifies the questionable intentions of those who manage Clyde's past, for though commendable, his strategizing on behalf of Clyde's defense at times appears ruthless. He is described at one point, "his harebell eyes showing only cold, eager, practical," his manner "like a spider spinning a web, on his own plan" (609). Although Jephson's professional intensity can hardly be faulted, and Clyde benefits from his personal strength at the trial, there are hints that he is so caught up in his own machinations that he objectifies and effaces Clyde as harshly as his trial foes. And some of his judgments seem actually harmful to Clyde.[19] At least a few of Jephson's trial tactics are suspicious. We

[19] In one striking description, Jephson's plottings take on Clyde's demeanor at the moment of Roberta's death. "So interested [is] he in his own plot" that his eyes look "for all the world like windless, still pools." Jephson's eyes reflect the "still dark water," seemingly "bottomless," of Big Bittern, as well as "the stillness" and "balanced immobility" of Clyde's mood at the moment of Roberta's death (612–13, 489, 492). The similarities between Clyde just prior to Roberta's drowning and Jephson plotting Clyde's defense suggest the difference between one who uses transcendent inspiration to delay acting to aid another, and one who uses it in an attempt to save another's life. Yet there may be another point here: that Clyde might

never receive an explanation for why Jephson reverses the "original plan" to have the stately and respectable Belknap cross-examine Clyde (672). Nor, more curiously, do we learn why Jephson suppresses a letter from the former captain of the bellboys at the Green-Davidson that would have supported Clyde's own testimony. Jephson's judgment that such a disclosure is "irrelevant" seems mysteriously misguided and arbitrary (676).

The boldness and rationality of others' approaches to Clyde's past provide a striking contrast to his own timorousness. Clyde's narrative befuddlement—his inability to narrate his past experiences—allows others to empower themselves through it. Clyde's role as a political pawn is replicated in his role as a literary pawn, the main character in the proliferating versions of his life. Thus, political and narrative power become one, as Clyde is shown to be a protagonist whose lack of control over his own tale proves fatal.

Repeated references to Clyde's poor plotting and scheming relate his downfall to his ineptness as a systematic narrator. Contemplating the trail of evidence left by Clyde, Mason wonders silently, "What sort of a plotter and killer would that be?" (520). And the narrator describes Clyde at his capture, his "shrunk" form revealing the "effects of his so poorly conceived and executed scheme" (559). The publicity pamphlets offering for a penny "an outline of 'the great plot'" (630) provide an ironic contrast to Clyde's own plotting deficiencies. Mason quickly deduces Roberta's pregnancy from the bits of information extracted from "the broken and gloomy Titus" (522). All the evidence, which tumbles out with astounding ease, "seemed to unescapably point to [Clyde] as the murderer of Roberta Alden" (526). Though he is prepared to recognize some "trace of truth" in Clyde's version, Mason is more intent on seizing it in his own instinctive grasp (573). But while Mason's entirely intuitive detailing of Clyde and Roberta's shared life is stunningly accurate, there is an element missing in

---

have been better served had Jephson helped him to discover his own explanation. There is an analogy to be made here between Jephson's cold-hearted scheming and plotting, his superintending of Clyde's past, and Clyde's role in Roberta's death.

CHAPTER SIX

"facts" so starkly represented (640). Mason's seamless portrait of
Clyde is a distortion not unlike his characterization of Clyde's plotting: "how shrewd and deep must be that mind that would foresee
and forestall all the accidents and chances of life" (646).
The novel's greatest irony is that despite the appearance of intentional plotting and murder, Clyde's actions ultimately recoil
back upon themselves as haphazardly as unplanned chaos. Clyde's
experiences present an epistemological dilemma—how to treat a
situation that in every way points to a certain reality, but that fundamentally swerves away from that reality? It is not surprising
that Clyde cannot convey his past coherently either to himself or
to Mason. Forced to hedge about a plot he has been too ineffectual
to carry out, Clyde becomes more and more implicated by Mason's whirling inquiries, trapped by fiction as well as by fact (572–
73).
In its own way, the defense version of Clyde's experience is no
more viable. It even seems more threatening to his sense of self in
its disregard for the potential truths of Clyde's experiences due to
the urgent necessity of crafting a salvational fiction. Doubting that
Clyde can save himself, Belknap and Jephson shape a "straightened story," thereby entrenching his impotence. Sitting in passive
contemplation as they plot his past, without any sense of participation or control in its recreation, Clyde seems to embody the idea
of reification. "They talked as though he was not present or could
have no opinion in the matter, a procedure which astonished but
by no means moved him to object, since he was feeling so helpless"
(604). Clearly, their dismissiveness serves to alienate him the more
from his own past. He repeats the greater part of his testimony
mindlessly, from a page "written out for him" by Jephson and dutifully committed to memory (682). Dispossessed of his memories,
Clyde's capacity for self-defense seems doomed.
So removed is Clyde from the defense's version of his life that
he even fails to recognize a familiar childhood metaphor from the
Arabian Nights when Jephson alludes to it in his cross-examination. Though Clyde has continually envisioned his aspirations in

this fantasy framework, his response to Jephson's description of his life as "a case of the Arabian Nights, of the enscorcelled and the enscorceller," is a vague, "I don't think I know what you mean" (681). The "exotic" "romance" terms that have dominated his imaginative life since boyhood (14) are not even a dim memory.[20] And to emphasize further Clyde's estrangement from his aspiring self, one of Clyde's friends on Death Row, the lawyer Nicholson, is portrayed giving Clyde a copy of the Arabian Nights (776). Perhaps, this gift suggests, Clyde's final days will see a restoration of his earliest romantic self, the only, if sadly derivative, self he has felt a connection to. The paradox of Clyde's circumstances is that he becomes in Book 3 what he has willed for himself in Book 2—a passive observer of his own life. But this brings with it something he has not anticipated: he and his history become objectified and exploitable.

The superintending of Clyde's past implies that any life "artfully . . . recapitulated" and "recanvass[ed]" for its "fine points" (735–36) can be made to fulfill the needs and assumptions of present viewers. Reconstructed with his "crime" in mind, the chaotic details of Clyde's experience become significant clues to his later murderous intentions and actions. Indeed, the task of narrating the past serves as the ultimate example of determinism—in the work of retrospective signification, one is invariably fixed from the start. Clyde and Roberta's affair is socially deviant because she becomes pregnant and is unable to erase its consequences. Likewise, Roberta's drowning seems to drain much of the ambiguity and ambivalence from Clyde's actions leading up to it, so that even readers doubt whether it is not murder, the outcome of careful planning and clear intent.[21] Once it has achieved symbolic status,

[20] See for example, 53, 66, and Ellen Moers's fine discussion of the extensiveness of this metaphor, in *Two Dreisers*, 271–85.

[21] In sociological terms, the idea of "retrospective interpretation" is exemplified by "the organizational processing of deviators and involves the use of the 'case record,' or 'case history' . . . [which] seem . . . almost entirely to support current diagnoses." Edwin Schur, *Labelling Deviant Behavior* (New York: Harper and Row, 1971), 52–56. Schur then quotes Erving Goffman's claim that "almost anyone's

Clyde's life is no longer the disconnected and arbitrary events of his experience, but a rationalized and reified tale with crucial meanings for others.

Yet Clyde's own inability to articulate his past, like his inability to devise an effective plan for coping with Roberta's pregnancy, arises from an inner confusion that is in great part attributable to his unthinking incorporation of society's myths. Rather than the enactment of the doom of humanity at the hands of fate, or the requisite downfall of a character psychologically unsuited to his desired position, Clyde's life is more fully seen in terms of a social hegemony that overregulates his aspirations. The novel's narrative features a discrepancy between a social rhetoric that insists that nature (both biological and universal) is everything, the all-encompassing factor predetermining human destiny, and its own underlying political revelations, which expose how such rhetoric masks the social and political particulars governing and constricting Clyde's life. Clyde's alienation from his own actions in history, and his related inability to narrate his past, can be seen to result from his excessive belief in society's tales. The novel reveals narrative itself to be the means by which a social determinism is entrenched.

Clyde's passive tendencies are cultivated and affirmed by those

---

life's course could yield up enough denigrating facts to provide grounds for the record's justification of commitment." The philosopher Thomas Nagel considers the issue of retrospective interpretation as a problem of individual responsibility. He writes, "As the external determinants of what someone has done are gradually exposed, in their effect or consequences, it becomes gradually clear that actions are events and people things. Eventually nothing remains that can be ascribed to the responsible self." ("Moral Luck," in *Mortal Questions* [New York: Oxford University Press, 1981], 37–38. This is the paradox of the novel's third book. Clyde's "murder" of Roberta has become a public event, and Clyde himself is objectified to the point that his own past is personally meaningless. William James wrestled with similar questions of how human beings could be held accountable for their actions in a predetermined world. The novel's insight into the political ramifications of this question and into suggestions that human beings are made *differentially* responsible is illuminating. See "The Dilemma of Determinism," in *A William James Reader*, ed. Gay Wilson Allen (New York: Houghton Mifflin, 1971), 16–40.

who exploit him for the purposes of their operative systems. Samuel Griffiths uses Clyde as a test case for his survival of the fittest philosophy (158). Sondra Finchley toys with Clyde as a test of her seductive powers (305–309). Jephson sees Clyde's case as the testing ground for his judicial powers (598). Repeatedly, Clyde encounters fixed systems of thought that he only mildly understands, whose operators seek to tailor him to their uses. Perhaps the ultimate example of such a systematic hegemony is the public opinion of Bridgeburg, which typecasts Clyde as an evil deviant irreverently challenging their rigorous moral code. Belknap and Jephson's treatment of Clyde's case, which turns him into an ineffectual participant in the narrative defense of his life, serves similarly to efface Clyde. In each case, Clyde's own lack of an effective governing paradigm makes him vulnerable to exploitation.

Thus, understanding how all of these relationships form a pattern that reveals Clyde's overall experience of society is as important as understanding the psychological complexities of Clyde's interactions with various other characters.[22] Clyde's condition in the novel's third book might be seen to typify Lukács's view of the human absorption by time in the increasingly reified world of twentieth-century Western society. No longer possessed of a *relation* to time, Clyde *incarnates* it. Because of his inability to account for his past actions in an acceptably rational form, Clyde is given a past by various authorities. Defined by his "crime," he is stilled thereby in others' imaginations. Each view of Clyde—the prosecution's "mature" and "bearded man," the defense's "mental" and "moral coward," the Bridgeburg public's "little devil," and the "astonishingly youthly slayer" of the press and anonymous crowds (642, 669, 739, 754)—fails to see him as a specific human being in history.

The fixture of Clyde's image also allows for his incorporation into others' reified systems of thought. Thus, the lawyers see

---

[22] Lukács writes in his description of "concrete analysis" that the key is to focus on "the relation to society as a whole . . . not those between one individual and another." See *History and Class Consciousness*, 50.

Clyde legalistically, judging his responsibility for his actions; the public sees him moralistically, insisting on the necessary repression of human instincts and passion in society; the press sees him sensationally, as a figure to incite and feed a bored public's desire for intimacy with lives seemingly more romantic than their own. Clyde comes to fulfill the rationale of each of these systems, literally "take[n] . . . up" (310) in Sondra's phrase, his identity "incarnating" its adherents' governing concerns. The death house ideology that Clyde encounters near the novel's close proves the logical extension of all its ruling perspectives.

Following Roberta's death, Clyde's life becomes the province of the novel's death instrument, the camera. Frozen in a single moment of the past, it is pictured over and over in innumerable press and pamphlet versions for the satisfaction of public voyeurs. The inhabitants of Bridgeburg, and the nation as a whole, are gripped by this sensational case, their obsession fueled and fed by publicity on Clyde's life in newspaper stories and photographs. Their view allows sufficient distance from the unsettling though glamorous object, while it yields a feeling of intimacy.[23] The novel's central agents of modern technology, the newspaper and the camera, provide a false illusion of familiarity with the exceptional being, guiding the community to define him or her in its own terms. Lives captured within the pages of the daily press in a written or photographic form are inevitably viewed as public property to be exploited.

Everyone associated with Clyde siphons the celebrity of his de-

[23] The phenomenon of the public's attraction and repulsion toward celebrated crime figures was borne out in the Atlanta trial of Wayne Williams. At a critical moment in the trial, jurors were invited to touch the defendant, to test his physical strength. Murray Kempton recalls that he knew Williams was convicted when he saw how no "juror would reach out and touch the real Williams." *New York Review of Books* (March 14, 1985), 31. Also pertinent here is Richard Sennett's analysis of the developing quest for intimacy with those defined as public figures in nineteenth- and twentieth-century society. This desire is seen in tandem with the obsessive emphasis placed on "personality" and appearances. *The Fall of Public Man* (New York: Vintage, 1978).

viant act. Mason is a "true hero," his departure from the court-
room like the exit of a movie idol, "a heavy, baggy overcoat thrown
over his shoulder," a "worn soft hat pulled low over his eyes," followed by his "royal train" of assistant district attorneys (740).
Clyde's life comes to seem less and less his own as public versions
of it synthesized from witnesses' testimonies (637, 658) overtake
his already tenuous self-image. The clearer Clyde appears in the
frameworks of others, the more shadowy he becomes in his own.
En route to the death house, he is "astonished" by the response of
crowds encountered at every train stop, all desiring to "achieve a
facile intimacy with this daring and romantic, if unfortunate figure" (754). He is "heartened" but profoundly disconcerted by the
familiarity of anonymous strangers. And upon his arrival at the
death house, Clyde is dismayed by the extent to which things
"concerning him [were] known here" (756–57).

In the face of this overwhelming public seizure of his identity
and of the brutally exposed procedures of death row, Clyde turns
to the spiritual preachings of his mother and Reverend McMillan
in an attempt to discover a past narrative that more closely expresses his experience of his past. Yet she and McMillan are as intent as his legal advisors on fitting Clyde's history into their own
schemes of judgment. Clyde's mother must know the facts of the
case: "Were those things as contended by Mason true or false?"
She bewails Clyde's dumbfoundedness, finding him "not positive
enough" (749). Absorbed by binomial oppositions of truth and
falsehood, faith or deception, she denies Clyde the ranging exploration that might allow him to recuperate his past. Her thirst for
"all the data which was the ultimate, basic truth in regard to her
son" (752), a thirst shared by Clyde's previous examiners, paradoxically sacrifices Clyde in the name of a system she believes
might save.

Reverend McMillan likewise inhibits Clyde's ability to confront
his past. Another representative of a rational system, his religious
terms are no more adequate for accommodating ambiguity. Following Clyde's narration, McMillan's face reflects the same horri-

fied confusion Clyde has seen in other listeners. "McMillan's face was gray and drawn . . . he had been listening, as he now felt, to a sad and terrible story—an evil and cruel self-torturing and destroying story," a story that troubles his "reason" as it moves his heart (794). His reason triumphs over his heart as McMillan adheres to rational judgment in refraining from supporting Clyde's appeal before the governor (803). Yet as the scene closes on Clyde's execution, it is implied that McMillan may forever be hounded by his heart for allowing such a victory.

The novel's final image of Clyde as storyteller is striking. "In his uniform—his hair cropped so close, Clyde sat there, trying honestly now to think how it really was (exactly) and greatly troubled by his inability to demonstrate to himself even—either his guilt or his lack of guilt" (795). So caught up is Clyde in the persistent demands of his various audiences that his own terms have now become exclusively binomial oppositions. Incapable of reenacting or recapturing a sense of how "it" was for himself, his only framework is right or wrong, guilt or innocence. The severity of these limited frames is reflected in his close-cropped hair and sterile prison uniform.

Despairing that he will ever "get the whole thing straightened out in his own mind," Clyde awaits his execution, absorbed in biblical texts. Compulsively "reading and re-reading the psalms," he hopes thereby to achieve "peace and strength" but never "quite catch[es] it" (798–99). Like his Jewish counterpart on Death Row, who seeks absolution in ceaseless repetition of the Kol Nidre, Clyde finds that conventional narratives, religious or legal, do not serve those who have strayed beyond the boundaries of acceptable conduct. Moreover, society's terms are rational and uniform, Clyde's past is to be "taken all together and considered as a connected whole." And within this frame, the court concludes, Clyde's experiences "make such convincing proof of guilt that we are not able to escape from its force by any justifiable process of reasoning" (799).

But the various versions of Clyde's life told in Book 3 lack the

authority that characterizes a story originally told from the heart of its experiencer. The novel's plot closes on the "dazed" eyes of a protagonist who has been unable to shape a text of his life that would allow him some degree of self-expression or power. Clyde, however, does attain a certain awareness of his needs by the novel's end, paradoxically through his inability to find himself in others' versions of his past. At the opening of Book 3, Clyde's mind is caught in "fear and confusion . . . as to whether he did or did not bring about [Roberta's] untimely end" (527). A character who has all along feared his connection to his past, Clyde doubts he "would . . . ever be able to shake [it] off" (529). His view of the "single bundle" of clothes worn on the boat, noting "sickeningly" the "odds and ends he had worn that day," leads him to wonder at the fragmented mystery of his own past, "all he had contacted since his arrival in the east, how little he had in his youth. How little he had now, really" (534). So severely alienated is Clyde here that he can envision himself as no more than miscellaneous threads of cloth. By the book's close, however, he has achieved some insight.

The closing description of Clyde, finally aware that he can never make his mother understand him, reveals his recognition of his inability to locate a self that can be made known to others.

But how strange it was, that to his own mother, and even now in these closing hours, when above all things he craved sympathy—but more than sympathy, true and deep understanding—even now—and as much as she loved and sympathized with, and was seeking to aid him with all her strength in her stern and self-sacrificing way,—still he could not turn to her now and tell her, his own mother, just how it all happened. It was as though there was an unsurmountable wall or impenetrable barrier between them, built by the lack of understanding—for it was just that. She would never understand his craving for ease and luxury, for beauty, for love—his particular kind of love that went with show, pleasure, wealth, position, his eager and immutable aspirations and desires. . . . And she would and did expect him to be terribly sorry and wholly repentant, when, even now, and for all he had said to the Reverend McMillan and to her, he could not feel so—not wholly so—although great was his desire

287

now to take refuge in God, but better yet, if it were only possible, in her own understanding and sympathetic heart. (806)

Clyde desires recognition above all: to have his cravings and impulses corroborated by another human being. Wracked with guilt over the possible profanity and excessiveness of his desires, he needs them acknowledged as not monstrous. Yet Clyde discovers only walls between himself and that formidable other, his mother. This "insurmountable wall or impenetrable barrier . . . built by the lack of understanding" seems an intentional edifice, erected brick-by-brick through a process of complicity that both have shared. To his mother, Clyde's desires have always been slightly monstrous.

But he has come to recognize needs that will never be rationalized out of existence, the set of fluid desires he cannot reason away. Apart from "all he had said to Reverend McMillan," despite his fears of the afterlife, Clyde seems to know that he will never completely accept the repression of desire. He can be seen to have reached this awareness through his inability to recognize others' pictures of him. Nevertheless, only coherent and very specific kinds of narratives provide for survival in Clyde's society. And the possibility that human beings are incapable of perceiving anything that falls outside the boundaries of their governing paradigms points to the subject of ideological hegemony, and the links between narrative and political power.

Conclusion: The "Fractional" Determinism of An American Tragedy

Many critics have recognized the extent to which the novel questions the American social system that creates, nurtures, and eventually condemns Clyde Griffiths. Irving Howe has been especially responsive to the novel's political perspective, and, in an afterword to the novel, terms it a "parable of our national experience" (821), a portrait of "the passivity, rootlessness, and self-alienation of urban man . . . [in which] the problem of human freedom becomes critically acute through a representation of its decline [and] the problem of awareness is brought to the forefront through a portrait of its negation" (826). But Howe's insistence on the novel's unequivocal determinism seems to belie its most complex political vision.

Rather than exemplifying the human condition in a predetermined universe, Clyde's "fractional awareness" (819) represents the specific conditions of a lower-class youth in a society where some lives are more predetermined than others, and where the conception of a world ruled by impersonal forces might precisely serve the interests of that society's elite. *An American Tragedy* is more accurately conceived to ponder uncertainly its deterministic philosophy, in light of the social and political uses to which this philosophy is often put in the novel's world.

The use of determinism as a containment strategy that allows social authorities to deny their role in the creation and perpetuation of an oppressive social order can be seen in the discussion of the Auburn execution system. As the narrator pointedly informs us at the outset, the new death house is a place "for which no one primarily was really responsible" (758). Erected "by degrees and without anything worthy of the name of thinking on anyone's part," it is "all that could possibly be imagined in the way of unnecessary and really unauthorized cruelty" (758–59). With no one accepting responsibility for its existence, the death house, like some pure product of nature, seems to have emerged from the workings of eternal law. Yet the narrative irony here is undisguised, and the denial of any human agency or intent is immediately overriden by the allusion to "the thoughtful and condescending authorities" who have "devised" this "newer and better" death house. Alleviating the intense solitude of the previous model, this more open and "brightly lighted" death house renders its inhabitants' impending executions an excruciatingly public affair (759–60). Each inmate is now "actually if not intentionally compelled to hear if not witness the final preparations" (761) of the soon-to-be-executed. Contrary to the opening rhetoric of botched inevitability, the denial of privacy in this new execution system seems remarkably consistent with the slim divide between public and private spheres in the novel's society.

The features of the new death house, in other words, are linked to an identifiable set of assumptions about the best means of social organization, reflecting a social ideology built upon the mutual policing of society's members. As the narrative implies, the links between the new death house's spotlight aura and the relentlessly public nature of self-perceptions portrayed throughout the novel—from Clyde's street-corner anguish over the shabby appearance of his family to his late embarrassment about the shearing of his hair in prison—are too precise to be accidental. For a world of selves increasingly swallowed up by their social milieu, a death house with floodlights and open cells seems entirely appropriate. As was true for the "captive bear" at Starlight Park, the lack of privacy is indeed part of the punishment.

The narrator's own stance in this passage is more difficult to assess. His waffling in first describing the new death house as "unauthorized" (however ironic), and then referring to its elaboration by "thoughtful authorities," perhaps betrays his reluctance to pin responsibility on anyone. Though he consistently unmasks others' efforts to deny responsibility for their historical actions, this does not preclude his own denials. Yet there are even more important ways in which determinism functions as a containment strategy in the novel.

Central among these is the issue of Clyde's suitability for success. The question of the primary determinants of success in the novel's society is a complex one. But an understanding of the issue is critical for assessing the interaction of psychological and socio-political factors in Clyde's downfall. Throughout *An American Tragedy*, allusions to the importance of education or vocation as means by which one gains entrance into the ranks of America's elite war mysteriously with references to "connections." Indeed, the obsessive repetition of this word in the novel has eluded the attention of critics.[24]

The novel's early chapters emphasize Clyde's resentment toward his parents for their mismanagment of their children's educational and vocational training (14, 17, 18, 19, 27, 170). Other mentions of Clyde's attitudes toward success, however, seem to contradict this anxiety. Seen as representative of "American youth," Clyde appears to disdain most kinds of occupational training. "True to the standard of the American youth, or the general American attitude toward life, [Clyde] felt himself above the type of labor which was purely manual. What! Run a machine, lay bricks, learn to be a carpenter, or a plasterer, or plumber, when boys no better than himself were clerks and druggists' assistants?" (18). Clyde's perspective seems generally to deny process, to belie the work of achieving a goal. He conceives of ends without means, success without the expenditure of effort in attaining it.

But this air of impracticality or lack of initiative and commitment, the narrator assures us, is not peculiar to Clyde. Nor, more crucially, does it seem inconsistent with the American success ethic as the novel portrays it. Samuel and Gilbert repeatedly refer to Clyde's lack of training as an explanation for his low placement in the factory hierarchy, contradicting the larger social picture

[24] Critics have identified the word "dream" as appearing more frequently than any other word in the novel; see Lehan, *Dreiser*, 187; Moers, *Two Dreisers*, 277. The word "connection," used almost exclusively in its meaning of social contact, appears at least 207 times. Clyde is from youth obsessed with his lack of "contacts and connections" (30). The word appears in quotation marks early in Book 2 to indicate the idiom of Dillard, who is envious of Clyde's "class and connections" (196). The most important aspect of its use is that it increases over the novel's course, particularly following Clyde's fixation with his social aspirations in Lycurgus. The word appears 186 times in Books 2 and 3 as compared to 21 times in Book 1, a considerable difference even allowing for the different page lengths of the three books. "Connection" appears on the average of once every seven pages in Book 1, and once every three and a half pages in Books 2 and 3—that is, with twice the frequency. The differing rates of the word's usage correspond significantly to Clyde's growing absorption into the hegemony of the American class structure, a process ruled by an obsession with connections. The frequency of the word is a crucial index to the novel's underlying political concerns.

their rhetoric inscribes (158, 181–82, 216). Though the society's Horatio Alger story of business success seemingly paints the road to wealth and position as open to any American youth through hard work and self-belief, the tale's underlying message suggests otherwise. The Griffithses' continual alignment of worldly success and spiritual favor, and condonation of exploitative business practices with elevated rhetoric, implies that success cannot be pursued. Rather, success is a state or condition that one achieves naturally, by merely being a certain type of individual. Whether the outcome of predetermination or chance, success is possessed, not made.

The issue is complicated by Clyde's resentment toward Gilbert Griffiths, whose manner claims wealth and respect as his rightful due, but whose past does not justify it. While Samuel Griffiths's superiority is legendary, Gilbert effects "airs and superiorities which, but for his father's skill before him, would not have been possible" (181). Clyde resents Gilbert's criticisms of his lack of vocation, while Gilbert's success is determined by blood alone. Of course, Clyde's own reception by Lycurgus's lower classes is based on this similarly unearned premise of high birth.

Success to the increasingly worldly Clyde of Book 2 comes to appear as a miraculous election into "a company of seemingly mentally and socially worldly elect" (168), or a chance result of having "the right sort of contacts . . . a connection" (169). This developing vision of success reveals its growing separation from the possibility of personal initiative. Thus, Clyde's view of success comes to accord with the prevailing deterministic ideology of the social systems he encounters. From his employment at the Green-Davidson and the Union League, Clyde begins to view success as a predestined or arbitrary phenomenon. His response to the inexplicable downpour of coins into his pocket at the Green-Davidson captures the contradictory terms of his perspective. He feels "a sense of luck and a sense of responsibility as to future luck" (53). Clyde's inappropriate sense of "responsibility" toward his luck merely highlights the remoteness of his desires from the plane of human action.

Like the reconstruction of Clyde's past at his trial, the life becomes separated from the human actor who lives it, as choices and actions in history become mere threads in a pattern. For well-placed individuals like Samuel or Gilbert Griffiths, such an immobilized view of the world is clearly beneficent. But for Clyde it can only lead to frustration and ultimately to self-annihilation.[25]

By the late nineteenth and early twentieth centuries, the rags-to-riches myth was beginning to seem more and more antedated, given growing perceptions of the expanding role of large institutions in American life.[26] The absence of a relation between means and ends in success narratives might well have felt more realistic to many Americans at this time.[27] Yet the element of futility in

[25] This view qualifies the Durkheimian paradigm applied to the novel by Bernard Rosenberg, though Durkheim's ideas are appropriate in a number of ways. Durkheim's theory of poverty as developed in his concept of anomie is illuminating to Clyde's experiences. "Poverty," Durkheim observes, "protects against suicide because it is a restraint in itself . . . the less one has the less he is tempted to extend the range of his needs indefinitely. . . . The less limited one feels, the more intolerable all limitation appears" (quoted in Rosenberg's Afterword, 818). It seems true that the closer Clyde comes to fulfilling his aspirations, the closer he comes to self-annihilation. (This is especially pertinent if one views Clyde's "murder" of Roberta as a form of suicide, as some critics have suggested.) And even Clyde's most characteristic facial expression, "his eyebrows and the skin of his forehead rising and falling as he talked—a form of contraction and expansion that went on involuntarily whenever he was nervous or thought deeply" (68), can be seen in terms of Durkheim's description of the contraction and expansion of human expectations. But Durkheim's social determinism is unequivocal, whereas Dreiser's seems to me less clear-cut. An American Tragedy ultimately implies that the vision of an omnipotent social rule beyond human control is an alienating projection, a collective evasion of human powers for social change. Also see Durkheim, Suicide (New York: Free Press, 1951), 254 and passim. Pierre Bourdieu and Jean-Claude Passeron offer an interesting perspective on this issue of social determinism in examining the French educational system. See The Inheritors, trans. Richard Nice (Chicago: University of Chicago Press, 1979), esp. 69–70, and passim.

[26] Two fine studies of the cultural and political impact of corporate and industrial growth in late-nineteenth-century America are Alan Trachtenberg's The Incorporation of America and David F. Noble's America by Design.

[27] A later example of the way in which American tales of success dispense with

Dreiser's portrait, and its links to the function of American ideology, registers a far sharper critique. For Dreiser's novel is precisely interested in how the dream creates the reality, aware that the perceptions that hem human beings in cannot be separated from any actual barriers in their way. *An American Tragedy* pictures its deterministic ideology as inevitably dragging the world along in its wake. But the novel's sustained reflection on the social and political effects of its own determinism stands as a form of resistance to that vision. And that resistance reveals, above all, a faith in human powers to change the world.

---

the specifics of process is found in Arthur Miller's *Death of a Salesman* (New York: Penguin, 1976). In the recurring exchange between Willy and his brother Ben, who is part myth, part man, Ben intones, "William, when I walked into the jungle, I was seventeen. When I walked out I was twenty-one. And by God, I was rich" (52). For social historians contemporary to Dreiser who discuss the discrepancy between the myth and the reality of rising, see Wyllie, *The Self-Made Man*, 154–67, and others in n. 13 above. And for contemporary views on the delusiveness of the American dream, see Gustavus Myers, *History of the Great American Fortunes* (New York, 1910), and William James Ghent, *Socialism and Success* (New York, 1908). Also pertinent here is Andrew Carnegie's "A Talk to Young Men," in *The Empire of Business* (New York, 1902).

Bibliography

Adams, Henry. *The Education of Henry Adams*. Boston: Houghton Mifflin, 1961.
———. *History of the United States*. 9 vols. New York: 1889–1891.
Adams, Herbert Baxter. "The New Historical Movement." *Nation* 39 (September 1884).
Adorno, Theodor, and Max Hortheimer. *The Dialectic of Enlightenment*. New York: Continuum, 1987.
"The Aim of History." *Princeton Review* 24 (April 1857).
Althusser, Louis. *For Marx*. Translated by Ben Brewster. New York: Vintage, 1970.
———. *Lenin and Philosophy*. Translated by Ben Brewster. London: New Left Books, 1971.
Anderson, Charles. "Introduction." In Henry James, *The Bostonians*. New York: Penguin English Library, 1984.
Anderson, Quentin. *The American Henry James*. New Brunswick, N.J.: Rutgers University Press, 1957.
Arac, Jonathan. *Commissioned Spirits*. New Brunswick, N.J.: Rutgers University Press, 1979.
———. "Reading the Letter." *Diacritics* (1979): 42–52.
"The Art of History-Making." *Littell's Living Age* 48 (January 1856).
Arvin, Newton. *Hawthorne*. Boston: Little, Brown, 1929.
Austin, J. L. *How To Do Things with Words*. New York: Oxford University Press, 1970.
Babbit, Irving. "The Critic of American Life." *Forum* 79 (February 1928): 161–76.
Bakhtin, Mikhail. *The Dialogic Imagination*. Austin: University of Texas Press, 1981.
Bancroft, George. *History of the United States*. Abridged and edited by Russell Nye. Chicago: University of Chicago Press, 1966.
———. *Literary and Historical Miscellanies*. New York: Harper and Bros., 1855.
Banner, Lois, and Hartman, Mary. eds. *Clio's Consciousness Raised*. New York: Harper and Row, 1974.

Bannister, Robert C. *Social Darwinism*. Philadelphia: Temple University Press, 1979.

Banta, Martha. "Beyond Post-Modernism: The Sense of History in *The Princess Cassamassima*." *Henry James Review* (Winter 1982), 96–107.

———. *Failure and Success*. Princeton: Princeton University Press, 1981.

Barthes, Roland. *A Barthes Reader*. Edited by Susan Sontag. New York: Hill and Wang, 1983.

———. *New Critical Essays*. New York: Farrar Straus and Giroux, 1980.

Baym, Nina. *The Novel in Antebellum America*. Ithaca: Cornell University Press, 1984.

———. *The Shape of Hawthorne's Career*. Ithaca: Cornell University Press, 1976.

Beard, Charles. *An Economic Interpretation of the Constitution of the United States*. New York: Macmillan, 1913.

Bell, Michael Davitt. *The Development of American Romance*. Chicago: University of Chicago Press, 1977.

———. *Hawthorne and the Historical Romance of New England*. Princeton: Princeton University Press, 1966.

Belsey, Catherine. *Critical Practice*. New York: Methuen, 1983.

Bendix, Reinhard, and Lipset, Seymour Martin, eds. *Social Mobility in Industrial Society*. Berkeley: University of California Press, 1959.

Benjamin, Walter. *Illuminations*. Edited by Hannah Arendt. Translated by Harry Zohn. New York: Schocken Books, 1969.

———. *Werke:* Volume 1. Frankfurt, 1955.

Bercovitch, Sacvan. *The American Jeremiad*. Madison: University of Wisconsin Press, 1978.

———. "The Problem of Ideology in American Literary History." *Critical Inquiry* 12 (Summer 1986): 631–53

———. *The Puritan Origins of the American Self*. New Haven: Yale University Press, 1975.

———, ed. *Reconstructing American Literary History*. Cambridge, Mass.: Harvard University Press, 1986.

Bercovitch, Sacvan, and Myra Jehlen, eds. *Ideology and Classic American Literature*. New York: Cambridge University Press, 1986.

Bernstein, Barton J., ed. *Towards a New Past: Dissenting Essays in American History*. New York: 1968.

Bersani, Leo. "The Narrator as Center in *The Wings of the Dove*." *Modern Fiction Studies* 6 (Summer 1960): 131–44.

Bewley, Marius. *The Eccentric Design*. New York: Columbia University Press, 1963.

Booth, Wayne. *The Rhetoric of Fiction*. Chicago: University of Chicago Press, 1961.

Borges, Jorge Luis. *Ficciones*. New York: Grove Press, 1962.

Bourdieu, Pierre, and Passeron, Jean-Claude. *The Inheritors*. Translated by Richard Nice. Chicago: University of Chicago Press, 1979.

Brainerd, Charles E. *New England Society Orations*. 2 vols. New York: Century Press, 1901.

Brooks, Peter. *Reading for the Plot*. New York: Knopf, 1984.

Buitenhuis, Peter. *The Grasping Imagination*. Toronto: Toronto University Press, 1970.

Burke, Kenneth. *Attitudes toward History*. Boston: Beacon Press, 1961.

Calcott, George. *History in the United States, 1800–1860*. Baltimore: Johns Hopkins University Press, 1970.

Canary, Robert, and Harry Kozicki, eds. *The Writing of History*. Madison: University of Wisconsin Press, 1978.

Carnegie, Andrew. "A Talk to Young Men." In *The Empire of Business*. New York, 1902.

Carter, Harold Dean. *Henry Adams and His Friends*. Boston: Houghton Mifflin, 1947.

Cawelti, John. *Apostles of the Self-Made Man*. Chicago: University of Chicago Press, 1976

Chambers, Ross. *Story and Situation*. Minneapolis: University of Minnesota Press, 1984.

Chase, Richard. *The American Novel and Its Tradition*. Garden City, N.Y.: Doubleday, 1957.

Chatman, Seymour. *The Later Style of Henry James*. Oxford: Basil Blackwell, 1972.

———. *Story and Discourse*. Ithaca: Cornell University Press, 1978.

Chiarmonte, Nicola. *The Paradox of History*. Philadelphia: University of Pennsylvania Press, reprint 1985.

Christian Examiner 52 (July 1863): 429.

Colacurcio, Michael. *The Province of Piety*. Cambridge, Mass.: Harvard University Press, 1984.

———. "The Sense of an Author: The Familiar Life and Strange Imaginings of Nathaniel Hawthorne." *A Journal of the American Renaissance* 27 (Fall 1981): 108–33.

Collingwood, R. G. *The Idea of History*. New York: Oxford University Press, 1946.

Cott, Nancy, ed. *Root of Bitterness*. New York: Dutton, 1972.

Crews, Frederick. *Sins of the Fathers*. New York: Oxford University Press, 1966.

BIBLIOGRAPHY

Crowley, J. Donald. *Hawthorne: The Critical Heritage*. London: Routledge and Kegan Paul, 1970.

Dauber, Kenneth. *Rediscovering Hawthorne*. Princeton: Princeton University Press, 1977.

Davis, Sara. "Feminist Sources in *The Bostonians*." *American Literature* 50 (December 1979): 570–603.

Davis, Walter, and Fish, Stanley. "An Exchange." *Critical Inquiry* 10 (June 1984), 695–718.

de Tocqueville, Alexis. *Democracy in America*. Translated by Henry Reeve. New York: Vintage, 1945.

"Domestic Histories of the South." *Southern Quarterly Review* 21 (January–April 1852).

Domhoff, G. William. *Who Rules America?* Englewood Cliffs: Prentice-Hall, 1967.

Donadio, Stephen. *Nietzsche, Henry James and the Artistic Will*. New York: Oxford University Press, 1978.

Douglas, Ann. *The Feminization of American Culture*. New York: Knopf, 1978.

Dreiser, Theodore. *An American Tragedy*. New York: Signet, 1964.

———. *Sister Carrie*. New York: Charles E. Merrill Standard Editions, 1969.

———. *The Financier*. New York: Harper and Bros., 1912.

Dryden, Edgar. "Hawthorne's Castles in the Air: Form and Theme in *The House of the Seven Gables*." *English Literary History* 38 (1971): 294–317.

Dupee, F. W. *The Question of Henry James*. New York: Henry Holt, 1945.

Durkheim, Emile. *Suicide*. New York: Free Press, 1951.

"Editor's Easy Chair." *Harper's Magazine* 24 (May 1862).

"Editor's Table." *Harper's Magazine* 10 (May 1855).

Elliott, Emory. *Revolutionary Writers*. New York: Oxford University Press, 1981.

Elson, Ruth Miller. *Guardians of Tradition*. Lincoln: Nebraska University Press, 1964.

Esch, Deborah. "A Jamesian About-Face: Notes on 'The Jolly Corner.' " *English Literary History* 50 (Fall 1983): 587–605.

Feidelson, Charles. *Symbolism and American Literature*. Chicago: University of Chicago Press, 1953.

Fisher, Philip. *Hard Facts*. New York: Oxford University Press, 1985.

———. "Looking Around to See Who I Am: Dreiser's Territory of the Self." *English Literary History* 44 (1977): 728–48.

Foucault, Michel. *Language, Counter-Memory, Practice: Selected Essays and*

Interviews, trans. by Donald F. Bouchard and Sherry Simon. Ithaca: Cornell University Press, 1977.

Fox, Richard, and Lears, Jackson, eds. *The Culture of Consumption*. New York: Pantheon, 1983.

Franzosa, John. "A Psychoanalysis of Hawthorne's Style." *Genre* 14 (Fall 1981): 383–409.

Freud, Sigmund. *Beyond the Pleasure Principle*. Vol. 18 of *The Standard Edition of the Complete Psychological Works of Sigmund Freud*. Translated by James Strachey. 24 vols. London: Hogarth Press, 1953–1974.

Friedman, Lawrence J. *Inventors of the Promised Land*. New York: Knopf, 1975.

Frye, Northrop. *Anatomy of Criticism*. Princeton: Princeton University Press, 1957.

Garner, Stanton. "Fact as Fraud in Herman Melville's 'Billy Budd.' " *San Jose Studies* (1977): 82–105.

Gatta, John. "Progress and Providence in *The House of the Seven Gables*." *American Literature* 50 (1978): 37–48.

Genette, Gerard. *Narrative Discourse*. Translated by Jane E. Lewin. Ithaca: Cornell University Press, 1980.

————. *Figures of Literary Discourse*. Translated by Alan Sheridan. New York: Columbia University Press, 1982.

Ghent, William James. *Socialism and Success*. New York, 1908.

Giddens, Anthony. *Central Problems in Social Theory*. Berkeley: University of California Press, 1979.

————. *The Class Structure of the Advanced Societies*. London: Hutchinson, 1973.

Gilmore, Michael. "The Artist and the Marketplace in *The House of the Seven Gables*." *English Literary History* 48 (1981): 172–89.

Gutman, Herbert G. *Work, Culture, and Society*. New York: Vintage, 1977.

Hall, Sallie. "Henry James and the Bluestockings." In *Aeolian Harps: Essays in Literature*, ed. Donna Fricke and Douglas Fricke. Bowling Green, Ohio: Bowling Green University Press, 1976.

Hartz, Louis. *The Liberal Tradition in America*. New York: Harcourt Brace, 1955.

Hawthorne, Nathaniel. *The Blithedale Romance*. Columbus: Ohio State University Press, 1964.

————. *The House of the Seven Gables*. Columbus: Ohio State University Press, 1965.

————. *The Marble Faun*. Columbus: Ohio State University Press, 1968.

Hawthorne, Nathaniel. *Miscellanies: Biographical and Other Sketches and Letters*. Boston: Houghton Mifflin, 1900.

———. *The Scarlet Letter*. Columbus: Ohio State University Press, 1962.

———. *Tales and Sketches*. New York: The Library of America, 1982.

Henderson, Harry. *Versions of the Past*. New York: Oxford University Press, 1974.

Higham, John. "Hanging Together: Divergent Unities in American History." *Journal of American History* 61 (1974): 5–28.

———. *History*. Englewood Cliffs: Prentice-Hall, 1965.

Hirsch, E. D. "Meaning and Significance Reinterpreted." *Critical Inquiry* 11 (December 1984): 202–225.

———. *Validity in Interpretation*. New Haven: Yale University Press, 1967.

Hirschman, Albert O. *The Passions and the Interests*. Princeton: Princeton University Press, 1977.

"Historical Studies." *Church Review* 4 (April 1851).

"History and Its Philosophy." *Putnam's Monthly* 11 (April 1868).

"History: Its Uses and Meaning." *Westminster Review* 62 (October 1854).

Hobsbawm, Eric. *The Invention of Tradition*. Cambridge: Cambridge University Press, 1983.

Hofstader, Richard. *The Progressive Historians*. New York: Knopf, 1968.

———. *Social Darwinism in American Thought*. Boston: Beacon, 1955.

Holland, Laurence. *The Expense of Vision*. Princeton: Princeton University Press, 1964.

Horwitz, Morton. *The Transformation of American Law, 1780–1860*. Cambridge, Mass.: Harvard University Press, 1977.

Howe, Irving. "Afterword." *An American Tragedy*. New York: Signet, 1964.

———. *Politics and the Novel*. New York: Horizon, 1957.

James, Henry. *The Art of the Novel*. Edited by R. P. Blackmur. New York: Scribner's, 1934.

———. *The Bostonians*. New York: Penguin Modern Classics, 1966.

———. *The Golden Bowl*. New York: Penguin, 1973.

———. *Hawthorne*. New York: Macmillan, 1966.

———. *The Portrait of a Lady*. New York: Penguin, 1979.

———. *The Sense of the Past*. New York: Scribner's, 1917.

———. *The Wings of the Dove*. New York: Norton, 1978.

James, William. "The Dilemma of Determinism." In *The William James Reader*. ed. Gay Wilson Allen, 16–40. New York: Houghton Mifflin, 1971.

Jameson, Fredric. *Marxism and Form*. Princeton: Princeton University Press, 1971.

———. "Marxism and Historicism." *New Literary History* 11 (Autumn 1979): 41–73.

———. *The Political Unconscious*. Ithaca: Cornell University Press, 1981.

———. "Reification and Utopia in Mass Culture." *Social Text* 1 (1979): 130–48.

Jameson, J. Franklin. *The History of Historical Writing in America*. Boston: Houghton Mifflin, 1891.

Jehlen, Myra. "New World Epics: The Novel and the Middle Class in America." *Salmagundi* 36 (Winter 1977): 49–68.

Johnson, Barbara. *The Critical Difference*. Baltimore: Johns Hopkins University Press, 1980.

Jordan, Gretchen. "Hawthorne's Bell: Historical Evolution Through Symbol." *Nineteenth Century Fiction* 19 (1964): 106–124.

Jordy, William H. *Henry Adams, Scientific Historian*. New York: Archon, 1970.

Kahn, Victoria. "Virtu and the Example of Agathocles in Machiavelli's *Prince*." *Representations* 13 (Winter 1986): 63–83.

Kammen, Michael, ed. *The Past Before Us*. Ithaca: Cornell University Press, 1985.

———. *A Season of Youth*. New York: Knopf, 1978.

Kempton, Murry. "The Trial of Wayne Williams." *New York Review of Books* (March 14, 1985), 31.

Kennedy, David. *Birth Control in America: The Career of Margaret Sanger*. New Haven: Yale University Press, 1970.

Kenner, Hugh. *The Pound Era*. Los Angeles: University of California Press, 1971.

Kermode, Frank. *The Sense of an Ending*. New York: Oxford University Press, 1966.

Kolb, Harold. *The Illusion of Life*. Charlottesville: University Press of Virginia, 1981.

Kraditor, Aileen. *The Ideas of the Woman Suffrage Movement, 1890–1920*. New York: Columbia University Press, 1965.

———. *Up from the Pedestal*. Chicago: Quadrangle Books, 1968.

Kraus, Michael. *The Writing of American History*. Norman: University of Oklahoma Press, 1953.

Krook, Dorothea. *The Ordeal of Consciousness*. Cambridge: Cambridge University Press, 1962.

Kundera, Milan. "Man Thinks, God Laughs." *New York Review of Books* (June 13, 1985), 11–12.

LaCapra, Dominick. *Rethinking Intellectual History*. Ithaca: Cornell University Press, 1982.

Lawrence, D. H. *Studies in Classic American Literature*. New York: Penguin, 1978.

Lears, Jackson. *No Place of Grace*. New York: Pantheon, 1981.

Leavis, Q. D. "Hawthorne as Poet." In *Hawthorne*, ed. A. N. Kaul, 25–63. Englewood Cliffs: Prentice-Hall, 1966.

Lee, Vernon. *The Handling of Words*. London: John Lane, 1923.

Lehan, Richard. *Theodore Dreiser: His World and His Novels*. Carbondale: Southern Illinois University Press, 1964.

Lentricchia, Frank. *After the New Criticism*. Chicago: University of Chicago Press, 1980.

Levin, David. *In Defense of Historical Literature*. New York: Hill and Wang, 1967.

———. *The Romantic Historians*. Stanford: Stanford University Press, 1959.

Lewis, R.W.B. *The American Adam*. Chicago: University of Chicago Press, 1955.

Littell's Living Age 24 (February 1850): 202.

Loewenberg, Bert James. *American History in American Thought*. New York: Simon and Schuster, 1972.

Lowi, Theodore J. *The End of Liberalism*. 2nd ed. New York: Norton, 1979.

Lukács, Georg. *History and Class Consciousness*. Translated by Rodney Livingstone. Cambridge, Mass.: MIT Press, 1971.

———. *The Theory of the Novel*. Translated by Anna Bostock. Cambridge, Mass.: MIT Press, 1971.

Lukes, Steven. *Power*. New York: Macmillan, 1974.

Lynd, Helen, and Lynd, Robert. *Middletown*. New York: Harcourt Brace and Co., 1929.

Mailer, Norman. *The Executioner's Song*. Boston: Little, Brown, 1979.

Male, Roy P. *Hawthorne's Tragic Vision*. Austin: Texas University Press, 1957.

Marsh, George. *The American Historical School*. Troy, N.Y.: Steam Press of J. C. Kneeland and Co., 1847.

Marx, Karl. *The Marx-Engels Reader*. Edited by Robert C. Tucker. New York: Norton, 1978.

———. "On America and the Civil War." In *The Karl Marx Library*, ed. Saul K. Padover. New York: McGraw-Hill, 1972.

Marx, Leo. *The Machine in the Garden*. New York: Oxford University Press, 1964.

Matthiessen, F. O. *American Renaissance*. New York: Oxford University Press, 1941.

———. *Henry James: The Major Phase*. New York: Oxford University Press, 1944.

———. *The James Family*. New York: Vintage, 1980.

———. *Theodore Dreiser*. New York: William Sloane, 1951.

McGann, Jerome. *Historical Studies and Literary Criticism*. Madison: University of Wisconsin Press, 1985.

Mellow, James. *Nathaniel Hawthorne in His Times*. Boston: Houghton Mifflin, 1980.

Melville, Herman. *Great Short Works of Herman Melville*. Edited by Warner Berthoff. New York: Harper and Row, 1969.

Michaels, Walter. "Romance and Real Estate in *The House of the Seven Gables*," *Raritan* 2 (1983): 66–87.

Miller, Arthur. *The Death of a Salesman*. New York: Penguin, 1976.

Miller, J. Hillis. *Fiction and Repetition*. Cambridge, Mass.: Harvard University Press, 1983.

Miller, William. "American Historians and the Business Elite." *Journal of Economic History* 9 (1949): 184–208.

Mills, C. Wright. "The American Business Elite: A Collective Portrait." *The Tasks of Economic History*, Supplement 5 (1945): 20–44.

Mitchell, W.J.T., ed. *On Narrative*. Chicago: University of Chicago Press, 1981.

Moers, Ellen. *Two Dreisers*. New York: Viking, 1969.

Montrose, Louis. "Renaissance Literary Studies and the Subject of History." *English Literary Renaissance* 16 (1986): 5–12.

Myers, Gustavus. *History of the Great American Fortunes*. New York, 1910.

Nagel, Thomas. *Mortal Questions*. New York: Oxford University Press, 1981.

Nietzsche, Fredrich. *The Use and Abuse of History*. Translated by Adrian Collins. Indianapolis, Ind.: Bobbs-Merrill, 1957.

Noble, David F. *America by Design*. New York: Oxford University Press, 1980.

North American Review 73 (October 1851): 411–47.

North American Review 74 (April 1852): 508.

North American Review 80 (April 1855): 390.

North American Review 93 (July 1862): 163.

North American Review 246 (April 1875): 424.

"Notes." *Nation* 5 (January 1877).

Nye, Russell B. *George Bancroft*. New York: Knopf, 1945.

Parker, Gail. *The Oven Birds*. Garden City, N.Y.: Doubleday, 1972.

Parkman, Francis. *The Conspiracy of Pontiac and the Indian War after the Conquest of Canada*. 3 vols. Boston: Little and Brown, 1898.

Parrington, Vernon. *Main Currents in American Thought*. 3 vols. New York: Harcourt, Brace, Jovanovich, 1927, 1930.

Pearce, Roy Harvey. "Hawthorne and the Sense of the Past Or, The Immortality of Major Molineux." *English Literary History* 21 (1954): 327–49.

———. *Historicism Once More*. Princeton: Princeton University Press, 1969.

Petrey, Sandy. "The Language of Realism, the Language of False Consciousness: A Reading of *Sister Carrie*." *Novel* (Winter 1977): 101–113.

"The Philosophy of History." *North American Review* 34 (July 1834): 36–57.

Pizer, Donald. *The Novels of Theodore Dreiser*. Minneapolis: University of Minnesota Press, 1976.

Plumb, J. H. *The Death of the Past*. London: Macmillan, 1969.

Poirier, Richard. *The Comic Sense of Henry James*. New York: Oxford University Press, 1967.

———. *A World Elsewhere*. New York: Oxford University Press, 1966.

Porter, Carolyn. *Seeing and Being*. Middletown, Conn.: Wesleyan University Press, 1981.

Poulet, Georges. *The Metamorphoses of the Circle*. Translated by Carley Dawson and Elliott Coleman. Baltimore: Johns Hopkins University Press, 1966.

Rank, Otto. *The Double*. New York: Meridian, 1971.

Ricoeur, Paul. *Time and Narrative*. 2 vols. Chicago: University of Chicago Press, 1984–85.

Robinson, James Harvey. *History*. New York: Columbia University Press, 1908.

———. *The New History*. New York: Macmillan, 1912.

Rodgers, Daniel T. *The Work Ethic in Industrial America, 1850–1920*. Chicago: University of Chicago Press, 1978.

Rowe, John Carlos. *Henry Adams and Henry James*. Ithaca: Cornell University Press, 1976.

———. *Through the Custom House: Nineteenth-Century Fiction and Modern Theory*. Baltimore: Johns Hopkins University Press, 1982.

Sacks, Oliver. "The Lost Mariner." *New York Review of Books* (February 16, 1984), 14–19.

Said, Edward. *Beginnings*. New York: Basic Books, 1975.

Schur, Edwin. *Labelling Deviant Behavior*. New York: Harper and Row, 1971.

BIBLIOGRAPHY

"The Science of History." *Hours at Home* 2 (February 1866).

Sears, Sallie. *The Negative Imagination*. Ithaca: Cornell University Press, 1968.

Seltzer, Mark. *Henry James and the Art of Power*. Ithaca: Cornell University Press, 1984.

Sennett, Richard. *The Fall of Public Man*. New York: Vintage, 1978.

Shaffer, Arthur H. *The Politics of History*. Chicago: Precedent, 1975.

Shaw, Peter, "Hawthorne's Ritual Typology of the American Revolution." *Prospects* 3 (1977): 483–98.

Shils, Edward. *Tradition*. Chicago: University of Chicago Press, 1981.

Showalter, Elaine. ed. *The New Feminist Criticism*. New York: Pantheon, 1985.

Simms, William Gilmore. *Views and Reviews in American History*. Edited by C. Hugh Holman. Cambridge, Mass.: Harvard University Press, 1962.

Singleton, Charles, ed. *Interpretations: Theory and Practice*. Baltimore: Johns Hopkins University Press, 1969.

Smith, Henry Nash. *Virgin Land*. Cambridge, Mass.: Harvard University Press, 1950.

Smith-Rosenberg, Carroll. "Beauty, the Beast, and the Militant Women," *American Quarterly* 23 (1971): 562–84.

Sochen, June, ed. *The New Feminism in Twentieth-Century America*. Lexington, Mass.: D. C. Heath, 1971.

Somkin, Fred. *Unquiet Eagle*. Ithaca: Cornell University Press, 1967.

Sontag, Susan. *Illness as Metaphor*. New York: Farrar, Straus and Giroux, 1977.

Sorokin, Pitirim. *Social and Cultural Mobility*. New York: Harper, 1927.

Stage, Sarah. "Out of the Attic: Studies in Victorian Sexuality." *American Quarterly* 27 (October 1975): 460–85.

Stern, Fritz, ed. *The Varieties of History*. New York: Meridian, 1956.

Stoehr, Taylor. *Hawthorne's Mad Scientists*. Hamden, Conn.: Archon Books, 1978.

Stone, Lawrence. "The Revival of Narrative." *Past and Present* 85 (1979): 1–24.

Struever, Nancy. *The Language of History in the Renaissance*. Princeton: Princeton University Press, 1970.

Sundquist, Eric, ed. *American Realism: New Essays*. Baltimore: Johns Hopkins University Press, 1982.

Terdiman, Richard. "Deconstructing Memory." *Diacritics* (Winter 1985): 13–36.

"Their Strength Was to Sit Still." *American Magazine* 108 (October 1929).

BIBLIOGRAPHY

Thomas, Brook. " 'Billy Budd' and the Judgment of Silence." *Literature and Ideology*, ed. Harry Garvin. East Brunswick, N.J.: Associated University Presses, 1982.

———. "*The House of the Seven Gables*: Reading the Romance of America." *Publication of the Modern Literature Association* (May 1981): 195–211.

Tobin, Patricia. *Time and the Novel*. Princeton: Princeton University Press, 1978.

Tompkins, Jane. *Sensational Designs*. New York: Oxford University Press, 1985.

Trachtenberg, Alan. *The Incorporation of America*. New York: Hill and Wang, 1982.

Trilling, Lionel. *The Opposing Self*. New York: Viking, 1955.

Tuveson, Ernest. *Redeemer Nation*. Chicago: University of Chicago Press, 1968.

The United States Magazine and Democratic Review 1 (October 1837): Introduction.

The United States Magazine and Democratic Review 26–29 (1849–1851). "The Uses of History." *New Englander* 22 (July 1863).

Van Leer, David. "Moonlight and Moonshine: The Irrelevance of Hawthorne's Prefaces." MLA Special Session, December 27, 1983.

Van Tassell, David. *Recording America's Past*. Chicago: University of Chicago Press, 1960.

Veblen, Thorstein. *The Theory of the Leisure Class*. New York: Mentor, 1953.

Vincec, Sister Stephanie. " 'Poor Flopping Wings': The Making of Henry James's *The Wings of the Dove*." *Harvard Library Bulletin* 24 (1976): 60–93.

Wade, Mason. *Francis Parkman, Heroic Historian*. New York: Viking Press, 1942.

Waggoner, Hyatt. *The Presence of Hawthorne*. Baton Rouge: Louisiana State University Press, 1979.

Warren, Robert Penn. "An American Tragedy." *Yale Review* 52 (October 1962): 1–15.

Wayne, Don E. "Power, Politics, and the Shakespearian Text: Recent Criticism in England and the United States," In *Shakespeare Reproduced: The Text in History and in Ideology*, ed. Jean Howard and Marion O'Connor. London and New York: Methuen, forthcoming.

Wegelin, Christof. *The Image of Europe in Henry James*. Dallas: Southern Methodist University Press, 1958.

White, Allon. *The Uses of Obscurity*. London: Routledge and Kegan Paul, 1981.

White, Hayden. "Getting Out of History." *Diacritics* (Fall 1982): 2–13.
———. *Metahistory*. Baltimore: Johns Hopkins University Press, 1973.
———. "Structuralism and Popular Culture." *Journal of Popular Culture* 7 (Spring 1974): 754–75.
———. *Tropics of Discourse*. Baltimore: Johns Hopkins University Press, 1978.
White, Morton. *Social Thought in America: The Revolt against Formalism*. Boston: Beacon, 1947.
Williams, Raymond. *Marxism and Literature*. New York: Oxford University Press, 1977.
Wilson, Major. "The Concept of Time and the Political Dialogue in the U. S., 1828–1848." *American Quarterly* 19 (1967): 619–44.
Wills, Garry. *Inventing America*. New York: Vintage, 1978.
Winsor, Justin. "The Perils of Historical Narrative." *Atlantic Monthly* (1890).
Wish, Harvey. *The American Historian*. New York: Oxford University Press, 1960.
Wyllie, Irvin G. *The Self-Made Man in America*. New Brunswick, N.J.: Rutgers University Press, 1954.
Yeazell, Ruth Bernard, ed. *The Death and Letters of Alice James*. Berkeley: University of California Press, 1981.
———. *Language and Knowledge in the Late Novels of Henry James*. Chicago: University of Chicago Press, 1976.

Index

INDEX

consumerism, 18, 85–86, 123–25, 142, 145. *See also* capitalism
Crews, Frederick, 114n
Crowley, J. Donald 105n

daguerreotype, 95–96
Darwin, Charles, 57, 70
Dauber, Kenneth, 105n
Davis, Sara, 155n
Davis, Walter, 31n
de Man, Paul, 108n
determinism, 21–22, 76, 87, 243, 246, 249–50, 262, 265–71, 276, 281, 289–90, 292–94. *See also* class structure and social class
Dewey, John, 57
Domhoff, G. William, 254n
Donadio, Stephen, 68n, 234n
double and doubling, 221–24, 262–63, 265–66
Douglas, Ann, 46n, 101n, 112n, 153n, 238n, 239
Draper, John William, 56–59
Dreiser, Theodore, xi, xii, xviii, 3, 7, 12, 16, 38, 43, 44, 70, 262, 277n, 294; WORKS: *An American Tragedy*, 20–23, 70, 79–81, 242–94; *Sister Carrie*, 252n
Dryden, Edgar, 131n
Dunne, Peter Finlay, 238n
Durkheim, Emile, 293n
Dwight, Timothy, 179n

eiron figure, 136n, 160
Eliot, T. S., 161n
Elliott, Emory, 179n
Emerson, Ralph Waldo, 8, 95
Esch, Deborah, 165n, 191n
evolution, theory of, 57

Faulkner, William, 8
feminism, 141–43, 155n, 156, 165, 172, 178; and authorship, 240–41. *See also* illness and death, and women
figuration, 164–65
Fisher, Philip, 51n, 251n
Foucault, Michel, xivn, 10n, 28, 29–30
Franzosa, John, 32
free will. *See* determinism
Freeman, Mary Wilkins, 239n
Freneau, Philip, 179n

Freud, Sigmund, 151
Friedman, Lawrence J., 56n
Frye, Northrop, 136n, 160

Garner, Stanton, 66n
Gatta, John, 119n
Genette, Gerard, 11n, 106n, 111, 138n, 164n, 188n, 213n, 262n
Ghent, William James, 294n
Giddens, Anthony, 4n, 7n, 193n
Gilman, Charlotte Perkins, 238n
Gilmore, Michael, 90n
Glasgow, Ellen, 238n
Goffman, Erving, 281n
Gossman, Lionel, 12n, 42n, 63n
Gramsci, Antonio, xviin
Gutman, Herbert G., 247n, 257n

Hall, Sallie, 136n
Hartz, Louis, 146n
Hawthorne, Nathaniel, ix, xi–xii, xviii, 3, 5, 7, 9, 12, 16, 21, 24, 29n, 32, 36, 38, 43–44, 54–55; and history, 119n, 122n; and social novel, 5; WORKS: *The Blithedale Romance*, 83, 100, 176, 220n; "The Custom-House Preface," 92; *The House of Seven Gables*, x, 13, 26–27, 33–34, 42, 54, 83–134, 176, 185, 205; *The Marble Faun*, 100; *The Scarlet Letter*, xv, 15–16, 83, 100, 128, 228
Henderson, Harry, 8n
hero, heroism, 17, 101n, 186, 261, 285
Higham, John, 56n, 57, 69n
Hildreth, Richard, 43, 48–50, 55
Hirsch, E. D., 28–29
Hirschman, Albert O., 39n, 254n
historical change and process, 21–22, 105, 138, 145, 156, 169
historical consciousness, 3, 23–24, 33, 40, 45, 81, 93–95, 106, 139, 141, 169, 182, 183, 218, 244, 260–61
historical knowledge, xviii, 53, 57, 64, 80–81, 84, 272
historical narration, xi, xii, xvin, 4, 11, 19, 41, 60, 63, 78, 82; and power, 65, 67, 244, 261; in *An American Tragedy*, ix, xviii, 20, 79–81, 245, 250–51, 252–53, 261, 268–69, 278–79, 281, 285; in *Billy Budd*, 65–67; in *The Bostonians*, ix, 16, 20, 137, 143, 152n, 176; in *The*

310

INDEX

House of Seven Gables, ix, xviii, 16, 20,
28, 44, 127–30; in *The Scarlet Letter*, 16;
in *The Wings of the Dove*, ix, 20, 183,
189–91, 199, 211, 213. *See also* past
historiography, 11, 46–47, 50, 53, 57–61,
77, 183n, 190
history, x, 42, 88–89, 131, 140, 149–50,
152–53, 197n, 199, 205, 208–209, 224,
231, 244, 272, 281; "antiquarian,"
141n, 153n; certainty of, 69; "critical,"
141n; definition of, xvi; and economic
theory, 74; emblems of, 91, 96; erasure
of, 145–46; evasion of, 83, 101, 104,
110; evolutionary, 70; familial, 187,
259; historical evidence, 52; individual
vs. collective, 13–15; and institutions,
59–60; interpretation of, xviii, 4; ironic
historian, 262–69; and literature, 9,
169; "monumental," 141n; and morality, 54–55; and mystification, xvii;
nineteenth-century attitudes toward,
12n, 46n, 55; and politics, xviii; philosophy of, 41n; reconstruction of, 183,
209, 212, 281, 293; representation of,
xi; repression of, xii, 20n, 25, 66; role
of, 47, 83; responses to, 141n; scientific, 43, 44, 57–59, 62; of self, 23n;
and social science, 9, 73–75, 169, 281n;
writing, 58, 62–63, 72. *See also* determinism; historical consciousness; historical knowledge; historical narration;
historiography; modernism; myth;
New History; reification; temporality
and time
Hobsbawm, Eric, 56n
Hofstadter, Richard, 5n, 77n, 247n
Holland, Laurence, 233
Horwitz, Morton, 39n, 254n
Houton, Frank, 257n
Howe, Irving, 135n, 242n, 288–89
Huxley, Thomas H., 58

identity, 157–59, 277; public vs. private,
166, 285
Ideology: American, 6–7, 45, 239n, 243,
246, 253–54, 294; conservative, 152–
53; hegemony, 117–19, 288; of individualism, 15; liberal, 254; and literature,
4, 28, 40, 169; and narration, 25, 81,
84–85, 117–18; and society, 114–15,

117, 248, 272, 284, 290. *See also* capitalism; class structure and social class; determinism
illness and death: and power, 220, 225,
238–40; and women, 237–38, 239, 264;
in *An American Tragedy*, 263–64, 278n,
279; in *The Wings of the Dove*, 196, 201,
205, 225, 234–40
imagination, 45, 69, 194, 199–200, 202,
207, 209, 236, 267

Jackson, Andrew, 47
James, Henry, ix, xi–xii, xviii, 3, 5, 7, 8,
9, 12, 16, 21, 23, 25, 29n, 32, 34, 38,
43, 44, 67–69, 135, 162n, 170n, 192,
193n, 211, 231–33; and social novel, 5,
8; WORKS: *The American*, 202; *The Awkward Age*, 69; *The Bostonians*, 13, 24,
135–81, 185, 213; *The Europeans*, 170n;
The Golden Bowl, 67; *Hawthorne*, ix, 83,
168, 170n; *Portrait of a Lady*, 45, 214,
215n, 265–66; *The Wings of the Dove*,
xvii, 13, 42, 68, 182–241
James, William, 3, 57, 216, 282n
Jameson, Fredric, xi, 4n, 11n, 13n, 14,
16n, 20n, 38, 42n, 104, 105n, 123,
124n, 142n, 170n, 183n, 246n
Jehlen, Myra, xiii, 7n
Jewett, Sarah Orne, 238n
Johnson, Barbara, 66n
Jones, Ann Rosalind, 241
Jordan, Gretchen, 119n
Jordy, William H., 60n, 63n
journalism, 262
Joyce, James: *Ulysses*, 243n

Kammen, Michael, 10n, 45n, 46n, 56,
140n
Kant, Immanuel, 197n
Kennedy, David, 238n
Kenner, Hugh, 30, 31
Kermode, Frank, 99n
Kolb, Harold, 57n
Kozicki, Henry, 42n
Kraditor, Aileen, 157n, 238n
Krook, Dorothea, 186n
Kundera, Milan, 35n

LaCapra, Dominick, 10n
Lawrence, D. H., 102n

311

Library of Congress Cataloging-in-Publication Data

Mizruchi, Susan L. (Susan Laura)
The power of historical knowledge : narrating the past in Hawthorne,
James, and Dreiser / Susan L. Mizruchi.
p. cm.
Bibliography: p.
Includes index.
ISBN 0–691–06725–2 (alk. paper)
1. Historical fiction, American—History and criticism. 2. Narration
(Rhetoric) 3. Hawthorne, Nathaniel, 1804–1864. House of the seven gables.
4. James, Henry, 1843–1916. Bostonians. 5. James, Henry, 1843–1916.
Wings of the dove. 6. Dreiser, Theodore, 1871–1945. American tragedy.
7. Literature and history. I. Title.

PS374.H5M59 1988   813′.081′09—dc19   87–21877